Letting Business Premises

AUSTRALIA
Law Book Co.
Sydney

CANADA and USA
Carswell
Toronto

HONG KONG
Sweet & Maxwell Asia

NEW ZEALAND
Brookers
Auckland

SINGAPORE and MALAYSIA
Sweet & Maxwell Asia
Singapore and Kuala Lumpur

Letting Business Premises

Eighth Edition

Trevor M Aldridge Q.C. (Hon)
M.A. (Cantab) Solicitor

London
Sweet & Maxwell
2004

First Published 1985
Eighth edition 2004

Published in 2004 by
Sweet & Maxwell Ltd, 100 Avenue Road
Swiss Cottage, London NW3 3PF
http://www.sweetandmaxwell.co.uk

Typeset by Servis Filmsetting Ltd, Manchester
Printed in Great Britain by Creative Print & Design,
Harmondsworth, Middlesex

No natural forests were destroyed to make this product;
only farmed timber was used and replanted.

A CIP catalogue record for this book is available from the
British Library

ISBN 0 421 881 801

Contents

Part II: Renewing Business Tenancies

CONTENTS

Preface

There have been major changes to the procedure for renewing tenancies or business premises. The Regulatory Reform (Business Tenancies) (England and Wales) Order 2003, taking effect on June 1, 2004, makes the first major changes in the legislation since 1969. Largely following recommendations which the Law Commission made in 1992, the main reforms are:

- No court application is needed to contract out of the statutory right to renew. Instead, a notice procedure must be followed.
- In deciding entitlement to renew a lease or to oppose a renewal, the position of a company and a controlling shareholder are effectively equated.
- If the landlord gives notice to end the current tenancy, the tenant no longer has to give a counter-notice stating whether or not he agrees to give up possession.
- The landlord, as well as the tenant, is entitled to apply to the court for an order to renew a lease. He may also seek an order ending the current tenancy without renewal.
- Recognising that an interim rent will not necessarily be more than the current rent, the tenant may apply for it to be fixed. In some cases, the interim rent will automatically be the same as the rent under the new lease.
- The maximum term of a new lease ordered by the court is 15 years, instead of 14 years.

These changes and other, mainly consequential, amendments to Pt II of the Landlord and Tenant Act 1954 are fully dealt with in this new edition.

At the same time, it has been possible to cover many of the other changes in the law which, since the last edition was prepared, have affected the matters with which this book deals. As well as decisions of the courts, these have included these innovations: stamp duty land tax, limited liability partnerships, terms implied into leases to enable tenants to adapt premises so that the disabled are not disadvantaged, commonhold, the fourth edition of the Standard Conditions of Sale and the second edition of the Standard Commercial Property Conditions.

The law is stated on the basis that the amendments to the Landlord and Tenant Act 1954 have taken effect, and that the Commonhold and Leasehold Reform Act 2002, Pt I, and the Licensing Act 2003 have come into force; in other respects it is stated as it applies on March 15, 2004.

Trevor M. Aldridge
March 2004

Table of Cases

Table of Statutes

Table of Statutory Instruments

Part I

Contents of Leases

Forms for use in connection with the transfer of the benefit and burden of lease covenants are prescribed by the Landlord and Tenant (Covenants) Act 1995 (Notices) Regulations 1995.

Chapter 1

Categories of Tenancy

1 Renewable business tenancy

The tenants of most commercial and industrial premises have the statutory right to renew their lease or tenancy under the Landlord and Tenant Act, Pt II. This renewal right is dealt with in Part II of this book. The tenancies to which it refers are defined in Chapter 10.

1–01

2 Farm business tenancy

A farm business tenancy is a category of tenancy letting agricultural property created by the Agricultural Tenancies Act 1995. It replaces the letting of agricultural holdings under the Agricultural Holdings Act 1986 and earlier legislation. The 1995 Act lays down the conditions with which a farm business tenancy must comply.

1–02

For this purpose 'agriculture' is defined to include (Agricultural Tenancies Act 1995, s.38(1)):

> horticulture, fruit growing, seed growing, dairy farming and livestock breeding and keeping, the use of land as grazing land, meadow land, osier land, market gardens and nursery grounds, and the use of land for woodlands where that use is ancillary to the farming of land for other agricultural purposes.

This definition is the same as the one used in the Agricultural Holdings Act 1986. Accordingly, the decisions that letting land for certain uses is not for agriculture, with the result that the Landlord and Tenant Act 1954, Pt II, applies, are still valid.

(a) Tenancy

A farm business tenancy must be a tenancy (Agricultural Tenancies Act 1995, s.1(1)), so a licence does not come into this category. It may be any type of tenancy, other than a tenancy at will (s.38(1)).

(b) Start date

A farm business tenancy must begin on or after September 1 1995 (Agricultural Tenancies Act 1995, s.2(1)(a)). For this purpose, a tenancy begins on the day when the tenancy terms entitle the tenant to possession (s.38(4)).

(c) Conditions

1–03   There are certain conditions with which a farm business tenancy must comply (Agricultural Tenancies Act 1995, s.1). The effect is that some part of the demised land must be commercially farmed, but part of the property can be used for other purposes either at the outset or later. The tenancy must satisfy:

(1)   The business conditions; and
(2)   *Either* the agriculture condition *or* the notice conditions.

Business conditions There are two business conditions, both of which must be satisfied. First, all or part of the demised land must be farmed for the purposes of a trade or business. Secondly, this must have been the case since the beginning of the tenancy.

Agriculture condition The character of the tenancy is primarily or wholly agricultural. This is judged having regard to the terms of the tenancy, the use of the land (other than any in breach of covenant), the nature of any commercial activities carried out there and any other relevant circumstances.

Notice conditions Landlord and tenant give each other written notice that each intends that the tenancy of the demised land, which must be identified, be and remain a farm business tenancy. The parties have to give this notice, which must be separate from the instrument creating the tenancy, on or before the day the tenancy is granted or the day on which the tenant is entitled to possession (whichever is earlier).

1–04   It will generally be best where possible to rely on the notice conditions, rather than the agriculture condition, because if the notices are correctly given they leave no room for argument. However, that necessarily means taking action when the tenancy is granted; it is possible to satisfy the agriculture condition later.

3 Tenancy of commonhold unit

A commonhold unit used for business purposes, or part of one **1–05** (Commonhold and Leasehold Reform Act 2002, s.21(2)(b)), can be let in the same way as other business premises. Legislation of general application—*e.g.* relating to consent to assignment and sub-letting, the benefit and burden of lease covenants, compensation for improvements and the tenant's right to renew—applies to such lettings.

What is different is that the tenancy is subject to any provision of the commonhold community statement (Commonhold and Leasehold Reform Act 2002, s.18). The current version of the statement is registered at HM Land Registry, from which copies may be obtained. The commonhold community statement may limit the period for which a unit may be let, restrict the use to which it is put, impose other conditions which an occupier must observe, including repairing duties, and may allow the commonhold association to enforce obligations and recover money due for services (commonhold assessments) directly from the tenant (Commonhold and Leasehold Reform Act 2002, ss.14, 19). A tenant is not eligible for membership of the commonhold association which is responsible for managing the development, but a lease can contain a proxy giving him the right to vote.

4 Sub-lease

The distinctive feature of a sub-lease is the fact that the tenant's **1–06** title is dependent on the validity and continued existence of the head lease. If the head lease ends, even before the sub-lease was due to come to an end, in principle the sub-lease falls with it (*Re Cater & Ellis Ex p. Savill Brothers* [1905] 1 K.B. 735). This effect has, however, been alleviated by statute. If the head lease is surrendered or merged with a superior title, the sub-lease continues as a direct tenancy from the superior title (Law of Property Act 1925, s.139(1)). If the head landlord seeks to forfeit the head lease, a sub-tenant may apply to have the property vested in him until the sub-lease would have expired (Law of Property Act 1925, s.146(4)).

A sub-lease must be granted for a term less than the residue of **1–07** the head lease term, so that the head tenant retains a reversionary interest. A purported sub-lease for the same period as the head lease or longer takes effect as an assignment of the head lease (*Beardman v Wilson* (1868) L.R. 4 C.P. 57; *Wollaston v Hakewill* (1841) 3 Man. & G. 297). However, this does not apply where there is merely the possibility that the sub-letting will exceed the length of the head lease, *e.g.* because it may be extended under the statutory provisions for renewing business leases (*William Skelton & Son Ltd v Harrison & Pinder Ltd* [1975] 1 Q.B. 361).

Chapter 2

Benefit and Burden of Covenants

The Landlord and Tenant (Covenants) Act 1995 made fundamental changes to the rules governing who is responsible for obligations undertaken in a lease and for how long, and to the corresponding rules concerning who is entitled to the benefit of those covenants. The changes were not retrospective. Accordingly, two sets of rules now apply: one to the category of 'new tenancies' created by the 1995 Act, the other to the remaining lettings which may conveniently be dubbed 'old tenancies'. **2–01**

1 New tenancies

(a) Definition
A new tenancy is, generally, one granted on or after January 1, **2–02** 1996. To this there are a few exceptions. A lease granted after that date is an old lease if it is granted under an agreement made before that date. The same applies to a lease granted pursuant to a court order taking effect or an option granted before that date and to an overriding lease granted because of the default of the tenant under an old lease (Landlord and Tenant (Covenants) Act 1995, ss.1, 20(1)).

(b) General rule
On the assignment of a new lease, or the reversion to it, the general principle is that the burden and benefit of all the landlord covenants and tenant covenants passes. A 'landlord covenant' is one falling to be complied with by the landlord for the time being, rather than only by the original landlord (*BHP Petroleum Great Britain Ltd v Chesterfield Properties Ltd* [2002] Ch. 194). Presumably, a similar definition applies to a 'tenant covenant'.

There are some exceptions to the general principle and they are dealt with below.

(c) Tenant and tenant's surety

2–03   When a tenant—whether the original tenant or an assignee—assigns, he is released from the tenancy covenants from the date of the assignment. If he only assigns part of the demised property, the release applies, but only to the covenants which fall to be complied with in relation to the part assigned. When, and to the extent that, a tenant is released from his covenants under a tenancy he ceases to be entitled to the benefit of the landlord's covenants (Landlord and Tenant (Covenants) Act 1995, s.5). Necessarily, the release of the tenant automatically releases any surety who has agreed to guarantee his compliance with the covenants.

This does not apply in the case of an 'excluded assignment' (s.11). There are two cases which do not trigger the release of the tenant. They are: first, an assignment in breach of covenant, and secondly, an assignment by operation of law. The second category certainly includes a transfer to personal representatives on the death of a tenant and one to a trustee in bankruptcy on the insolvency of a tenant who is an individual. It is suggested that it does not extend to assignments on compulsory purchase: they are involuntary, but not, in the sense normally understood, by operation of law.

Although an excluded assignment does not release the tenant, the next assignment which is not an excluded assignment does. Say, a tenant *T* dies, the lease vests in his executor *E*, who then sells and assigns it to *P*. The assignment from *T* to *E* is an excluded assignment and *T* is not released at that point. However, when *E* assigns to *P*, the assignment is not an excluded one, and the result is that both *T* and *P* are then released.

(d) Authorised guarantee agreement

2–04   In some circumstances, a former tenant may continue to have some liability in relation to the lease covenants, notwithstanding having been released by the assignment. This happens when he enters into an authorised guarantee agreement (Landlord and Tenant (Covenants) Act 1995, s.16). Such an agreement is possible when the lease contains an absolute or qualified bar against assignment, consent is given on condition that the tenant enters into an agreement and that condition is lawfully imposed.

Technically, this does not extend his responsibility under the covenants. He becomes a surety for the assignee, although, as is the case with many tenants' sureties, his liability may be that of a principal debtor. The agreement can also oblige the former tenant to take a new tenancy (on no more onerous terms) if the lease is disclaimed on the assignee's insolvency.

Under an authorised guarantee agreement, the former tenant guarantees the performance of the covenants by the immediate assignee, but nobody else. It cannot therefore be used to extend the tenant's liability after there has been a further assignment. The guarantee can apply to only some of the tenant's covenants, but that is unlikely.

(e) Tenant's assignee

When a lease is assigned, the assignee becomes bound by the tenant covenants and is entitled to the benefit of the landlord covenants (Landlord and Tenant (Covenants) Act 1995, s.3). Presumably, however, this does not mean that the assignee becomes liable to perform a covenant which was intended to bind only the original tenant. **2–05**

There are some tenant covenants which do not bind the assignee:

(i)   The assignee does not become bound by any covenant which did not bind the tenant immediately before the assignment, disregarding, however, any waiver or release which was personal to the assignor;

(ii) The assignee is not bound by, and does not have the benefit of, any covenant to the extent that it falls to be complied with in relation to any part of the demised property which is not assigned;

(iii) The assignee is not bound by any covenant expressed, in whatever terms, to be personal to someone else.

When the assignee himself comes to assign, the provisions concerning the release of a former tenant apply to him.

(f) Former landlord

The landlord is not automatically released from his covenants in a lease when he assigns the reversion. He may, however, apply to the tenant to be released (Landlord and Tenant (Covenants) Act 1995, ss.6–8). If the tenant agrees or does not react, or if the court considers that it would be reasonable, the landlord is released with effect from the assignment. On an assignment of the reversion to part of the property let, the provisions for release apply to the extent that the covenants fall to be complied with in relation to the part of the property affected by the assignment. **2–06**

The landlord can apply, by serving a prescribed notice (whole reversion: form 3; part of reversion: form 4; subsequent assignment:

form 5 (whole) or 6 (part)), on the tenant, before the reversion is assigned or within four weeks afterwards. He also has a further chance to apply for release on each subsequent assignment of the reversion. The tenant has four weeks within which to reply. If he objects the landlord is not released, but may apply to the county court for a declaration that it is reasonable that he should be.

The result of these provisions is that one or more former landlords may remain liable in parallel with the current landlord. Also, some former landlords may be released while others are not, either because they did not apply for release or because it was resisted.

(g) Landlord's assignee

2–07   When the reversion to demised property is assigned, the assignee becomes bound by the landlord covenants. A 'landlord covenant' is one which is to be complied with by whoever is for the time being entitled to the reversion; a covenant to be performed personally only by the original landlord does not fall within the definition (*BHP Petroleum Great Britain Ltd v Chesterfield Properties Ltd* [2002] Ch. 194). The landlord's assignee is also entitled to the benefit of the tenant covenants (Landlord and Tenant (Covenants) Act 1995, s.3).

This does not apply in certain cases:

(i)   The assignee does not become bound by any covenant which did not bind the landlord immediately before the assignment, disregarding, however, any waiver or release which was personal to the assignor;

(ii)   The assignee is not bound by, and does not have the benefit of, any covenant to the extent that it falls to be complied with in relation to any part of the demised property which is not assigned;

(iii)   The assignee is not bound by any covenant expressed, in whatever terms, to be personal to someone else.

2 Old tenancies

2–08   Two forms of liability can bind the original landlord and the original tenant. The first arises from privity of contract, which recognises that a lease is a contractual document under which obligations last for the duration agreed. The second liability arises from privity of estate, which acknowledges that a lease creates an estate in land involving obligations binding those currently affected by it.

There are four other classes of people who may have an obligation to comply with lease covenants:

(i)   a tenant's surety (theoretically, the landlord's compliance can also be guaranteed, but this is rare);

(ii)   an assignee who joins in the licence to assign to covenant to comply with the lease covenants for the remainder of the term;

(iii) an assignee's surety; and

(iv)   an additional party to the lease, *e.g.* a management or maintenance company.

(a) Privity of contract

The liability of an original landlord or an original tenant normally extends for the whole of the lease term, whether or not he has parted with his interest in the property (*Stuart v Joy* [1904] 1 K.B. 362; Law of Property Act 1925, s.142(2)). So, *e.g.* if an assignee falls into arrears with the rent, the original tenant is liable to pay even if the amount due reflects a rent review which took place after he assigned (*Centrovincial Estates plc v Bulk Storage* (1983) 46 P. & C.R. 393). However, a former tenant is not liable for any part of a rent payment to the extent that it is increased on review to reflect a variation in the lease terms after he parted with the property (*Friends' Provident Life Office v British Railways Board* [1995] 2 E.G.L.R. 55).

The original tenant is a principal debtor and is not in the position of a guarantor of the current tenant. This means that he is not released by any indulgence given to the current tenant, and the landlord has no obligation first to enforce a covenant against the current tenant (*Norwich Union Life Insurance Society v Low Profile Fashions Ltd* [1992] 1 E.G.L.R. 86). The landlord is, however, obliged to give notice before seeking to recover arrears of rent, service charge or other fixed payments from a former tenant. **2–09**

Because this liability is contractual, the parties may agree to vary it. Some leases provide that a party (or perhaps only a landlord or only a tenant) who assigns his interest in the property has no further obligation to comply with the covenants. That is perfectly valid (*Bath v Bowles* (1905) 93 L.T. 801). Similarly, a party can negotiate his release from the covenants.

(b) Privity of estate

The enforceability of lease covenants between the current landlord and the current tenant depends on two matters: the ownership of the property and the nature of the covenants. **2–10**

Privity of estate exists between the current owner of the reversion and the current tenant. This includes a contracting purchaser of the reversion (*Jaeger v Mansions Consolidated Ltd* (1903) 87 L.T. 690), but the lease must be legally assigned (*Stratford-upon-Avon*

Corporation v Parker [1914] 2 K.B. 562). There is no privity of contract between a head landlord and a sub-tenant (*Bryant v Hancock & Co Ltd* [1898] 1 Q.B. 716), although, under the doctrine of *Tulk v Moxhay* (1848) 2 Ph. 774, a sub-tenant may be bound by a restrictive covenant in a superior lease (*e.g. Hill v Harris* [1965] 2 Q.B. 601).

The covenants which privity of estate makes binding on assignees of the reversion or the lease are those which have 'reference to the subject-matter of the lease' (Law of Property Act 1925, s.142(1)) or 'touch and concern the land' (*Spencer's Case* (1583) 5 Co. Rep. 16a). These categories are the same (*Breams Property Investment Co Ltd v Stroulger* [1948] 2 K.B. 1).

(c) Examples

These covenants have been held to be enforceable by and against parties bound by privity of estate:

(i)   To pay rent (*Williams v Bosanquet* (1819) 1 Brod. & Bing. 238);

(ii)   To repair premises and yield them up in repair (*Martyn v Clue* (1852) 18 Q.B. 661);

(iii) To insure the premises against fire (*Vernon v Smith* (1821) 5 B. & Ald. 1);

(iv)   To use premises for a particular purpose (*Wilkinson v Rogers* (1863) 9 L.T. 434);

(v)   Not to assign without the landlord's consent (*Hooper v Clark* (1867) L.R. 2 Q.B. 200);

(vi)   To provide services (*Barnes v City of London Real Property Co* (1918) 2 Ch. 18);

(vii) To accept a surrender (*System Floors Ltd v Ruralpride Ltd* [1995] 1 E.G.L.R. 48).

The following covenants have been held not to be enforceable as a result of parties being bound by privity of contract:

(i)   To pay a premium by instalments (*Hill v Booth* [1930] 1 K.B. 381);

(ii)   To repay a tenant's deposit at the end of the lease (*Hua Chiao Commercial Bank Ltd v Chiaphua Industries Ltd* [1987] A.C. 99).

(d) Sureties and assignees

2–11   The extent of the liability of sureties who are parties to the lease, and of assignees and sureties who later enter into covenants with the landlord, is a matter of interpretation of the covenant in question. It does not, *e.g.* extend to the tenant's liability in tort: so a surety has no liability for the tenant's failure to pay mesne profits, but he might be responsible for damages if the tenant fails to perform his covenant to yield up possession at the end of the term (*Associated Dairies Ltd v Pierce* (1982) 265 E.G. 127). Frequently, the obligation continues for the remainder of the term of the lease, but it can equally be limited to the period of a particular party's ownership (*Johnsey Estates Ltd v Webb* [1990] 1 E.G.L.R. 80). Whether a surety is a principal debtor or only a guarantor is also relevant.

If the surety is a true guarantor, he is released by a substantial increase in the tenant's liability or a change in the tenancy terms which is prejudicial to the surety. An example was the landlord agreeing to the use of the premises as an off-licence which increased their rental value (*Howard de Walden Estates Ltd v Pasta Place Ltd* [1995] 1 E.G.L.R. 79).

(e) Additional lease party
The extent of the liability of an additional party to the lease,   **2–12** and its ability to enforce covenants in the lease, *e.g.* its obligation to provide services and its right to collect service charges, will depend on the lease wording. The entitlement and liability of the owner of an interest in the property (*e.g.* a tenant's right to the benefit of services and his duty to pay a service charge) will normally run with the property, because each will be 'a covenant relating to … land of the covenantee/covenantor' (Law of Property Act 1925, ss.78, 79).

Chapter 3

Rent

1 Amount of rent

The amount of rent reserved by a lease must be certain (*Parker v* **3–01**
Harris (1692) 1 Salk. 262), or ascertainable with certainty (*Selby v*
Greaves (1868) L.R. 3 C.P. 594). The amount need not, therefore,
be stated in cash in the lease, but can be left to be ascertained by a
third party (*e.g. Lloyds Bank v Marcan* [1973] 1 W.L.R. 1387), or
be variable in some other way. The rent can fluctuate on the happening of future events (*Fawke v Viscount Chelsea* [1980] Q.B. 441:
rent to increase when repairs effected).

A lease which reserves no rent is perfectly valid (*Lynes v Snaith*
[1899] 1 Q.B. 486; Law of Property Act 1925, s.205(1) (xxvii)). So
the omission of rent from a lease gives rise to no particular impli-
cation, *e.g.* there can be no assumption that a reasonable rent is to
be paid. If the lease accidentally omits or understates the rent,
rectification is available in appropriate circumstances to correct
that mistake (*Garrard v Frankel* (1862) 30 Beav. 445). The error
must be about the effect of the lease, not merely whether it accords
with a preliminary agreement (*London Regional Transport v*
Wimpey Group Services Ltd (1987) 53 P. & C.R. 356).

A rent expressed as a sum in sterling is satisfied by a payment of
that amount of currency at the date of payment, notwithstanding
fluctuations in the value of money (*Treseder-Griffin v Cooperative*
Insurance Society [1956] 2 Q.B. 127). That case ruled out the possibility of a rent reserved in a foreign currency, or linked to the
value of gold, but this is presumably now possible (see Treaty of
Rome, art. 106; *Miliangos v George Frank (Textiles) Ltd* [1976]
A.C. 443; *Multiservice Bookbinding Ltd v Marden* [1979] Ch. 84).

Rent involving a fraction of a pound reserved before the cur- **3–02**
rency was decimalised (on February 15, 1971) is converted on the
whole penny table (Decimal Currency Act 1969, s.5, Sch.1).

Payments for specific purposes (*e.g.* insurance or services) are sometimes expressed in leases to be reserved as rent. The object is to give the landlord the right, on a default, to use the remedies for non-payment of rent. An additional payment is made rent by a statement to that effect; it does not have to be formally reserved in a reddendum (*Sinclair Gardens Investment (Kensington) Ltd v Walsh* [1995] 2 E.G.L.R. 23). However, these payments will only count as rent if they are reserved to the landlord. Payments reserved to a third party (*e.g.* a management company) are not rent.

2 Variable rents

3–03   Both because of the erosion of fixed rents by inflation, and the desire of the landlords to share increases in the benefit that tenants obtain from the demised premises, various means have been used to obtain automatic variations in rent. These are valid provided the rent payable on any particular occasion can be definitely ascertained, even though not until later (*C H Bailey Ltd v Memorial Enterprises Ltd* [1974] 1 W.L.R. 728). The common rent review clause is separately dealt with in the next chapter.

The traditional method of maintaining the value of a rent was to reserve it in kind, rather than money—this course is still open, but it is rarely practicable—or to link the amount of rent to the price of a commodity, like a corn rent. One difficulty in doing that today is official intervention by means of price fixing and subsidies (*e.g. Re Scremby Corn Rents* [1960] 1 W.L.R. 1227). A modern example adjusted a hotel rent according to the movement of the average nightly room rate (*Nikko Hotels (UK) Ltd v MEPC plc* [1991] 1 E.G.L.R. 103). A service may also be rendered as a rent (*e.g.* cleaning a synagogue: *Montagu v Browning* [1954] 1 W.L.R. 1039). But this cannot extend to an uncertain number of hours' work as demanded by the landlord (*Barnes v Barratt* [1970] 2 Q.B. 657).

3–04   Rent may be linked to a regularly published index, such as the Index of Retail Prices (*e.g. Blumenthal v Gallery Five Ltd* (1971) 220 E.G. 31). If that method is chosen, provision should be made for the possible revision, or even abandonment, of the publication of the index (*e.g. Cumshaw Ltd v Bowen* [1987] 1 E.G.L.R. 30). A clause linking rent to changes in the cost of living, measured not by a published index, but by 'accepted methods' has been upheld (*Griffiths & Diggens v Great Universal Stores* [1953] C.L.Y. 2107), but it is suggested that the validity of such a clause could not always be guaranteed, and that the practical difficulties of evidence in such cases would be great.

In mining leases, a royalty rent, linked to the quantity of mineral won, is common. This is often reserved with a basic rent payable in any event, a 'dead rent'. A provision that the royalty rent can be a minimum figure is effective, and if worded appropriately can continue even if the minerals have been worked out (*Marquis of Bute v Thompson* (1844) 13 M. & W. 487). But a royalty rent payable only on minerals gained, linked to a covenant to extract a minimum quantity, yields nothing once the mineral reserves have been exhausted (*Lord Clifford v Watts* (1870) L.R. 5 C.P. 577).

There is express power to grant mining leases of settled land at **3–05** variable rents, according to the acreage worked or the quantities obtained (Settled Land Act 1925, s.45(1)). The different methods of calculation of price to which the rent can be linked are interesting: sale price, price in a trade price list, fixed by arbitration, or by any such method averaged over a period.

For retail and catering premises particularly, some modern leases have linked all or part of the rent to the profit or turnover of the tenant's trade on the premises (*e.g.* 10 per cent of gate receipts at a football ground: *SB Property Co Ltd v Chelsea Football and Athletic Co Ltd* [1990] E.G.C.S. 132). Again, it must be possible on each occasion to determine what rent is due, and the lease should provide for the production of adequate accounts enabling the landlord to check. A variation on this was a rent of a livestock market expressed as a percentage of the tenant auctioneer's gross commission (*Naylor v Uttoxeter* UDC (1974) 231 E.G. 619). Similarly, rent payable under a head lease may vary with the amount reserved to the tenant in subleases that he grants, but care must be exercised in regulating the position where the tenant himself occupies instead of subletting (*British Railways Board v Elgar House Ltd* [1969] E.G.D. 235). Without express provision, it may not be possible to imply an alternative formula for calculating the rent (*Fraser Pipestock Ltd v Gloucester City Council* [1995] 2 E.G.L.R. 90).

'Rent formulae can often be expressed more simply and unambiguously in algebraic form [than verbally]' (*London Regional Transport v Wimpey Group Services Ltd* (1986) 53 P. & C.R. 356 at 360 *per* Hoffman J.).

3 When payable

(a) Period
Normally, rent is payable from the commencement of the term **3–06** of the lease, or the date the tenant takes possession under it (*i.e.* assumes the position of tenant, not when he goes into physical

occupation), whichever is the later. A lease can validly provide for payment of rent for a period before it was executed when the tenant was in possession (*Bradshaw v Pawley* [1980] 1 W.L.R. 10). Rent reserved 'from the date hereof' by a lease executed in escrow is not payable until the condition of the escrow is satisfied but then dates back to the date of the execution in escrow (*Alan Estates Ltd v WG Stores Ltd* [1982] Ch. 511).

(b) Date

If no date is specified for payment of rent, it is due at the end of the year, or other period for which it is reserved (*Coomber v Howard* (1845) 1 C.B. 440). Where, as is normal, dates for payment are specified, rent may be paid at any time during that day, and is not in arrear until the following day (*Re Aspinall, Aspinall v Aspinall* [1961] Ch. 526). Rent due on a bank holiday is payable on the following day (Banking and Financial Dealings Act 1971, s.1(4)), but rent due on a Sunday is payable on that day (*Child v Edwards* [1909] 2 K.B. 753).

Most leases now reserve rent as payable in advance, but in the absence of an express provision, it is payable in arrear (*Holland v Palser* (1817) 2 Stark. 161). It should be borne in mind that such rent is not normally apportionable once it has accrued due. So, for instance, a tenant who surrenders a term during a rent period is not entitled to credit for any part of the rent paid in advance for that period, unless he makes a bargain to that effect (*William Hill (Football) Ltd v Willen Key and Hardware Ltd* (1964) 108 S.J. 482).

Rent paid before it is due does not immediately count as a payment of rent (*Lord Cromwel v Andrews* (1583) Cro. Eliz. 15). This means that if the reversion changes hands between the date of payment and the date the rent is due, and the tenant is duly notified, the new landlord can still require payment from the tenant, if the assignor of the reversion did not account to him for the sum paid (*De Nicholls v Saunders* (1870) L.R. 5 C.P. 589). Advance payments of rent are subject to the automatic condition that the landlord apply them towards rent when the rent day comes. That condition does not apply to other payments, *e.g.* an accidental overpayment of arrears, which the landlord need not apply against the rent due (*Morris Gore Ltd v Westbourne Hill Properties Ltd* (1982) 126 S.J. 135).

4 Interest

3–07   Many leases now require the tenant to pay interest on rent paid late. That charge, or an increased rent in such circumstances, is only recoverable if it is not a penalty, which it will not be if the rate of interest is reasonable. The interest on each overdue instalment of rent is calculated separately, from the date on which the rent was due to be paid (*Allied London Investments Ltd v Hambro Life Assurance Ltd* (1985) 50 P. & C.R. 207). The court can award interest on a judgment for outstanding rent (Supreme Court Act 1981, s.35A; Administration of Justice Act 1982, Sch.1; County Courts Act 1984, s.69). An extra rent payment related to the breach of particular covenants in a lease, and linked to the extent of the default, is normally enforceable (*Lord Elphinstone v Monkland Iron and Coal Co Ltd* (1886) 11 App. Cas. 332).

5 Deductions from rent

Except in the case of the deductions authorised by statute, the **3–08**
lease may, and often does, expressly prohibit deductions from rent (*Bradbury v Wright* (1781) 2 Doug (K.B.) 624). A lease that reserves a 'net rent' has the same effect (*Bennet v Womack* (1828) 7 B. & C. 627 at 629). Subject to that, the tenant may deduct the following from his rent payments:

(a) income tax assessed on the landlord, but, on his default, recovered from the tenant (Income and Corporation Taxes Act 1988, s.23(2)) and income tax at the basic rate on the current instalment of rent (*Tenbry Investments Ltd v Peugeot Talbot Motor Co Ltd* [1993] 1 E.G.L.R. 71) payable to a landlord whose usual place of abode is outside the UK (Income and Corporation Taxes Act 1988, s.43(1));

(b) owner's drainage rate (Land Drainage Act 1930, s.26; Land Drainage Act 1976, s.72(5)(d)). The rate must have been paid, not merely due (*Sloan Stanley Estate Trustees v Barribal* [1994] 2 E.G.L.R. 8);

(c) a proportion of certain payments to a highway authority (Highways Act 1980, ss.152, 153, 212, 236, 305) and any instalment of coast protection charge recovered from the tenant (Coast Protection Act 1949, s.10(3));

(d) rent paid by a sub-tenant to a head landlord (*O'Donoghue v Coalbrook and Broadoak Co Ltd* (1872) 26 L.T. 806). A sub-tenant can avoid distress on his goods for non-payment of the head rent, by serving on the head landlord, or the bailiff, a declaration containing *inter alia* an undertaking to pay rent due from the subtenant to the head landlord (Law of Distress Amendment Act 1908, s.1);

3–09   (e)   sums payable by the landlord and charged on the premises, so that non-payment threatens the tenant's peaceable enjoyment of the property;

    (f)   the cost of repairs undertaken by the tenant to make good the landlord's default in complying with his repairing obligations (*Lee-Parker v Izzet* [1971] 1 W.L.R. 1688), or the unquantified estimated cost (*Melville v Grape Lodge Developments Ltd* (1978) 39 P. & C.R. 179);

    (g)   other amounts arising from the lease and directly connected, so that the tenant can claim an equitable set-off. A tenant was able to set-off, against a claim for arrears of rent originally due to the landlord's predecessor, damages resulting from that predecessor's unreasonable conduct in carrying our works on the premises (*Muscat v Smith* [2003] 1 W.L.R. 2853;

    (h)   compensation due to the tenant from the landlord for improvements (Landlord and Tenant Act 1927, s.11(2)).

6 Method of payment

3–10   Like any other debt, rent is primarily payable in legal tender (*Henderson v Arthur* [1907] 1 K.B. 10). The lease, or the practice of the parties, may require some other method, or make it acceptable. Rent is frequently paid by cheque. Strictly, the rent is not discharged until the cheque is cleared (*Official Solicitor v Thomas* [1986] 2 E.G.L.R. 1). A cheque that appears to have been honoured by the banker upon whom it was drawn is evidence of payment (Cheques Act 1957, s.3).

  A remittance of rent by post is at the tenant's risk unless expressly or impliedly authorised by the landlord (*Pennington v Crossley & Son* (1897) 13 T.L.R. 513). Even if payment by post is authorised, the tenant must still take all proper precautions, *e.g.* sending cash by registered post (*Mitchell-Henry v Norwich Union Life Insurance Society* [1918] 2 K.B. 67).

  An established course of dealings between the parties establishes the tenant's right to pay rent by cheque (*Day v Coltrane* [2003] 1 W.L.R. 1379). The rent is paid when the cheque is put in the post, provided it is honoured. Payment is not, however, backdated to the date of posting if the cheque lacks a signature (*Luttenberger v North Thoresby Farms Ltd* [1993] 1 E.G.L.R. 3) or if it is not honoured on first presentation (*Hannaford v Smallacombe* (1993) 69 P. & C.R. 399).

7 To whom payable

Rent must normally be paid to the landlord. The tenant can   **3–11**
equally discharge his obligation by paying to:

(a)   the landlord's agent, authorised expressly or by implica-
      tion. This might be someone who would normally be enti-
      tled to receive money on his principal's behalf and give
      receipts (*e.g.* an estate agent), or a banker nominated for
      the purpose (*Breed v Green* (1816) Holt N.P. 204);
(b)   the assignor of the reversion, before the tenant has
      received notice of the assignment (Law of Property Act
      1925, s.151(1));
(c)   a mortgagee who takes possession of the reversion (*De
      Nicholls v Saunders* (1870) L.R. 5 C.P. 589 at 594);
(d)   a judgment creditor of the landlord, pursuant to a form
      of execution (*Lord Ashburton v Nocton* [1915] 1 Ch. 274).

There is no implied covenant by a landlord to accept rent
(*Preston v Lindlands* (1976) 239 E.G. 653).

8 By whom payable

Rent must be paid by the tenant, or someone on his behalf. In this   **3–12**
context, the tenant includes a permitted assignee (*Re House
Property and Investment Co Ltd* [1954] Ch. 576 at 586). However,
the landlord is not bound to accept payment from a stranger (see
Smith v Cox [1940] 2 K.B. 558), even if he had expressly covenanted
with the landlord to guarantee the rent (*London and County (A &
D) Ltd v Wilfred Sportsman Ltd* [1971] Ch. 764). Once a third party
has paid, however, the tenant is discharged from liability (*Milverton
Group Ltd v Warner World Ltd* [1995] 2 E.G.L.R. 28).

9 Limitation

Arrears of rent may not be recovered (even from a guarantor: **3–13**
Romain v Scuba TV Ltd [1995] E.G.C.S. 176) more than six years
after they become due, notwithstanding that the rent is reserved by
deed (Limitation Act 1980, s.19). Part payment on account does
not extend the period (s.29(6)), but time starts running again from
a written, signed acknowledgment of the debt (s.29(2)). The fact
that the right to recover the rent is statute barred does not of itself
prejudice the landlord's right to the reversion.

10 Recovery from former tenant or guarantor

3–14 A former tenant may remain liable for arrears of rent, either by privity of contract (old tenancies) or under an authorised guarantee agreement (new tenancies). Similarly, the liability of a surety who guaranteed the former tenant's compliance with the covenants can continue. There are, however, statutory restrictions on the extent of their liability.

(a) Notice

A former tenant only has to pay arrears of rent, which should have been made by a successor, if the landlord gives him notice (on form 1) during the six months after the rent becomes due (Landlord and Tenant (Covenants) Act 1995, s.17). That notice states that the sum is due and that the landlord intends to recover it from the former tenant, with interest on a specified basis if applicable. If the amount due could rise, *e.g.* as a result of a pending rent review, the landlord can recover any additional sum if his original notice gives warning of this and he serves a further notice (on form 2) within three months of the amount being determined.

Similar provisions apply to a former tenant's guarantor. The landlord must serve him with a separate notice, within the time limit, if he is to be made liable.

(b) Variation in lease terms

If the terms of the lease are varied after the former tenant parted with it, and the result is to increase the rent, he is not responsible for any amount referable to that later variation (Landlord and Tenant (Covenants) Act 1995, s.18). He is not discharged from the duty to pay rent; the extent of his liability is reduced. A parallel provision applies to a former tenant's guarantor, and similarly restricts his liability.

3–15 This only applies to a variation which the landlord has an absolute right to refuse, or one for which he had that right of refusal when the former tenant assigned. Accordingly, it does not apply to a case where the tenant has an option to require variation (*e.g.* an option to have the user clause extended, possibly on payment). Nor does it apply where the court exercises its statutory power to modify the terms of the lease of a shop which would otherwise prevent the tenant doing structural work required under the Offices, Shop and Railways Premises Act 1963.

There is no statutory provision for establishing what part of any rent is attributable to a variation in the lease terms. It may, therefore, be a matter for negotiation whenever there are arrears. This provision does not protect a former tenant from having to pay a rent which is higher merely as a result of a rent review carried out after he parts with the property. If the lease terms have remained the same, the review is not a variation but an implementation of a provision in the lease.

Chapter 4

Rent Reviews

1 Generally

The normal kind of contractual rent review in a lease takes the **4–01** form of a revision of the rent reserved to a sum equivalent to the amount for which the premises were originally let. This will normally be the market rent, although it is now commonly more closely defined. This is the type of review clause dealt with in this chapter. The rent reserved by a head lease can be subject to a review designed to maintain its relationship to the sublease rents. To ensure that the rent remains the same proportion of the rack rental value of the premises, the clause must deal with the possibility of all or part of them not being sub-let (*British Railways Board v Elgar House Ltd* [1969] E.G.D. 235).

Rent reviews under farm business tenancies are governed by statute. They are dealt with separately at the end of this chapter.

(a) Construction

A rent review clause is construed like any other contractual pro- **4–02** vision. If there is no ambiguity its clear terms will be applied. Where a clause is not clear, there is a move towards purposive interpretation, as in *British Gas Corporation v Universities Superannuation Scheme Ltd* [1986] 1 W.L.R. 398 at 401 *per* Browne-Wilkinson V.C.:

> ... the general purpose of a provision for rent review is to enable the landlord to obtain from time to time the market rental the premises would command if let on the same terms on the open market at the review dates. The purpose is to reflect the changes in the value of money and real increases in the value of property during a long term ... the lease should be construed so as to give effect to the basic purpose of the rent review clause and

not to confer on the landlord a windfall benefit which he could never obtain on the market.

These principles have been said to produce 'a presumption of reality' (*Co-operative Wholesale Society Ltd v National Westminster Bank plc* [1995] 1 E.G.L.R. 97 at 99 *per* Hoffman LJ).

(b) Rectification

4-03   Rectification is available both to include a rent review in a lease which lacks one (*Central & Metropolitan Estates Ltd v Compusave* (1982) 266 E.G. 900), and to insert part of the clause, *e.g.* a provision for arbitration, which was accidentally omitted (*Thomas Bates & Son Ltd v Wyndham's (Lingerie) Ltd* [1981] 1 W.L.R. 505). There is no presumption that a commercial lease should contain a rent review clause (*Philpots (Woking) Ltd v Surrey Conveyancers Ltd* [1986] 1 E.G.L.R. 97), so the normal prerequisites for rectification are needed: a preliminary agreement not properly reflected in the final lease, and entitlement to equitable relief. An original landlord's successor in title has successfully claimed to rectify a rent review clause which gave the wrong interval between reviews (*Boots the Chemist Ltd v Street* (1983) 268 E.G. 817).

(c) Form of new rent

The only form of new rent which the normal rent review clause allows to be determined is a fixed money rental. Even though the review pattern laid down by the lease does not conform to modern practice, this cannot be altered unless the lease expressly gives authority (*National Westminster Bank Ltd v BSC Footwear Ltd* (1981) 42 P. & C.R. 90). How far unusually infrequent rent reviews increase the new rent is uncertain. Suggestions that they may not do so (*Lear v Blizzard* [1983] 3 All E.R. 662) have been widely doubted.

Similarly, a differential rent—increasing on the happening of a pre-determined event—cannot result from a rent review (*Clarke v Findon Developments Ltd* (1983) 270 E.G. 426).

2 Procedure

(a) Trigger notice

4-04   Most rent review clauses specify that the procedure should be triggered by a notice served by the landlord, or sometimes by either party. Some clauses do not require service of a notice, but in practice one party must necessarily take some action if the procedure is to be activated. A notice triggering a rent review must be unequivocal. One inappropriately marked 'without prejudice' was ineffective (*Norwich Union Life Insurance Society v Tony Waller Ltd* (1984) 128 S.J. 300).

Some rent review clauses require the landlord to suggest a new rent in his trigger notice, and make that the new rent if the tenant does not serve a counter-notice, refer the matter to arbitration or do whatever else is specified, within a strict time limit. A landlord's notice omitting a new rent figure which it should have contained is effective to initiate the review (*Dean and Chapter of Chichester Cathedral v Lennards Ltd* (1977) 35 P. & C.R. 309). The figure quoted does not have to be a bona fide estimate of the correct new rent (*Amalgamated Estates Ltd v Joystretch Manufacturing Ltd* (1980) 257 E.G. 489). So, if the tenant does not challenge it in the required manner within the time limit, the landlord's proposal becomes the contractual rent.

(b) Time limits

The general rule is that time is not of the essence for the pur- **4-05**
poses of triggering or operating a rent review (*United Scientific Holdings Ltd v Burnley Borough Council* [1978] A.C. 904). This means that no delay on the landlord's part prejudices his chance of a review (*Amherst v James Walker Goldsmith & Silversmith Ltd (No. 2)* [1983] Ch. 305). However, time can be made of the essence either for starting the rent review, or for all or some of the other parts of the procedure. As the question whether time is of the essence is a matter of substance not form, it is not material where in the lease the timetable is set out (*Pembroke St Georges Ltd v Cromwell Developments Ltd* [1991] 2 E.G.L.R. 129). When time is of the essence for claiming a review, the court will not intervene to impose a review when the notice was served out of time (*Weller v Akehurst* [1981] 3 All E.R. 411).

Time can be of the essence in these circumstances: **4-06**

(i) When the lease expressly states that it is;
(ii) When the language of the clause imposing the time limit is sufficiently firm. It is not clear just what wording will satisfy this test (*Touche Ross & Co v Secretary of State for the Environment* (1983) 46 P. & C.R. 187: '...but in any event not later than three months after ...' did not make time of the essence). A precise procedural timetable stating what happens if it is not adhered to can make time of the essence (*Henry Smith's Charity Trustees v AWADA Trading & Promotion Services Ltd* (1984) 47 P. & C.R. 607), so can a clause stating that the old rent continues unless by a certain date a new one is agreed or it is referred

to arbitration (*Greenhaven Securities Ltd v Compton* [1985] 2 E.G.L.R. 117);

(iii) Where connected wording in the lease makes it clear. For example, in the absence of a tenant's counter-notice, the landlord's proposal 'conclusively fixes' the rent (*Mammoth Greetings Cards Ltd v Agra Ltd* [1990] 2 E.G.L.R. 124); where written notice a specified time in advance was 'a condition of precedent' (*Chelsea Building Society v R&A Millett (Shops) Ltd* [1994] 1 E.G.L.R. 148);

(iv) When another clause in the lease means it must necessarily be so. A tenant's option to terminate, exercisable at the review date, will normally have this effect (*Al Saloom v Shirley James Travel Services Ltd* (1981) 42 P. & C.R. 181);

(v) When a time limit has passed, and one party gives notice to the other who should have taken action, giving a reasonable final period for compliance. But the tenant does not make time of the essence by serving notice to require the landlord to go to arbitration when he could himself have gone (*Factory Holdings Group Ltd v Leboff International Ltd* [1987] 1 E.G.L.R. 135).

4–07 A time limit for applying for the appointment of an arbitrator can be extended by the court (Arbitration Act 1950, s.27), whether the application should have been made by one party or could have been made by either (*Pittalis v Sherefettin* [1986] Q.B. 868). This power is not commonly exercised, although a tenant might be successful in a case where a landlord's proposed rent would otherwise take effect, because avoiding arbitration could present the landlord with an unwarranted windfall (*Chartered Trust plc v Maylands Green Estate Co Ltd* (1984) 270 E.G. 845). The court has no power to extend the time for applying for the appointment of an independent expert (*Fordgate Bingley Ltd v Argyll Stores Ltd* [1994] 2 E.G.L.R. 84).

To avoid missing the time limit, without incurring unnecessary expense on arbitration when negotiations are continuing, a practice has grown up of applying for the appointment of an arbitrator but asking that it should not be acted upon until further notice. A so-called 'in time only' application, not accompanied by the fee charged for making an appointment, was held to be effective to avoid missing the time limit (*Staines Warehousing Co Ltd v Montagu Executor & Trustee Co Ltd* (1987) 54 P. & C.R. 302).

(c) Disputes

4–08 Every rent review clause must provide some machinery which finally and conclusively settles the amount of the new rent in the event of failure to agree, because only in that way can it be rendered certain. This is normally achieved by providing for determination by an independent third party, by arbitration or expert valuation. If arbitration is used, it will be governed by the Arbitration Acts. They provide for an appeal to the courts in certain circumstances, and give the arbitrator the power to award interest on outstanding sums unless the lease withdraws that power (Arbitration Act 1950, s.19A). Interest from the date of the award runs at the rate payable on judgment debts (s.20). An arbitrator cannot be sued for negligence. An expert, by contrast, can be sued for negligence (except, possibly, if he gives reasons for his decision: *Burgess v Purchase & Son (Farms) Ltd* [1983] Ch. 216), although to show negligence one must go further than simply showing that another valuer would have come to a different conclusion (*Zubaida v Hargreaves* [1995] 1 E.G.L.R. 127). There is no appeal to the court from an expert's decision, although the courts will intervene in cases of fraud, mistake and miscarriage (*Dean v Prince* [1954] 1 Ch. 409 at 426 *per* Denning L.J.).

Normally the rent review clause provides that if the parties do   **4–09**
not agree on who should act as arbitrator or expert, he should be nominated by a third party, *e.g.* the President of the Royal Institution of Chartered Surveyors. If an upward and downward review only gives the landlord the right to apply for the appointment of a third party, the court will oblige him to apply if the tenant wants to operate the review (*Royal Bank of Scotland plc v Jennings* [1995] 2 E.G.L.R. 87). An alternative is for each party to nominate an arbitrator, and for those arbitrators to appoint an umpire. If, in that type of case, one party declines to name his arbitrator, the court will intervene (*Sudbrook Trading Estate Ltd v Eggleton* [1983] A.C. 444).

The generally accepted view is that a rent review clause can specify whether disputes are to be settled by an arbitrator or an expert, or may even give one party the right to choose when the dispute arises. This has received some support (*Langham House Developments Ltd v Brompton Securities Ltd* (1980) 256 E.G. 719; *Safeway Food Stores Ltd v Banderway Ltd* (1983) 267 E.G. 850). However, it is considered that this is contrary to established authority. Third parties appointed as experts can in fact be arbitrators (*Arenson v Casson Beckman Rutley & Co* [1977] A.C. 405 at 424 *per* Lord Simon). The determining factor is whether the third parties are settling a dispute, which is arbitration, or merely fixing the level of a rent which has not been agreed, which is the work of an expert.

(d) Evidence

4–10   The nature of the evidence considered by an arbitrator or an expert must necessarily depend on the nature of the case. An expert is not obliged to receive representations from the parties, unless the lease expressly stipulates that he should. Evidence normally consists of 'comparables', *i.e.* current rents agreed for other premises. An earlier arbitrator's award cannot be used as evidence in a later arbitration (*Land Securities plc v Westminster City Council* [1993] 4 All E.R. 124), and an arbitrator cannot take account of his own information, effectively giving evidence to himself (*Segama NV v Penny le Roy Ltd* (1983) 269 E.G. 322).

An expert is appointed so that he may exercise his expertise, and he may do so to supplement the evidence. This means that he may make an award which is higher than the landlord's asking rent, at least where the tenant has made no representations (*Rajdev v Becketts* [1989] 2 E.G.L.R. 144). An arbitrator may also be entitled to use his own expertise, at least where the lease stipulates that he should be drawn from a class with professional expertise. However, even an expert is not entitled to conduct research into the particular case, without the knowledge of the parties, and rely on the results (*Top Shop Estates Ltd v Danino* [1985] 1 E.G.L.R. 9).

(e) Appeals

4–11   There is an appeal to the High Court from an arbitrator's award on questions of law, either with the consent of the parties or leave of the court (Arbitration Act 1979, s.1(3)). The court will not give leave unless the outcome will substantially affect the parties' rights (s.1(4)). For this reason, it has been refused where the amount at issue was small (*Duvan Estates Ltd v Rossette Sunshine Savouries Ltd* (1981) 261 E.G. 364). However, the criteria for granting leave in rent review cases are less restrictive than in other cases. Leave will be granted if there is real doubt that the arbitrator was wrong in law and if the decision is likely to affect the future relationship between the parties, particularly in the determination of future reviews (*Lucas Industries plc v Welsh Development Agency* [1986] Ch. 500; *Ipswich Borough Council v Fisons plc* [1990] Ch. 709).

Preliminary points of law can be referred to the court, with the consent of the arbitrator or of all the parties (Arbitration Act 1979, s.2(1)). The court is reluctant to assume the role of arbitrator on valuation questions, and so is unlikely to give leave in rent review cases (*Chapman v Charlewood Alliance Properties Ltd* [1981] 260 E.G. 1041).

3 Amount of new rent

(a) Definition
    Normally a rent review clause defines with some care the **4-12**
formula by which the new rent is to be fixed. Nevertheless, in a case
where the lease gave no guidance, the review clause was not void;
rather the arbitrator had an unfettered discretion (*Store Property
and General Investments Ltd v Darrington (Rustington) Ltd* (1978),
unreported).
    Decided cases give some guidance on the interpretation of some
expressions commonly found in formulae defining the new rent:

(i)   *'market rent'*: The rent fixed on the grant of a new lease
under the Landlord and Tenant Act 1954, but not ignoring the factors which the Act requires to be disregarded
(*Brown v Gould* [1972] Ch. 53);

(ii)   *'rack rent'*: The full rent (*London Corporation v Cusack-
Smith* [1955] A.C. 337), but restricted by any rent control
legislation (*Newman v Dorrington Developments Ltd*
[1975] 1 W.L.R. 1642). *'Fair rack rent'* ignored the effect of
temporary restrictions on raising rents (*Compton Group
Ltd v Estates Gazette Ltd* (1979) 43 P. & C.R. 336);

(iii)   *'reasonable rent'*: Rent which is reasonable between the
parties, and may therefore take into account subjective
factors (*Thomas Bates & Son Ltd v Wyndham's (Lingerie)
Ltd* [1981] 1 W.L.R. 505);

(iv)   *'rent which a willing tenant would pay a willing landlord'*: A
market rent not influenced by any subjective factors
affecting the actual parties, and making the assumption
that there is a market for the premises (*F R Evans (Leeds)
Ltd v English Electric Co Ltd* (1977) 36 P. & C.R. 185).

(b) Assumptions
    A lease can validly require that specified assumptions be made **4-13**
in fixing the new rent, although in the absence of clear words the
'presumption of reality' is likely to be applied.
    If a lease says nothing expressly, there are certain assumptions
which decided cases direct should be made:

(i)   *Date*: The new rent will normally be assessed as at the rent
review date (*Glofield Properties Ltd v Morley (No.2)*
(1990) 59 P. & C.R. 14);

(ii)   *Vacant possession*: Rent is assessed on the assumption that
the premises are being let with vacant possession;

(iii)   *Term*: Rent will normally be assessed for a term equal in

CONTENTS OF LEASES

length to the remainder of the term the lease granted (*Norwich Union Life Insurance Society v Trustee Savings Bank Central Board* [1986] 1 E.G.L.R. 136). The likelihood of the lease being renewed under the Landlord and Tenant Act 1954 is to be taken into account (*Pivot Properties Ltd v Secretary of State for the Environment* (1980) 41 P. & C.R. 248);

(iv) *User*: If the lease directs that authority to use the premises for a particular purpose is to be assumed, the grant of planning consent is also to be assumed (*Bovis Group Pension Fund Ltd v G C Flooring & Furnishing Ltd* (1984) 269 E.G. 1252). An assumption that premises are 'available for use' for a certain purpose does not mean that one must also assume that the physical adaptation which would be required has been carried out (*Trusthouse Forte Albany Hotels Ltd v Daejan Investments Ltd* (1980) 256 E.G. 915);

(v) *Repairs*: Any decrease in rent resulting from the tenant's failure to comply with his repairing obligations in the lease is to be ignored (*Harmsworth Pension Funds Trustee Ltd v Charrington Industrial Holdings* (1985) 49 P. & C.R. 297);

(vi) *Improvements*: Premises must be valued as they stand, including any improvements which may have been paid for by the tenant, in the absence of any special provision in the rent review clause (*Ponsford v H M S Aerosols Ltd* [1979] A.C. 63);

(vii) *Sub-letting*: The new rent is on the basis that the premises are let as a whole, and disregards the possibility of a higher return from letting a number of smaller units (*F R Evans (Leeds) Ltd v English Electric Co Ltd* (1977) 36 P. & C.R. 185). If the premises are so large that they will inevitably be let to an investor to sub-let, the investor's profit is taken into account (*Royal Exchange Assurance v Bryant Samuel Properties (Coventry) Ltd* [1985] 1 E.G.L.R. 84).

4 Effect of review

(a) New rent

4-14 The date from which the new rent takes effect is a matter of contract to be determined from the lease. Most leases make the new rent date back to the review date, even if not agreed or determined until later, and this is effective (*C H Bailey Ltd v Memorial Enterprises Ltd* [1974] 1 W.L.R. 728). That is how the amount due is calculated; it does not affect when payment has to be made. In the absence of any special provision, the first payment at the new rate, and any arrears, are due on the first rent day after the arbitrator's award is published (*South Tottenham Land Securities Ltd v R & A Millett (Shops) Ltd* [1984] 1 W.L.R. 710).

Whether or not VAT is charged on the new rent does not depend on the terms of the rent review clause, but rather on the answer to the general question whether it is payable on rent under that lease. The function of a rent review clause is merely to quantify the rent reserved from the review date so that it does not affect the tax status of that rent.

(b) Parties bound

When the lease has changed hands while the rent is being reviewed, and the new rent dates back to before the assignment, it is the liability of the tenant for the time being (*Parry v Robinson-Wyllie Ltd* (1987) 54 P. & C.R. 187). But it can go further than that. A new rent determined under a rent review clause is a quantification of the rent reserved by the lease for the period in question. This means that, in the case of an old tenancy, that determination is binding on the original tenant who is liable to the landlord by privity of contract (*Centrovincial Estates plc v Bulk Storage Ltd* (1983) 46 P. & C.R. 393). A former tenant may also become liable under the terms of an authorised guarantee agreement.

Similarly, a guarantor of the tenant's obligations underwrites the rent at the new rate, even though he had no part in fixing it.

To the extent that an increased new rent includes an element reflecting the effect of a variation in the lease terms made after the former tenant parted with the property, that part of the new rent is not recoverable from the former tenant (Landlord and Tenant (Covenants) Act 1995, s.18).

(c) Surrender

If the lease is surrendered after a review date has passed, but before the new rent has been determined, the review can continue to determine the amount of the liability of the tenant or his guarantor for the period until the surrender (*Torminster Properties Ltd v Green* [1983] 1 W.L.R. 676).

5 Farms

Rent payable under a farm business tenancy can normally be reviewed every three years. However, this is not the case if the lease expressly states that the rent is not to be reviewed. Nor does it

4–15

4–16

apply where the tenancy terms are that at one or more specified times the rent is to vary in one of two ways. Either it is to change by or to a specified amount, or in accordance with a formula which does not give anyone a discretion and which does not preclude a rent reduction, but otherwise the rent is to stay fixed (Agricultural Tenancies Act 1995, s.9).

(a) Procedure

A statutory review of the rent reserved by a farm business tenancy is triggered by a notice given by either party to the other. This specifies a review date and requires that the rent payable from the review date is referred to arbitration (Agricultural Tenancies Act 1995, s.10).

The review date must be at least 12 months, but no more than 24 months, after the date the notice is given. The parties may have agreed the review date(s) in writing; if not they will be the third anniversary of the start of the tenancy or an anniversary three years after the previous review took effect.

4–17   The parties are at liberty, by agreement after the trigger notice is given, to refer the rent to an arbitrator or independent expert of their choice. If they have not done so by six months before the review date, either party may apply to the President of the Royal Institution of Chartered Surveyors for him to appoint an arbitrator (s.12).

(b) New rent

4–18   The statutory review is upward or downward. The new rent is to be the rent 'properly payable' in respect of the property on the review date. This means the rent at which it 'might reasonably be expected to be let on the open market by a willing landlord to a willing tenant, taking into account ... all relevant factors, including (in every case) the terms of the tenancy', including any term fixing the review date(s) but excluding any prescribing criteria by which the new rent is to be determined (Agricultural Tenancies Act 1995, s.13).

Certain matters are to be disregarded:

(i)   the rental value of any tenant's improvement, except where the tenant was obliged to do the work, or to the extent that he had been given a benefit or compensated for it;

(ii)   any effect on rent of the fact that the tenant is in occupation;

(iii) any reduction in rent by reason of dilapidations, deterioration or damage to buildings or land caused or permitted by the tenant.

Chapter 5

User

1 Generally

It is now normal for leases of commercial and industrial premises 5–01
to place some restriction on the use to which they are put. If there
is no such restriction, the tenant may make whatever use of them
he chooses, so long as he complies with the provisions of the law
(*Yelloly v Morley* (1910) 27 T.L.R. 20). The use to which a commonhold unit may be put can be restricted by the commonhold
community statement (Commonhold and Leasehold Reform Act
2002, ss.14(1), 18).

Restrictions in leases commonly take four forms: limitation to
a particular business, restriction against carrying on specified businesses leaving the tenant free to choose between the remainder,
prohibition against certain classes of trade defined in such terms
as 'offensive, noxious and dangerous', and a general proscription
of any action on the property causing a nuisance or annoyance
which would include carrying on certain trades.

A restriction may take the form of a covenant simply not to do 5–02
something specified, or an obligation not to allow others to do so
may be added. A simple covenant 'not to permit' a particular activity carries with it an obligation on the covenantor not to do it
himself (*Oceanic Village Ltd. v United Attractions Ltd* [2000] Ch.
234).

The tenant is also subject to restrictions, even though they are
not mentioned in the lease, which are related to the tenure of that
property or which are imposed by law of general application. In
the first category, the tenant is bound by enforceable restrictive
covenants affecting the freehold, of which he is either deemed to
have notice by reason of their registration, or, if they are not registrable (*e.g. Cleveland Petroleum Co Ltd v Dartstone Ltd* [1969] 1
W.L.R. 116), of which he has notice under the equitable rules. He

is also bound by the restrictive covenants in any head lease which extend to use by a subtenant, even though he has no knowledge of its contents (*Hill v Harris* [1965] 2 Q.B. 601).

The general provisions of the law include the prohibition of immoral user and the statutory control of use under the Town and Country Planning Acts.

Covenants in leases limiting the use to which the premises are put are not affected by the rule against perpetuities (*MacKenzie v Childers* (1889) 43 Ch. D 265).

2 Uses required or prohibited

(a) Limitation to specific use

5–03   The limitation of the use of premises to one or more specific uses is effected by a tenant's covenant. Normally, this is negative in form ('not to use the premises otherwise than for ...'). This is not of itself a warranty by the landlord that the tenant is entitled to do so (*Hill v Harris* [1965] 2 Q.B. 601).

A covenant prohibiting a particular trade prevents the tenant from carrying on part only of it, but if the tenant carries on a different business which incidentally overlaps with the prohibited one, that is not a breach (*A Lewis & Co (Westminster) Ltd v Bell Property Trust Ltd* [1940] Ch. 345). Such a covenant is construed restrictively, to place the minimum limitation on the tenant consistent with the words of the covenant (*Rother v Colchester Corporation* [1969] 1 W.L.R. 720: a case of a restriction on the landlord). Whether or not there is a new trade, or the same trade extended, may be a question of degree (*St Marylebone Property Co Ltd v Tesco Stores Ltd* [1988] 2 E.G.L.R. 40).

Leases sometimes define permitted uses by reference to a Town and Country Planning (Use Classes) Order; an express reference to the 1972 Order is not to be construed by reference to the 1987 Order which replaced it (*Brewers Company v Viewplan plc* [1989] 2 E.G.L.R. 133). A covenant restricting use to a single trade does not of itself prohibit residential use (*Levermore v Jobey* [1956] 1 W.L.R. 697).

The interpretation of the extent of a particular trade should be judged in accordance with the way the term used in the lease was understood when the lease was granted (*Texaco Antilles Ltd v Kernochan* [1973] A.C. 609), although minor extensions to the use which are analogous to the original one are permitted (*Wadham v Postmaster General* (1871) L.R. 6 Q.B. 644).

In some leases the restriction is to the tenant's particular business ('not to use the premises otherwise than as offices for the tenant's business of …'). This means the business as carried on by the tenant for the time being (*London Scottish Properties Ltd v Council of Professions Supplementary to Medicine* (1977), unreported). The permitted use does not extend to the business of a sub-tenant, except in the rare case that the sub-tenant carries on its immediate landlord's business (*e.g.* when a tenant sub-lets to its service company). So, a head lease containing a covenant in this form means that a landlord's licence to change the use will necessarily be required on sub-letting.

Even more restrictive, but still valid, is a covenant only to use   **5–04** the premises for the business of the original tenant, identified by name (*Law Land Co Ltd v Consumers' Association Ltd* (1980) 255 E.G. 617).

The simple tenant's covenant, 'not to use … ', does not affect the tenant with any liability if the subtenant uses the premises in some other way. To make the head tenant responsible for a sub-tenant's use of the premises, the tenant's covenant in the head lease must prohibit his 'permitting' or 'suffering' a use contrary to that specified. An act is 'permitted' by a tenant if he can, but does not, prevent it, and it is an act he could reasonably have foreseen might have been done (*Norton v Charles Deane Productions Ltd* [1970] E.G.D. 268 at 270). A tenant who serves preliminary notice to forfeit on a sub-tenant, on the ground of the latter's immoral use of its sub-let premises, but who takes no further action and continues to accept rent, 'permits' the immoral user (*GMS Syndicate Ltd v Gary Elliott Ltd* [1982] Ch. 1).

(b) Specific use required

Less usually, a lease may contain a positive tenant's covenant to   **5–06** use the premises for a specific purpose (*Wadham v Postmaster General* (1871) L.R. 6 Q.B. 644). A positive covenant is generally used to maintain the value of the premises let or neighbouring properties, particularly in retail developments. This type of covenant involves a number of problems: enforcement by mandatory injunction is possible (*Cooperative Insurance Society Ltd v Argyll Stores (Holdings) Ltd* [1998] A.C.1), but might be refused if the landlord is dilatory or would be adequately compensated by damages; the changing nature of trades may make performance difficult after a time; and the landlord's objective of maintaining value may not be achieved if the tenant trades reluctantly. Nevertheless, a landlord has been awarded damages where the value of his reversion was reduced by a breach of the tenant's covenant to trade (*Costain Property Developments Ltd v Finlay & Co Ltd* [1989] 1 E.G.L.R. 237).

(c) Offensive trades and nuisances

5–07   Prohibitions of classes of trades or businesses are commonly found in leases, by such classifications as 'offensive', 'noisy', 'noisome', 'noxious', 'dangerous', or some combination of these and other words. Each case involves the interpretation of the wording of the particular lease, so that although reported decisions can assist in deciding when there is a breach of covenant, caution is required. In construing covenants, it should be remembered that 'trade' only covers buying and selling and 'business' is a wider term.

There has been judicial interpretation of 'offensive', from which perhaps the most important conclusion is that (as in deciding whether an act is a nuisance) surrounding circumstances will affect whether a particular trade is offensive. 'The word "offensive" is, I think, to be construed relatively to the person contemplated as enjoying the benefit of the stipulation, that is to say, relative to such a person as would be the purchaser of such a plot upon such an estate as this estate is by the conditions and plans shown to be ... A man may be legitimately offended by an annoyance which does not amount to a legal nuisance' (*Nussey v Provincial Bill Posting Co and Eddison* [1909] 1 Ch. 734 at 739 *per* Cozens-Hardy M.R.).

5–08   Statutory definitions may also help, although they can only be of persuasive force in interpreting a lease which does not incorporate that definition (which would be unusual). Offensive trades for the purposes of the Public Health Act 1936 are (s.107): blood boiler, blood drier, bone boiler, fat extractor, fat melter, fellmonger, glue maker, gut scraper, rag and bone dealer, size maker, soap boiler, tallow melter and tripe boiler. The definition also extends to any other trade, business or manufacture previously declared to be offensive by an order of local application, with the exception that references in some of them to fish frying are cancelled.

The London Building Act 1930 defines dangerous businesses as the manufacture of matches and other substances liable to sudden explosion, inflammation or ignition, or of turpentine, naphtha, varnish, tar, resin, or Brunswick black or any other manufacture dangerous on account of the liability of substances employed therein to cause sudden fire or explosion.

It is also common to find in leases a prohibition against any activity on the demised premises which is or might become a nuisance (which may well be interpreted in the technical sense) or annoyance to neighbouring occupiers.

Examples may be given, with the caution that the circumstances of a particular case may vary the result. Lime burning is noisome (*Wiltshire v Cosslett* (1889) 5 T.L.R. 410). Selling fried fish may be offensive (*Duke of Devonshire v Brookshaw* (1899) 81 L.T. 83). A fencing academy over a professional office would be a nuisance (*Jenkins v Jackson* (1888) 40 Ch. D 71). Music from a restaurant can be a 'nuisance or annoyance' to the occupiers of flats above (*Hampstead & Suburban Properties Ltd v Diomedous* [1969] 1 Ch. 248). Go-kart racing caused noise which was a nuisance (*Tetley v Chitty* [1986] 1 All E.R. 663).

(d) Enforcement
A tenant's covenant as to user may be enforced in three ways: **5–09** by an injunction, by damages or by forfeiture. An injunction is normally granted without question to restrain the breach of a negative covenant—not to use the premises in a certain way— although the court will consider all the circumstances before exercising its discretion to grant an interlocutory injunction (*Harlow Development Corporation v Cox Bros (Butchers) Ltd* (1975) 119 S.J. 99). The landlord may opt for an injunction even though he may be entitled to forfeit.

To obtain damages, the landlord must show loss measurable in financial terms, otherwise they will be nominal (*Katzler v Campbell* [1972] E.G.D. 494). An alternative is for the lease to provide that additional rent be payable on breach of covenant (*Weston v Metropolitan Asylum District Managers* (1882) 9 Q.B.D. 404). This does not mean that a tenant prepared to pay the extra rent can simply ignore the terms of the covenant (*Bray v Fogarty* (1870) 4 Ir. Eq. 544).

(e) Sunday trading
A lease of retail premises may require the tenant to keep the shop open for business 'during normal business hours' or during hours decided in some way which does not require his consent. If the lease was granted before August 26, 1994 and not subsequently varied, a provision in that form does not require the tenant to open the shop on a Sunday, except in a case where Sunday trading would have been legal before that date (Sunday Trading Act 1994, s.3).

3 Change of use

(a) Landlord's consent
The lease may expressly require the landlord's consent before **5–10** the use of the premises is changed, but he may agree to vary the terms of the lease even if nothing is mentioned about variation. Consent may be implied from long acquiescence by the landlord. However, a tenant's covenant as to user is a continuing covenant.

A contravention is a recurring breach: the landlord's right to forfeit is not lost by accepting rent. If the lease requires specific formalities (*e.g.* a written licence), they must be complied with unless waived by the landlord, expressly or by acquiescence.

Even where there is no express restriction against the change of use that a tenant wishes to make, a landlord can restrain him where the proposals involve substantial structural alterations, on the ground that the tenant would be committing waste (*Lambert v F W Woolworth & Co Ltd* [1938] Ch. 883).

A prohibition against altering the user without the landlord's consent restricts the landlord's rights. If the change involves no structural alterations, no fine or similar sum may be charged, nor may the rent be increased (Landlord and Tenant Act 1927, s.19(3)). This applies notwithstanding any express condition to the contrary, but does not extend to farm business tenancies. The landlord may charge a reasonable sum for any damage to or diminution in the value of the premises, or any neighbouring premises of his, and legal and other expenses. A landlord who volunteers consent without being asked cannot thereby gain an advantage on a rent review (*C & A Pensions Trustees Ltd v British Vita Investments Ltd* (1984) 272 E.G. 63).

5–11   There is no statutory proviso that consent to change of user may not unreasonably be withheld. If such a proviso is written into the lease, the county court has jurisdiction to determine whether the landlord has been unreasonable and to make a declaration (Landlord and Tenant Act 1954, s.53). A landlord who seeks to withhold consent to gain an advantage he would not otherwise have had, acts unreasonably. But he is entitled to take account of the effect on other property which he owns (*Sportoffer Ltd v Erewash Borough Council* [1999] 3 E.G.L.R. 136). However, a refusal to consent to the use of premises being changed to a building society office, on the grounds that the value of nearby retail property would be halved, was held unreasonable when the previous use of the premises as an employment agency had already prejudiced the value (*Anglia Building Society v Sheffield City Council* (1982) 266 E.G. 311).

The test is not subjective—depending on what the landlord knows—but rather whether the refusal is objectively reasonable. So, a landlord who in good faith accepted hopelessly flawed professional advice and refused consent, acted unreasonably for this purpose (*Luminar Leisure Ltd v Apostole* [2001] 3 E.G.L.R. 23).

(b) Varying restrictions

5–12   The Lands Tribunal has jurisdiction to discharge or modify restrictions on the use of premises contained in certain long leases

(Law of Property Act 1925, s.84; Law of Property Act 1969, s.28). Its jurisdiction does not extend to varying positive covenants (*Westminster City Council v Duke of Westminster* [1991] 4 All E.R. 136). The lease must have been granted for at least forty years, of which at least twenty-five (calculated from the date of the lease in a case where the term is expressed to run from an earlier date: *Earl of Cadogan v Guinness* [1936] Ch. 515) must have expired. A restriction may be discharged or modified where the Tribunal is satisfied on one of the following grounds:

(i)   that it is obsolete, *i.e.* that its original purpose is no longer served (*Re Truman, Hanbury, Buxton & Co Ltd's Application* [1956] 1 Q.B. 261);

(ii)   that it impedes the reasonable user of land and either fails to secure to those entitled to benefit any practical benefits or is contrary to the public interest: planning considerations are to be taken into account here;

(iii)   that those of full age and capacity entitled to the benefit of it have agreed;

(iv)   that the proposed discharge or modification will not injure those entitled to the benefit of it.

Proceedings to enforce a restriction may be stayed to enable the defendants to apply to the Lands Tribunal for a discharge or modification (Law of Property Act 1925, s.84(9)), but this does not apply to forfeiture proceedings because they are not brought to enforce the covenant (*Iveagh v Harris* [1929] 2 Ch. 142).

(c) Planning control
'The making of any material change in the use of any buildings   **5–13**
or other land' is development for which planning permission is required (Town and Country Planning Act 1990, s.55(1)). The change must be 'material'. This will normally exclude alterations to the use of a subsidiary part of the premises, even if for planning purposes the new use is quite different from the main one, provided it is ancillary to the principal use.

As planning control is generally enforced against the occupier of premises, it is of concern to a tenant even though the terms of his lease may not prohibit his changing the use of the property. But an enforcement notice can also be served on the landlord (Town and Country Planning Act 1990, ss.172(6), 336(1)). Many modern leases contain a tenant's covenant to comply with the Planning Acts, so adding to the statutory enforcement procedures the sanction of forfeiture. The landlord should also reserve a right of entry to take steps to comply with an enforcement notice. In default, he may have to seek the authority of a magistrates' court order (Public Health Act 1936, s.289; Town and Country Planning Act 1990, s.178).

5–14   The lease may also contain a tenant's covenant not to carry out any development. This offers the landlord the additional advantage of being able to prevent the premises from losing an authorised use he considers valuable, even though the tenant obtains planning permission so that a change of use is legal. Another safeguard landlords may want is an indemnity against expenditure required by a planning consent that the tenant obtains but which is not incurred until after the lease terminates. For example, a tenant with a seven-year term may obtain permission to change the use and carry out ancillary works for the period of ten years and subject to the condition that the premises are reinstated at the end of that period. Without some contrary provision, this could give the tenant the right to carry on his chosen use, leaving the landlord with the obligation to reinstate. It appears that to abandon an authorised use and do nothing with the property is a material change of use (*Hartley v Minister of Housing and Local Government* [1970] 1 Q.B. 413).

The landlord under a farm business tenancy may become liable to compensate the tenant who obtains a planning permission for a change of use which has not been implemented when the tenancy ends (Agricultural Tenancies Act 1995, s.18). This applies to cases where the landlord gave written consent to the making of the application for permission.

4 Restraint of trade

5–15   It has been said on the authority of *Esso Petroleum Co Ltd v Harper's Garage (Stourport) Ltd* [1968] A.C. 269, that the doctrine of restraint of trade, which can make contractual obligations unenforceable, does not apply to leases. This would mean that the reasonableness or otherwise of restrictions on the use to which premises may be put cannot be called into question (as it can be, for instance, in the case of mortgages), and would therefore open the door to the 'tied house' type of restriction where the tenant is obliged to buy his stocks for resale exclusively from the landlord.

However, in *Amoco Australia Pty Ltd v Rocca Bros Motor Engineering Co Pty Ltd* [1975] A.C. 561, the Privy Council accepted that the doctrine does apply to leases. It is probably possible to sever parts of the lease which offend against the doctrine, and are therefore illegal, except where they go to the essence of the transaction.

Nevertheless, the doctrine of restraint of trade does not invalidate normal user covenants (*Alec Lobb (Garages) Ltd v Total Oil GB Ltd* [1983] 1 W.L.R. 87, 108), even, it is assumed, if for other reasons, *e.g.* planning control, the tenant cannot use the premises for the permitted purpose. Also, exceptionally, a covenant in restraint of trade is valid, if imposed to require compliance with regulations made in the public interest (*Young v Evans-Jones* [2002] 1 P. & C.R. 14).

5 Farms

One aim of the Agricultural Tenancies Act 1995 was to facilitate **5-16** the diversification of the use of tenanted farms. At the start of the lease the character of the tenancy must be primarily or wholly agricultural, and throughout the term at least part of the premises must be farmed as a business (to comply with the 'business conditions': (s.1). Nevertheless, part of a farm can be used for other purposes.

The tenant's user covenant should ensure that farming continues on part of the premises, but may otherwise reflect the bargain between the parties. The statutory restriction preventing the landlord charging for giving consent to a change of use which does not involve any structural alterations does not apply, but a lease provision could give the tenant similar protection. The tenant may be well advised to obtain the landlord's written consent to his applying for planning permission to change the use, even if the lease does not require him to do so. If the permission is granted but not implemented, the consent may entitle the tenant to compensation for an improvement when the tenancy ends.

6 Licences and registration

Many businesses cannot lawfully be conducted without an appro- **5-17** priate licence. In many other cases, registration of the premises is required. As between landlord and tenant, it will generally be the tenant whose direct concern this is, but he may need to ensure in the lease or agreement for it that the licence or benefit of any registration is transferred to him to enable him to trade. In some cases, the tenant is not concerned with the previous licence or registration as long as he makes his own application. The landlord will also have a real interest in ensuring compliance with the statutory requirements. If the premises are structurally adapted for, or planning consent is restricted to, use for a particular trade, the loss of the licence authorising that trade to be carried on there could seriously depreciate the value of the landlord's interest in the property. Even where another use were possible, the letting value for the alternative might be less.

It is suggested that the matter should be covered in the lease in two ways. First, a tenant's covenant can be included to obtain, maintain and renew as necessary the licence or registration, and to do nothing to prejudice its continuance or transfer or future grant to any other person. The appropriate terms will vary according to the statutory control applicable. Secondly, the tenant's covenant commonly found requiring compliance with all statutory requirements relating to the premises can usefully be extended to cover such requirements relating to the manner in which and the persons by whom the business is there conducted.

A list of requirements for licences or registration follows. Although extensive, it is not exhaustive. In particular, a number of local Acts impose licensing and registration obligations on certain trades in certain areas only. Those given are intended to be those where the obligations concern the premises rather than, or as well as, the person involved. So, for example, the case of the doctor, who must be a registered medical practitioner, but whose surgery does not have to be licensed or registered, is not included. However, there are borderline cases, where the obligation primarily attaches to the person but the licence or registration is authority to carry on business at a particular place. Some of these cases are included.

(a) Manufacture

5–18   *Prescribed processes*: Many processes are prescribed under the Environmental Protection Act 1990 as having the potential to pollute the environment. They include many heavy industrial processes. These processes may only be carried on if an authorisation has been obtained (s.6).

Explosives: A licence is required to manufacture gunpowder and other explosives (Explosives Act 1875). Factories with a limited output of fireworks require a small firework factory licence (1875 Act, amended by Fireworks Act 1951, s.7).

Upholstery materials: A licence is required by a manufacturer of rag flock and other upholstery materials, including wool, jute, hair, feathers, down, kapok and straw (Rag Flock and Other Filling Materials Act 1951, s.6). Premises on which those materials are used in stuffing or lining bedding, toys and baby carriages must be registered (s.2).

Whale oil: The owner of a factory used for treating whales must have a licence (Whaling Industry (Regulation) Act 1934, s.4).

(b) Storage and sale

Petrol: a licence is required for storing petroleum spirit **5–19** (Petroleum (Consolidation) Act 1928, s.1). This does not apply to the storage of petrol for motor vehicles either in the vehicle or in metal cans not exceeding two gallons capacity up to a total of 60 gallons in one place.

Scrap metal: A dealer in scrap metal is required to register with the local authority, specifying his place(s) of business (Scrap Metal Dealers Act 1964, s.1).

Gunpowder: Premises used for retailing gunpowder must be registered (Explosives Act 1875, s.21).

Firearms: Dealers in firearms (all lethal barrelled weapons firing shot, bullets or other missiles) must register with the police, furnishing particulars of all their places of business (Firearms Act 1968, s.33).

Upholstery materials: A licence must be obtained for storing, on premises for which a manufacturing licence has been granted, the upholstery materials to which manufacturing licences apply.

Pharmacies: Premises from which National Health Service pharmaceutical services are provided must, along with the person providing them, be included in a pharmaceutical list prepared by a Family Practitioner Committee (see the National Health Service (Pharmaceutical Services) Regulations 1992, reg.4).

Pet shops: See under Animals.

Sex shops: Sex shops must be licensed in areas where the local authority has so resolved (Local Government (Miscellaneous Provisions) Act 1982, Sch.3, para.6).

Intoxicating liquor: Premises where alcohol is sold by retail must **5–20** have a licence granted by the local authority. A members' club serving alcohol must have a certificate (Licensing Act 2003, ss.11, 60, 136).

Late night refreshment houses: Late night refreshment houses, *i.e.* premises kept open for public refreshment, resort and entertainment at any time between 10pm and 5am, but excluding premises licensed for the sale of intoxicating liquor, must be licensed annually (Late Night Refreshment Houses Act 1969, s.2). This does not include premises from which refreshments are served, but which the public does not enter, like a coffee stall (*Frank Bucknell & Son Ltd v London Borough of Croydon* [1973] 1 W.L.R. 534).

Game: A wholesale or retail dealer in game must have a licence from the local authority (Game Act 1831, s.18) and an excise licence (Game Licences Act 1860, s.14).

(c) Services

5–21   *Betting offices*: A licence is required to authorise the collection or payment of winnings on a bet on the premises, known when licensed as a betting office (Betting, Gaming and Lotteries Act 1963, s.9).

Tattooing, ear piercing and electrolysis: Premises in which a business of tattooing, ear piercing or electrolysis is carried on must be registered, if the local authority has decided that the provision applies to its area (Local Government (Miscellaneous Provisions) Act 1982, s.15).

Marriage: Civil marriages may be solemnised on private premises which have been approved (Marriage Act 1949, s.46A; Marriage Act 1994, s.1).

(d) Entertainment

Cinemas: Sex cinemas need a licence in an area where the local authority has resolved to apply the provision (Local Government (Miscellaneous Provisions) Act 1982, Sch.3, para.6).

Activity centres: Centres providing adventure activities wholly or partly for people under 18 must be licensed (Activity Centres (Young Persons' Safety) Act 1995, s.1).

Football grounds: Premises to which spectators are admitted to see designated football matches must be licensed by the Football Licensing Authority (Football Spectators Act 1989, s.10).

Public hypnotism demonstrations: Music and dancing licences may be issued subject to conditions regulating or prohibiting hypnotism demonstrations, and demonstrations must be authorised by the licensing authority when the public are admitted, whether or not they pay (Hypnotism Act 1952, ss.1, 2).

Gaming: Gaming establishments (*i.e.* where games of chance are played for winnings in money or money's worth) must be licensed (Gaming Act 1968, s.11). Clubs and miners' welfare institutes where there is gaming have to be registered.

(e) Welfare

5–22   *Nursing homes*: Private nursing homes and mental nursing homes must be registered (Registered Homes Act 1984, s.23). Residential homes for the disabled, for old people and for those needing care by reason of past or present drug or alcohol dependence or mental disorder also have to be registered (s.1). A home may have to be registered under both provisions.

Child minders and nurseries: Child minders and those providing day care for children under the age of eight must register, and as part of the registration the premises where they propose to offer those services must be approved (Children Act 1989, s.71).

Children's homes: A children's home as defined by statute must be registered (Children Act 1989, s.63). A home run by a voluntary organisation ('voluntary home') is in a different category, but must also be registered (s.60).

Agencies: Any of the following agencies must be registered with the National Care Standards Commission or the National Assembly for Wales: domiciliary care agency, independent medical agency, fostering agency, nurses agency, voluntary adoption agency (Care Standards Act 2000, s.11).

Independent schools: An independent school must be registered with the Department of Education and Skills or the National Assembly for Wales (Education Act 2002, s.158) and may also be a children's home (Education Act 1993, s.292).

Houses in multiple occupation: A house in multiple occupation must be registered with the local authority, if a registration scheme has been established for the area (Housing Act 1985, s.346; Housing Act 1996, s.65).

Anatomy: Premises used to carry out anatomical examinations (except for post mortems) and for keeping anatomical specimens have to be licensed under the Anatomy Act 1984 (s.3).

(f) Animals

Meat processing: Premises used as slaughterhouse, cutting premises, a cold store, a farmed game handling facility or a farmed game processing facility must be licensed (Fresh Meat (Hygiene and Inspection) Regulations 1995). **5–23**

Laying hens: An establishment in England where 350 or more hens are kept for producing eggs which are not intended for hatching must be registered with the Secretary of State (Registration of Establishments (Laying Hens) (England) Regulations 2003).

Knackers' yards: Premises for the slaughter of animals otherwise than for human consumption must be licensed (Slaughterhouses Act 1974, s.1).

Kennels: The keeper of a boarding establishment for dogs or cats must have a licence for it (Animal Boarding Establishments Act 1963, s.1), as must anyone housing guard dogs (Guard Dogs Act 1975, s.2(1)). Commercial dog breeding establishments need a licence (Breeding of Dogs Act 1973, s.1).

Pet shops: A licence must be obtained for any premises (including a shop, dwellinghouse, stall or barrow in a market) used for the business of selling animals as pets (Pet Animals Act 1951, s.1).

Stables: Anyone keeping an establishment where a business is carried on of keeping horses for being hired out to ride and/or giving instruction in riding must have a licence (Riding Establishments Act 1964, s.1).

Zoos: A zoo, defined as a place where wild animals are kept for public exhibition but not a circus or a pet shop, must be licensed (Zoo Licensing Act 1981, s.1).

Experimental establishments: Premises which are used for scientific experiments on animals, or for breeding animals for this purpose, must be certificated (Animals (Scientific Procedures) Act 1986, ss.6, 7).

7 Advertising

(a) Control by landlord

5–24   Lessee's covenants usually control the use for advertising of premises let for business purposes in order to preserve the character and appearance of the property. In the absence of any restriction, the tenant is free to display any advertisements he wishes, whether or not they relate to the business conducted on the premises (*Clapman v Edwards* [1938] 2 All E.R. 507). The restriction may be against all advertisements, except with the landlord's consent. This is not a case in which statute implies a proviso that consent shall not unreasonably be withheld.

Other covenants, not expressly mentioning advertising, may also affect the position. If the facts warrant it, the display of advertisements may be a breach of a covenant not to carry on any offensive trade or calling (*Nussey v Provincial Bill Posting Co and Eddison* [1909] 1 Ch. 734). Similarly, it has been held arguable that using premises for bill posting is in breach of a covenant not to carry on any but a specified trade (*Heard v Stuart* (1907) 24 T.L.R. 104). If bill posting arrangements are subcontracted, they may constitute a breach of a covenant against subletting or parting with possession.

On the other hand, in the absence of specific controls of notices and advertisements, authority to use the demised premises for a particular purpose must include being allowed to advertise in the manner customary in that business.

(b) Statutory control

5–25   The Town and Country Planning (Control of Advertisements) Regulations 1992, as amended, impose planning control on advertisements. In effect, all outside advertising is controlled, although some common types do not need express consent. Anyone displaying an advertisement in contravention of the regulations is subject to a fine up to £1,000 (standard scale, level 3) and £40 a day for a continuing offence (Town and Country Planning Act 1990, s.224(3)).

What is of particular concern to many landlords is that not only the occupier but also the owner of land is deemed to be displaying an advertisement which contravenes the Act. It is, however, a defence for the landlord to prove that the offending advertisement was displayed without his knowledge or consent. To assist in this defence if necessary, and to avoid the offence being committed at all, it is useful for the lease to contain a tenant's covenant not to contravene these regulations. The point can generally be covered by a general covenant requiring compliance with the Town and Country Planning Acts and regulations made under them.

There are eleven classes of advertisements that may be dis- **5–26** played without consent, subject to the intervention of the local planning authority who may serve a discontinuance notice against which there is an appeal to the Secretary of State for the Environment. Except as mentioned, advertisements displayed without express consent may not be illuminated, and the permitted size of the lettering is limited. In summary the classes are:

Class 1: Functional advertisements of local authorities, statutory undertakers and public transport undertakers. These advertisements may be illuminated as reasonably required for their purpose.

Class 2: *(a)* Advertisements, of up to 0.3sq m in area, for identification, direction or warning in respect of the land or buildings, where they are displayed.

(b) One advertisement, of up to 0.3sq m in an area, for each person, partnership or company separately carrying on a profession, trade or business in the premises. One additional such advertisement is allowed for each entrance, provided that the premises have entrances on more than one road frontage.

(c) One advertisement, of up to 1.2sq m in area, relating to religious, educational, cultural, recreational or medical premises where it is displayed, or to any hotel, public house or block of flats, and an extra one on a different road frontage where the premises front more than one road.

Advertisements of medical and similar services and supplies may be illuminated.

Class 3: Certain advertisements of a temporary nature, *e.g.* a single 'to let' board, or two joined boards, of limited area.

Class 4: Illuminated advertisements on business premises, subject to conditions about size and brightness of illumination.

Class 5: Advertisements on business premises (an expression **5–27** which here excludes the forecourt of a petrol filling station: *Heron Service Stations Ltd v Coupe* [1973] 1 W.L.R. 502) which comply with the following conditions:

(i) they relate to the business or activity carried on there, the goods sold or services provided there or the name and qualifications of the person carrying on the business or supplying the goods and services;

(ii) they are not displayed on the wall of a shop which has no shop window in it;

(iii) the top of them is not above the bottom of any first floor window in the wall on which they are displayed;

(iv) in an area of special control, they do not cover more than 0.1 of the area of external face of the building on which they are displayed between ground level and 3.6 metres high (4.6 metres high in other cases).

5–28   Again, advertisements of medical and similar services and supplies may be illuminated.

Class 6: Advertisements on the forecourts of business premises (which includes any fence or screen wall) up to a limit of 4.5sq m. A building with a forecourt on two or more frontages is treated as having a separate forecourt on each frontage. A petrol service station forecourt comes into this class, with its limit on the amount of advertising displayed, notwithstanding that the greater part of its business area is forecourt (*Blakemore v Heron Service Stations Ltd* (1971) 115 S.J. 248).

Class 7: Flags displaying only the name or device of the occupier of the building.

Class 8: Advertisements on hoardings enclosing building operations or land primarily allocated on any development plan for commercial, industrial or business purposes.

Class 9: Advertisements on highway structures.

Class 10: Advertisements for neighbourhood watch schemes.

Class 11: Directional advertisements for house and building sites.

Class 12: Advertisements within buildings.

Class 13: Sites used for the display of advertisements on April 1, 1974, and continuously since.

Class 14: Advertisements displayed continuously after the expiry of an express consent, unless that consent was subject to a condition to the contrary or a renewal of the express consent has been applied for and refused.

8 Residential use

(a) Excluding residential use

5–29   Because of the special rights given to residential tenants, leases of business premises often expressly forbid the use of any part of the property as a residence. Indeed, a conversion to residential use, even if not prohibited by the lessee's covenants as to user or the Planning Acts, may be a breach of covenant not to make alterations. The reverse, the conversion of a house into business premises, albeit accompanied by physical alterations to the property, has been held to be such a breach (*Bonnett v Sadler* (1808) 14 Ves. 526).

However, for a tenancy to become a regulated tenancy (under the Rent Act 1977) or an assured tenancy (under the Housing Act 1988), the premises must have been 'let *as* a separate dwelling'. The parties' stated intention, *e.g.* in defining the use to which the premises are to be put, is conclusive (*Wolfe v Hogan* [1949] 2 K.B. 194, 204), unless that is not their true intention (*Grosvenor (Mayfair) Estates v Amberton* (1983) 265 E.G. 693). A restrictive user covenant is therefore useful in establishing that the property is not to fall within the residential tenancy legislation. Nevertheless, the parties can vary the position by later agreement (*Court v Robinson* [1951] 2 K.B. 60), but the tenant cannot do so unilaterally (*Russell v Booker* (1982) 263 E.G. 513).

(b) Mixed use
Where the premises are let for mixed business and residential use, the question is which predominates (*Royal Life Saving Society v Page*; *Cheryl Investments Ltd v Saldhana* [1978] 1 W.L.R. 1329). The Landlord and Tenant Act 1954, Pt II, may apply.

A short letting of property put to residential use which is within premises is licensed under the Licensing Act 2003 for the supply of alcohol does not come within the various forms of statutory protection. It cannot be a regulated, secure or assured tenancy (Rent Act 1977, s.11; Housing Act 1985, Sch.1, para.9; Housing Act 1988, Sch.1, para.5.)

(c) Exclusively residential use
A subletting for residential purposes of part of premises let for business purposes is different. The subletting has to be considered on its own, and as a letting in its own right, and then appears as an exclusively residential tenancy. The Rent Act then applies just as it would if there were no association with business premises. **5–30**

If an employee is let into occupation of part of business premises for the purposes of the business (*e.g.* a caretaker), he will not usually be a tenant, but rather a service occupier (*Glasgow City Corporation v Johnstone* [1965] A.C. 609). A licence cannot be an assured tenancy, but if it was granted before January 15, 1989 and furniture was provided for the employee, it may constitute a restricted contract (Rent Act 1977, s.19, Pt V).

5–31   Tax advantages attach to a tenancy or licence is granted to an employee for the actual performance of his duties, although there only applies to directors if certain conditions apply. For this reason, it can be useful for the document to set out the circumstances expressly.

The employee does not pay income tax on the benefit represented by the accommodation in either of two cases: first, if it is necessary for the proper performance of his duties; and secondly, if it is provided for the better performance of the duties and it is customary in that kind of business for living accommodation to be provided (Income Tax (Earnings and Pensions) Act 2003, s.99). In addition, where the employee is not charged to income tax, the consideration on which stamp duty land tax is charged is restricted to the actual consideration paid, if any (Finance Act 2003, Sch.4, para.12(1)).

Chapter 6

Alterations and Improvements

1 Landlord's consent

Leases of business premises usually contain a tenant's covenant **6–01** restricting the right to alter the premises. The covenant may be against making an alteration which is an absolute prohibition (*Daejan Properties Ltd v Holmes* [1996] E.G.C.S. 185). Or, the covenant may be not to make alterations without the landlord's consent, which puts the tenant under a duty to give the landlord sufficient information to enable him to reach an informed conclusion (*Kalford Ltd v Peterborough City Council* [2001] 12 E.G.C.S. 150). In the case of a commonhold unit, the commonhold community statement may restrict the right to make alterations and improvements (Commonhold and Leasehold Reform Act 2002, ss.14(2), 18).

In the absence of a restriction in the lease or under the general law, and subject to any other relevant term in the lease (*e.g.* a repairing covenant), the tenant is free to do what he pleases to the premises, subject only to the law of waste which is founded on tort rather than contract. Waste includes any act altering the nature of the premises. Lessees for years and periodic tenants are liable for voluntary waste (positive acts tending to the destruction of the premises) and lessees for years only are also liable for permissive waste (omissions resulting in damage to the premises). On the other hand, ameliorating waste (acts which are technically waste, but which improve the premises) may be permitted without penalty: damages, an injunction and forfeiture may often be refused to the landlord. This does not, however, go as far as permitting major alterations in the nature of the premises.

2 Commercial and industrial premises

6-02   Various statutory provisions modify the landlord's right to control alterations made by the tenant of commercial and industrial premises, and the terms of the lease governing who pays for them.

(a) Consent unreasonably withheld
    If the covenant is qualified by such words as 'not without the landlord's consent', the landlord is not entitled unreasonably to withhold that consent to improvements (Landlord and Tenant Act 1927, s.19(2)). In considering reasonableness, the possibility of disturbance to the landlord is not a major factor (*Haines v Florensa* [1990] 1 E.G.L.R. 33). If the landlord's refusal of consent is challenged, the question is whether a reasonable person could have reached that decision, not whether objectively the alteration was reasonable (*Estates Governors of Alleyn's College of God's Gift v Williams* [1994] 1 E.G.L.R. 112).
    Improvements must be distinguished from alterations, which is a more general term. For this purpose, improvements have to be considered from the tenant's point of view, not from the landlord's. They need not necessarily increase the value of the premises, indeed the result may be the reverse, but they must alter the premises in such a way as to confer positive benefit on the tenant as occupier.

6-03   The landlord is entitled to impose certain conditions on giving consent. He may require payment of a reasonable sum in respect of damage or diminution of the value of the demised premises or any neighbouring premises owned by him. In the case of an improvement which does not add to the letting value of the premises, he may impose a condition that they be reinstated, where that would be reasonable. He may also require payment of legal and other expenses in connection with this licence. The statutory proviso, that the consent shall not unreasonably be withheld, cannot be excluded by agreement.
    Both the High Court and the county court can make a declaration that the landlord's consent is being unreasonably withheld (Landlord and Tenant Act 1954, s.53). The onus of proving that the landlord is being unreasonable is on the tenant, except where the landlord offers no explanation. In that case he must show that his refusal was reasonable.

(b) Improvements
6-04   The provisions enabling the tenant of business premises to claim compensation for improvements allows the tenant to apply to the court for authority to carry out the work. The tenant must serve

notice of his intention on the landlord, with a specification and plan of the proposed improvement. If the landlord serves notice of objection within three months the matter must be determined by the court; otherwise it is deemed to be authorised. If the lease was granted on or after December 10, 1953, contracting out of these provisions is not possible (Landlord and Tenant Act 1954, s.49). In earlier cases, they may be excluded by the contract if adequate consideration was given (Landlord and Tenant Act 1927, s.9).

Improvements covered by the Act include not only additions to existing buildings, but the erection of new buildings, and demolition and reconstruction, even if the reconstructed building is used for a different business (*National Electric Theatres Ltd v Hudgell* [1939] Ch. 553).

Improvements may be authorised by the court if it is satisfied:

(i)   that they are calculated to add to the letting value of the property at the end of the tenancy;

(ii)   that they are reasonable and suitable to the character of the premises (which includes considerations of amenity and convenience of the neighbourhood); and

(iii) that they will not diminish the value of any other property of the landlord, or of any superior landlord.

The court may not authorise an improvement if the landlord offers to make it himself in consideration of a reasonable rent increase, or of such an increase as the court determines.

(c) Facilities for the disabled
The terms of a lease of premises occupied by an employer or   **6–05**
trade organisation are effectively modified, if that is necessary to enable the tenant to fulfil his duty to ensure that the physical features of the premises do not put disabled people who use them at a substantial disadvantage. This applies where the lease forbids the tenant to make the necessary alterations, if conditions are attached when alterations are made or if the landlord is entitled to impose conditions when granting consent. In such a case, to the extent that the lease does not make express provision, it has effect as if (Disability Discrimination Act 1995, s.16):

(i)   the tenant may make the alteration with the landlord's written consent,

(ii)   the tenant must make written application for consent,

(iii) the landlord is not entitled to withhold consent unreasonably, and

(iv)   the landlord may impose reasonable conditions.

Similar provisions apply to leases of educational institutions (Disability Discrimination Act 1995, s.28W). The following are reasonable conditions for the landlord to impose: to obtain planning consent, to carry out the work in accordance with plans and specifications approved by the landlord, to afford the landlord facilities to inspect, to pay the cost of the landlord's consent (Disability Discrimination (Educational Institutions) (Alteration of Leasehold Premises) Regulations 2002).

(d) Factories

6–06   The tenant of a factory who finds himself unable because of a restriction in his lease to carry out a structural or other alteration needed to comply with the Factories Act 1961, or any regulation or order made under it, may apply for relief to the county court (s.169). The court has power to avoid or modify the terms of the lease in whatever way it considers just and equitable in the circumstances. The county court may also make an order apportioning the cost of such alterations, even in the not uncommon case where the lease provides that the tenant is to bear the whole of the cost of complying with statutory requirements (s.170). The terms of the lease are not conclusive, but merely among the circumstances that the court must consider in reaching its conclusion (*Monk v Arnold* [1902] 1 K.B. 761).

(e) Fire escape work and fire precautions

6–06   A tenant whose lease prevents him doing structural or other alterations required for providing a fire escape or fire precautions may apply to the county court to modify its terms. This applies where the premises let are factories, including electrical stations and installations, offices, shops and railway premises, and premises subject to special fire risks (Fire Precautions Act 1971, ss.9A, 28; Health and Safety at Work, etc. Act 1974, s.78; Fire Certificates (Special Premises) Regulations 1976, reg. 14). The court may modify the terms of the lease, and apportion the cost of the works, as is just and equitable.

Anyone who has paid expenses or fees under the London Building Acts (Amendment) Act 1939, Pt V (relating to providing means of escape in case of fire from buildings in inner London) or has paid the cost of works required thereunder, may apply to the county court for an apportionment of the cost (s.107). The court may summon all those with any estate or interest in the premises and make such apportionment as is just and equitable in the circumstances, having regard to the terms of the lease. The terms of the lease are not, however, decisive. The extent of the expenses that the parties contemplated when the lease was granted will be taken into account (*Duke of Bedford v University College Medical School* [1974] C.L.Y. 2063 (*cc*)). The whole of the expense may, in appropriate circumstances, be apportioned to the tenant (*Monro v Lord Burghclere* [1918] 1 K.B. 291).

(f) Clean air work
    Where works are reasonably necessary in or in connection with   **6–07**
a building to allow it to be used without contravening the Clean Air
Act 1993, the county court may by order give consent which is withheld by the landlord, and may on the tenant's application order the
landlord to bear some or all of the cost of the works (s.54).

(g) Places of entertainment
    A local authority may by notice require the provision of sani-
tary appliances in places of entertainment open to the public,
places where food is served to members of the public and betting
offices. A party on whom a notice is served may appeal to the
county court to apportion the cost of the work, but there is no
power to modify the terms of a lease (Local Government
(Miscellaneous Provisions) Act 1976, ss.20, 21).

3 Farms

(a) Tenant's improvements
    Statute defines 'tenant's improvements' for the purpose of a   **6–08**
farm business tenancy (Agricultural Tenancies Act 1995, s.15).
They fall into two categories.

(i)   *physical improvements* made on the holding by the tenant
      by his own effort or wholly or partly at his own expense;
(ii) *intangible advantages* which become attached to the
      holding and which the tenant obtains for the holding by his
      own effort or wholly or partly at his expense. This would
      cover an easement of which the benefit can be enjoyed by
      future owners or a planning permission of which a future
      occupier is entitled to take advantage.

There are two other statutory definitions which are relevant
(Agricultural Tenancies Act 1995, s.19(10)):
    Fixed equipment 'includes any building or structure affixed to
land and any works constructed on, in, over and under land, and
also includes anything grown on land for a purpose other than use
after severance from the land, consumption of the thing grown or
its produce, or amenity'.

A *routine improvement* means a physical improvement made in the normal course of farming, but not consisting of fixed equipment or improving fixed equipment. No improvement which the tenancy prohibits can be a routine improvement.

(b) Landlord's consent

6–09   A tenant under a farm business tenancy is only entitled to statutory compensation for an improvement to which the landlord has consented, and in this context the Act gives the tenant a right to go to arbitration if consent to a physical improvement (but not a planning application) is not given within two months or is made conditional on a variation in the tenancy terms. However, as the consent must be given before the improvement is made and compensation is not payable until the tenant quits, the machinery can be used to give the tenant authority to make the improvement whether or not he intends or expects ultimately to claim compensation.

Before the tenant starts work on an improvement, other than a routine improvement, he may challenge a refusal of consent or the imposition of an unacceptable condition by referring the matter to arbitration. An arbitrator is appointed by agreement or in default by the President of the Royal Institution of Chartered Surveyors on the application of either party (Agricultural Tenancies Act 1995, s.19). There is a time limit for the reference to arbitration: two months from the date of the landlord's refusal or conditional grant was given to the tenant, or, if the landlord does not respond, four months from his request for consent.

The question for the arbitrator is whether it is reasonable, having regard to the terms of the tenancy and any other relevant circumstances (including the parties' circumstances), for the tenant to make the improvement. The arbitrator may give unconditional approval or withhold approval, but may not impose a condition. If he withholds approval that does not prejudice any conditional consent which the landlord has already given.

4 Taxation

6–10   A landlord is liable to be taxed where a lease for no more than 50 years requires the tenant to improve the premises. The obligation is treated in the same way as the payment of a premium, and a proportion is taxed as rent (Income and Corporation Taxes Act 1988, s.34). Tax is charged on the amount of the notional premium less two per cent for every year by which the length of the lease term exceeds one. The sum taxed is the increase in the value of the landlord's interest in the premises, which may differ substantially from the amount which the tenant actually pays.

5 Effect on future rent

(a) Improvements by the tenant
A tenant who improves the premises will generally avoid the **6–11** penalty of having his new rent assessed on the value of the improvement when he subsequently exercises his right to renew his lease under the Landlord and Tenant Act 1954, unless he was under an obligation to his immediate landlord to do the work concerned (s.34; Law of Property Act 1969, s.1). The improvement is ignored if it was carried out at any time during the term of the lease which falls to be renewed. It is also ignored if it was effected during the twenty-one years preceding the application for a new tenancy, and ever since the time it was carried out the premises, or any part of them affected by the improvement, have been subject to a tenancy to which Pt II of the 1954 Act did or would have applied and the then tenant did not quit at the end of any of those tenancies. An applicant for a new tenancy obtains the benefit of improvements satisfying these conditions even if carried out by one of his predecessors in title as tenant.

This provision is clearly equitable where the tenant made the improvements at his own expense, and the rental terms had not taken this into consideration, as they would have done if the lease had imposed an obligation to do the work. The statutory words are, however, 'any improvement carried out by a person who at the time it was carried out was the tenant'. It seems at least possible that this includes improvements carried out by or at the direction of the tenant pursuant to some statutory obligation in circumstances where he was able to persuade the court to order that some or all of the cost should be paid by the landlord. Although this can hardly be the Act's intention, the obligation on the court assessing the new rent to ignore the improvements is mandatory. On the other hand, the various Acts which give the court power to apportion the expense of carrying out works to comply with statutory requirements all confer a discretion. A landlord who was able to show that he would probably be deprived of all benefit of those improvements (because the tenant would claim a new lease, so that the reversion would not fall into possession, and yet no expenditure by him would be reflected in future rentals), might escape any liability to contribute.

On a rent being reviewed under the terms of a rent review **6–12** clause, the wording of the lease determines whether or not improvements made by the tenant are ignored. It is possible to have a situation where certain work done by the tenant increases the rent payable as a result of a review, but is subsequently ignored in determining the rent payable on a new lease of the premises granted on a statutory renewal.

On a statutory review of rent payable under a farm business tenancy, the arbitrator disregards any increase in the rental value of the property which is due to a tenant's improvement (Agricultural Tenancies Act 1995, s.13(3)). There are three exceptional cases, where an increase is not ignored. They are:

(i)   where the terms of the tenancy, or a previous tenancy, obliged the tenant to do the work at or before the start of the tenancy;

(ii)   to the extent that the landlord made or gave the tenant any allowance or benefit in consideration of the improvement;

(iii) to the extent that the landlord has paid the tenant any compensation in respect of the improvement.

6–13   Where the tenant makes an improvement authorised under the Landlord and Tenant Act 1927 and the result is an increase in the amount of rates payable by the landlord or an increase in the fire insurance premium he has covenanted to pay, the rent rises by the amount of those increases (s.16). Similarly, a landlord who granted or agreed to grant a reversionary lease of business premises before December 22, 1927 also has certain rights to adjust the rent to be reserved if in the meantime he becomes liable to pay compensation for an improvement (Landlord and Tenant Act 1927, s.15).

(b) Improvements by the landlord
Where the tenant seeks authority under the Landlord and Tenant Act 1927 to carry out improvements, the landlord has the option to offer to do the works himself (s.3). He may offer to do so in consideration of a reasonable increase in the rent, or of such increase as the court may determine. If the tenant accepts the offer and the work is carried out, the increase in rent becomes payable as a matter of contract. However, if the tenant withdraws his notice that ends the landlord's right to make the improvement (*Norfolk Capital Group Ltd v Cadogan Estates Ltd* (2004) *The Times*, March 12).

6 Compensation: commercial and industrial premises

6–14   The Landlord and Tenant Act 1927 entitles the tenant of business premises to compensation, to be paid by the landlord at the end of the term, for authorised improvements which the tenant carries

out and which benefit the landlord. Contracts depriving the tenant of the statutory right are ineffective if made after February 8, 1927, unless, in the case of those made before December 10, 1953, adequate consideration was given (s.9; Landlord and Tenant Act 1954, s.49).
The compensation provisions bind the Crown when it is in the position of landlord (s.24(1)).

A landlord who offers to do the proposed improvement himself, in consideration of a reasonable rent increase, or such increase as the court determines, defeats any claim for compensation, unless he fails to carry out his undertaking (s.3(1) proviso). To execute the work, the landlord and any person authorised by him may enter the premises at all reasonable times (s.10).

(a) Qualifications for compensation
The following conditions must be satisfied if the right to com- **6–15** pensation is to apply:

(i)   the premises must be used wholly or partly for a trade or business, or, regularly, for a profession (s.17). Lettings to employees, or those holding offices under the landlord, for their period of employment or office are excluded. Such a tenancy, if created after March 24, 1927, must, in order to be excluded, be in writing and expressly state the purpose for which the tenancy is created. Where premises are also used for other than business purposes, improvements only count so far as they are improvements for the trade or business;

(ii)   the improvement must have been carried out by the claiming tenant or his predecessor in title. Improvements by sub-tenants are not included, unless the tenant has paid or is liable to pay compensation to a sub-tenant.

An improvement does not qualify if (s.2):

(i)   it was made before March 25, 1928;
(ii)   it was begun before October 1, 1954, and was made in pursuance of a statutory obligation (Landlord and Tenant Act 1954, s.48(1));
(iii)   the tenant, or his predecessor in title, was under an obligation to make it under a contract for valuable consideration (even a contract with a subtenant: *Owen Owen Estate Ltd v Livett* [1956] Ch. 1). An obligation to do work in a certain way, which is really a condition imposed if the tenant decides to do the work at all, does not preclude

compensation (*Godbold v Martin the Newsagents Ltd* (1983) 268 E.G. 1202).

(b) Obtaining authority

6–16   The first thing the tenant must do is to serve written notice on his immediate landlord of his intention to make the improvement, with a specification and plan showing the proposed improvement and the part of the premises affected by it (s.3). That plan can be an outline one, if supplemented later (*Deerfield Travel Services Ltd v Leathersellers Company* (1983) 46 P. & C.R. 132). Service may be personal, by leaving the notice at the addressee's last known place of abode in England or Wales, or by sending it by registered or recorded delivery post addressed to him there (s.23; Recorded Delivery Service Act 1962, s.1). The place of abode includes a business address (*Price v West London Building Society* [1964] 1 W.L.R. 616). In the case of a local or public authority or statutory or public utility company, it may be addressed to the secretary or other proper officer at the principal office. The landlord's agent can be served if duly authorised. Actual receipt of the notice will be good service, even if one of the specified methods has not been used (*Stylo Shoes Ltd v Prices Tailors Ltd* [1960] Ch. 396). A notice may also be served on a limited company by sending it to the company's registered office by ordinary post (Companies Act 1985, s.725 (1)), and a local authority may be served at an office that it designates for receiving such notices (Local Government Act 1972, s.231(1)).

6–17   Where the landlord is himself a tenant he can claim compensation when his own term expires. However, to do so he must serve on his landlord those documents which were served on him (s.8).

The landlord (or any superior landlord to whom the tenant's notice is in effect passed on) is entitled to object, except where the improvement is made pursuant to a statutory obligation, by serving notice on the tenant within three months. Service is in the same manner as prescribed for serving the landlord, except that there is no provision for serving the tenant's agent. If the tenant starts work prematurely, without waiting for the three months to elapse, he does not forfeit his compensation if, in the event, the landlord does not object (*Deerfield Travel Services Ltd v Leathersellers Company* (1983) 46 P. & C.R. 132). The tenant must apply to the court if he wishes to pursue the matter.

The court may certify, before the work is done (*Hogarth Health Club Ltd v Westbourne Investments Ltd* [1990] 1 E.G.L.R. 89), that the improvement is a proper one:

> (i)   after ascertaining that superior landlords have been notified and giving them a chance to be heard;

(ii) if satisfied that the improvement is of a nature calculated to add to the letting value of the premises at the end of the tenancy, is reasonable and suitable to the character of the premises and will not diminish the value of any other property belonging to the landlord or any superior landlord. The court must take into account any evidence that the improvement is calculated to injure the amenity or convenience of the neighbourhood;

(iii) after making such modifications to the specifications or plan as it thinks fit, or imposing any conditions it thinks reasonable.

The tenant may execute a proposed improvement where no notice of objection was served within three months of the tenant's notice, or where the court has certified the improvement to be a proper one.

(c) Confirmation of completion
The tenant can require the landlord to certify the due execution **6–18** of any improvement that the tenant was authorised to execute (s.3(6)). The advantage of this to the tenant is that disputes are avoided at the end of the tenancy when the compensation becomes payable. If the landlord refuses, the tenant may apply to the court for a certificate. Where the landlord gives a certificate, the tenant must pay his reasonable expenses.

(d) Claim for compensation
The tenant must serve on the landlord a written notice claiming compensation. Service is effected by one of the means authorised for notices of intention to make an improvement, or by any means which results in actual receipt. The notice must be served within strict time limits that cannot be extended (*Donegal Tweed Co Ltd v Stephenson* (1929) 98 L.J. (K.B.) 657). The limits vary according to the manner in which the tenancy is brought to an end, and are as follows (Landlord and Tenant Act 1954, s.47):

(i) if the tenancy is terminated by notice to quit: three months from the day on which the notice is given;

(ii) if the tenancy is one to which the Landlord and Tenant Act 1954, Pt II, applies and is terminated by a tenant's request for a new tenancy: three months from the date the landlord gives notice opposing the tenant's request, or three months from the last day on which he could have done if he fails to do so;

    (iii)   if the tenancy comes to an end by effluxion of time: during the period from six months before it terminates to three months before;

    (iv)   if an order for possession is made following forfeiture or re-entry: three months from the date the order becomes effective according to its terms, or when it ceases to be subject to appeal, whichever is the later;

    (v)   if the tenancy is terminated by re-entry without an order for possession: three months from the date of entry.

No compensation is payable to a tenant under a new lease of a flat granted under statutory provisions, which the landlord terminates for redevelopment (Leasehold Reform, Housing and Urban Development Act 1993, s.61, Sch.14, para.6).

(e) Amount and payment of compensation

6–19 The compensation the tenant receives may not exceed either (s.1):

    (i)   the net addition to the value of the property as a whole directly resulting from the improvement, *i.e.* the benefit less any detriment (*National Electric Theatres Ltd v Hudgell* [1939] Ch. 553, 561); or

    (ii)   the reasonable cost of carrying out the improvement at the termination of the tenancy, less the reasonable cost (if any) of putting the improvement into a reasonable state of repair, unless the latter cost is covered by the tenant's liability under a repairing covenant.

In determining the amount of the net addition to the value of the property, the use to which the premises are to be put after the tenancy ends must be considered. If they are to be demolished, or structural alterations are proposed, or the use is to be changed, the effect of this on the additional value attributable to the improvement has to be taken into account. The length of time before the proposed change is also relevant. The compensation is reduced to take into consideration any benefits the tenant, or his predecessor in title, received from the landlord, or his predecessors in title, expressly or impliedly in consideration of the improvement (s.2(3)).

6–20 If the parties do not agree, the amount of the compensation is determined by the court. In applying to the court, the tenant must state the amount he claims (*British & Colonial Furniture Co Ltd v William McIlroy Ltd* [1952] 1 K.B. 107). If no compensation is awarded, or if it is reduced, by reason of an intention to demolish, alter or change the use of the premises, the court may authorise the tenant to make a further application if the intention is not carried into effect within a time fixed by the court. Either party may set compensation and other sums due under the tenancy off against each other (s.11). The landlord may obtain an order from the Secretary of State charging the premises, or any part of them, with repayment to himself or his successors in title of sums paid by way of compensation or costs incurred in connection with it (Sch.1). An order is registrable as a land charge, class A (Land Charges Act 1972, s.2(2)). Compensation and costs incurred are capital payments when made by trustees (s.13).

7 Compensation: farms

When a tenant under a farm business tenancy who has made   **6–21**
tenant's improvements quits the property at the end of his tenancy, he is entitled to compensation from the landlord for any physical improvement which remains there and any intangible advantage which remains attached to the property (Agricultural Tenancies Act 1995, s.16).

(a) Qualifications
A tenant is entitled to compensation for a physical improvement if the landlord gave written consent, in the tenancy agreement or elsewhere, or an arbitrator approved (Agricultural Tenancies Act 1995, s.17). In the case of a planning permission, the tenant qualifies for compensation if the landlord gave written consent to making the application for a specified physical improvement or a specified change of use. When the tenancy ends, the permission must still remain to be implemented (s.18).

(b) Amount
The amount of compensation for an improvement other than a   **6–22**
planning permission is a sum equal to the increase in the value of the property at the end of the tenancy, as land comprised in a tenancy (Agricultural Tenancies Act 1995, s.20). In two cases, the compensation is reduced:

(i)   if, under a written agreement between the parties, the landlord gave or allowed the tenant a benefit in consideration of making the improvement, by the proportion that the value of the benefit bears to the total cost of the improvement;

(ii) if the tenant has received a grant from public funds for the improvement, or will do so, by the proportion that the grant bears to the total cost of the improvement.

The formula is necessarily different where the improvement consists of an unimplemented planning permission. Here, the amount of compensation is a sum equal to the increase in the value of the property at the end of the tenancy as land comprised in a tenancy, so far as that increase is attributable to the authorisation of the development which the landlord specified in his consent to making the application (Agricultural Tenancies Act 1995, s.21). The compensation is reduced if, under a written agreement between the parties, the landlord gave or allowed a benefit to the tenant in consideration of obtaining the permission. The compensation goes down by the proportion which the benefit bears to the total cost of obtaining permission.

(c) Claims

6–23   The tenant must give the landlord written notice of his intention to claim for compensation, and of the nature of the claim, within two months after the end of the tenancy (Agricultural Tenancies Act 1995, s.22).

The parties have until four months from the end of the tenancy to settle the claim by agreement in writing or to refer it to an agreed arbitrator. In default, either party may apply to the President of the Royal Institution of Chartered Surveyors for him to appoint an arbitrator.

Should the tenant lawfully remain in possession of any part of the property after the end of the farm business tenancy, the time for making and settling a compensation claim in relation to that part runs from the date occupation ends.

Chapter 7

Assignment and Subletting

1 Landlord's consent

A tenant is free to assign (*Keeves v Dean*; *Nunn v Pellegrini* [1924]   **7–01**
1 K.B. 685) or sub-let (*Leith Properties Ltd v Byrne* [1983] Q.B.
433), unless his power is restricted by his lease. In the case of a
commonhold unit, the commonhold community statement may
place a restriction on a tenant who wishes to sub-let, but cannot
prohibit or restrict his assigning (Commonhold and Leasehold
Reform Act 2002, ss.18, 20(1)).

(a) Forms of covenant
Restrictions are normally included in leases as tenants' covenants, and commonly take one of the following forms:

(i)   *Absolute prohibition*: An unqualified prohibition against,
      e.g. assigning, validly bars any such transaction. Naturally,
      it is still open to the tenant to seek consent and for the land-
      lord to give it, although there is no compulsion except in
      the case of racial or sex discrimination. Such a covenant is
      not void as in restraint of trade (*Alec Lobb (Garages) Ltd
      v Total Oil Great Britain Ltd* [1983] 1 W.L.R. 87).

(ii) *Qualified prohibition*: The tenant's covenant against dealing   **7–02**
      with the premises may be qualified in a number of ways. It
      may simply require the landlord's prior consent. In this
      case there is an implied proviso that consent shall not be
      unreasonably withheld, and, in the case of some building
      leases, it is not required at all (Landlord and Tenant Act
      1927, s.19(1)). Some leases expressly state that the land-
      lord's consent is not to be unreasonably withheld, and this
      has the same effect as the statutory proviso. Other leases are
      more precise. A provision that consent is not to be withheld

'in the case of a respectable and responsible person' limits the landlord to refusal on the ground that the proposed assignee or subtenant is not respectable or responsible. He may not refuse consent on any other ground, however reasonable (*Moat v Martin* [1950] 1 K.B. 175). 'Responsible' refers to the assignee's financial capacity in relation to the lease concerned (*Re Greater London Properties Ltd's Lease* [1959] 1 W.L.R. 503).

7–03 (iii) *Prohibition against dealing with part*: It is now common in leases of business premises to find a qualified prohibition against dealing with the demised premises as a whole, but an absolute prohibition against dealing with part only of them. This is perfectly valid. Apart from any estate management reasons, statutory rules give two grounds for landlords to require such terms. First, the Landlord and Tenant Act 1954 gives renewal rights to the occupier of the premises. Subdivision by sub-letting can result, when the head lease comes to an end, in the head landlord having to grant new leases to each occupier, at least where the premises have been wholly sub-let. He may well wish to avoid the additional expense and management problems that that is likely to entail. Secondly, if the premises sub-let are used exclusively for residential purposes, there could be an assured tenancy, in which event the tenant would have protection against the head landlord even after the head lease came to an end (Housing Act 1988, s.18(1)).

(iv) *Preliminary offer of surrender*: A covenant that requires the tenant to offer to surrender his lease to the landlord before obtaining a licence to assign or sub-let is valid at common law (*Bocardo SA v S & M Hotels Ltd* [1980] 1 W.L.R. 17). However, while the tenant has the protection of the Landlord and Tenant Act 1954, no agreement to surrender pursuant to the covenant is enforceable (s.38(1); *Allnatt London Properties Ltd v Newton* [1984] 1 All E.R. 423). The unsatisfactory result for business leases seems to be that the tenant is bound to make the surrender offer, but need not surrender even if the landlord accepts. Yet the landlord who does not accept cannot be obliged to consent to the assignment

(b) When required

7–04 A tenant's covenant concerning dealings with the premises is strictly construed against the landlord, in determining precisely what is prohibited or restricted.

A covenant not to assign is not broken by sub-letting (*Sweet &*

Maxwell Ltd v Universal News Services Ltd [1964] 2 Q.B. 699), and similarly a covenant not to assign part only of the premises is not contravened by a sub-letting of part (*Russell v Beecham* [1924] 1 K.B. 525). A covenant against assignment does not bar the grant of an exclusive licence (*Edwardes v Barrington* (1901) 85 L.T. 650), a declaration of trust of the premises in favour of a third party (*Gentle v Faulkner* [1900] 2 Q.B. 267), nor the deposit of the lease as security (*Ex p. Drake* (1841) 1 Mont. D. & De G. 539).

No consent is needed in the case of involuntary assignments: under compulsory purchase powers (*Slipper v Tottenham and Hampstead Junction Railway Co* (1867) L.R. 4 Eq 112); on bankruptcy (*Re Riggs Ex p. Lovell* [1901] 2 K.B. 16); or on death (*Seers v Hinds* (1791) 1 Ves. 294).

A covenant not to part with possession of the premises prohibits assignment (*Marks v Warren* [1979] 1 All E.R. 20), but goes wider. Granting an exclusive licence contravenes it (*Stening v Abrahams* [1931] 1 Ch. 470). It is broken by letting a proposed subtenant into possession, subject to obtaining the landlord's consent to sub-let which was refused (*Abrahams v MacFisheries Ltd* [1925] 2 K.B. 18). It is however possible after the sale of a business to a company for the company to use the premises while the lessee still retains possession so that there is no breach of covenant (*Chaplin v Smith* [1926] 1 K.B. 198).   **7–05**

Sharing the premises may sometimes be forbidden or restricted. The tenant shares with someone who operates a separate business from the tenant (*Mean Fiddler Holdings Ltd v Islington London Borough Council* [2003] 2 P. & C.R. 7 at [41] *per* Sir Christopher Staughton).

A covenant not to underlet is broken if the lessee merely parts with exclusive possession of the premises (*Richards v Davies* [1921] 1 Ch. 90). If the covenant does not mention sub-letting part only of the premises, that does not constitute a breach (*Cook v Shoesmith* [1951] 1 K.B. 752), unless the part concerned is the only part not previously sub-let, so that the final subletting means that the whole is then sub-let (*Chatterton v Terrell* [1923] A.C. 578). Where the lease unusually referred to letting the premises 'for the whole of the term', the covenant precluded assignment (*Greenaway v Adams* (1806) 12 Ves. 395).

2 Qualified prohibition: landlord's duties

The Landlord and Tenant Act 1988 imposes statutory duties on a landlord whose tenant makes a written application for consent to assign or sub-let if the lease contains a qualified prohibition   **7–06** (s.1(1)). The Act does not apply where the lease contains an absolute prohibition or, necessarily, if it contains no restriction at all. The duties are (ss. 1(3), 2):

(i)   to give consent within a reasonable time, unless it is reasonable not to. To justify withholding consent, the landlord can only rely on what he knew at the time he took the decision and not on anything which he learned later (*CIN Properties Ltd v Gill* [1993] 2 E.G.L.R. 97). But he does not have to justify those matters as facts (*Air India v Balabel* [1993] 2 E.G.L.R. 66);

(ii) to serve notice of his decision on the tenant within a reasonable time. The notice must specify any conditions to which the consent is subject, or give his reasons for refusal;

(iii) if he knows of anyone else whose consent may be needed, to take reasonable steps to secure that that other person receives the application or a copy of it. This will normally mean sending a copy of the application to, *e.g.* a superior lessor, but not if it is clear that the tenant has already applied directly.

The landlord's time for giving consent ends when he gives a decision on the tenant's request. So, if he unreasonably refuses it quickly when he could have taken longer he is in breach of duty. Subsequent correspondence with the tenant, during which he acts reasonably, does not change the position (*Go West Ltd v Spigarolo* [2003] Q.B.1140).

7–07   If the landlord and tenant under a new tenancy have made an agreement which, in specified circumstances, modifies the tenant's right to receive consent to an assignment, the landlord's statutory duty (i) under the 1988 Act (as stated above) does not apply in those circumstances. However, the statutory duties (ii) and (iii) continue to apply.

The 1988 Act gives a special meaning to withholding consent unreasonably in two ways. First, if the landlord gives consent but attaches an unreasonable condition, he has not fulfilled his duty to give consent when it is reasonable to do so (s.1(4)). Secondly, it can never be reasonable to withhold consent if the tenant could have completed the transaction without being in breach of covenant (s.1(5)), *i.e.* the landlord has a duty to give consent in these cases: where it would be reasonable under the general law rules; and in a circumstance in which the lease specifies he has no discretion, even though it might otherwise be reasonable for him to withhold it.

3 Other statutory intervention

(a) Unreasonable withholding

Any lease containing a covenant, condition or agreement   **7–08**
against underletting, charging or parting with possession of the
demised premises or any part of them, without consent or licence
is deemed to be subject to an implied proviso (Landlord and
Tenant Act 1927, s.19(1)(a)). This proviso is that the licence or
consent is not to be unreasonably withheld. This brings covenants
to which it applies into the qualified prohibition category.
When the proviso applies, the landlord may nevertheless charge
a reasonable sum for legal or other expenses he incurs.
Neither this, nor the following statutory proviso, can be
excluded or curtailed by agreement of the parties. Any provision
purporting to give the landlord additional discretion is void
(*Creery v Summersell and Flowerdew & Co Ltd* [1949] Ch. 751).

(b) Building leases

A further proviso is implied into certain building leases, *i.e.*   **7–09**
leases granted wholly or partly in consideration of the erection, or
the substantial improvement, addition or alteration of the buildings (Landlord and Tenant Act 1927, s.19(1)(b)). In this case, no
consent at all is required where the dealing takes place more than
seven years before the end of the term, but notice of it must be
given to the landlord within six months. This does not, however,
overrule a lease term which requires an assignee to covenant
directly with the landlord and to provide a guarantor (*Vaux Group
plc v Lilley* (1991) 61 P. & C.R. 446).
This applies, with three exceptions, to all building leases granted
for more than forty years. The exceptions are: first, where the landlord is a government department, local or public authority, or a
statutory or public utility company; secondly, mining leases; and
thirdly, assignments of new tenancies of commercial and industrial premises.

(c) Payment

A further proviso is implied into leases containing a qualified
prohibition against underletting or parting with consent (Law of
Property Act 1925, s.144). In the absence of express provision to
the contrary in the lease, no fine or sum of money in the nature of
a fine is payable for the licence or consent. This does not preclude
payment of a reasonable sum for legal or other expenses incurred.
Provisions in leases requiring payment are not usual, and to insist
on payment might constitute an unreasonable withholding of
consent.

This provision (before re-enactment) was held to preclude a landlord from demanding an increase in rent where he believed that the proposed assignment would reduce the value of the premises (*Jenkins v Price* [1907] 2 Ch. 229: appeal decided on other grounds).

(d) Racial and sex discrimination

7–10   It is unlawful for a landlord to withhold his consent to assign, underlet or grant a licence to occupy premises either on grounds of the colour, race, nationality or ethnic or national origins of the proposed assignee, sub-tenant or occupier (Race Relations Act 1976, s.24), or on the ground of his or her sex (Sex Discrimination Act 1975, s.31). These provisions apply 'where the licence or consent of the landlord ... is required'. It is submitted that this is not limited to cases of qualified prohibitions against dealings, where such consent is expressly mentioned. Where there is an absolute prohibition, it is just as true to say that before there is a dealing, the landlord's consent is needed. Accordingly, although normally where there is an absolute prohibition the landlord's discretion is totally unfettered, he may not now decline consent exclusively on one of these discriminatory grounds.

The only sanction for unlawful discrimination in withholding consent is an action in tort in the county court, in which the damages may include compensation for injury to feelings (see Sex Discrimination Act 1975, s.66; Race Relations Act 1976, s.57).

4 Form of consent

7–11   The landlord's consent need not be in writing, unless the lease so requires. The landlord may by his conduct waive the requirement of writing (*Millard v Humphreys* (1918) 62 S.J. 505). A letter written 'subject to contract' may constitute consent, because that term does not necessarily suspend the effect of a unilateral act (*Next plc v National Farmers Union Mutual Insurance Co Ltd* [1997] E.G.C.S. 181).

Increasingly, leases of business premises require the proposed assignee, and sometimes the proposed sub-tenant, to join in a deed of licence to covenant directly with the landlord, or head landlord, to comply with the terms of the lease. Such covenants are often made to extend for the whole of the remainder of the term of the lease, so that the assignee does not escape liability when he assigns further and (in the case of an old lease) privity of estate with the landlord ceases. The benefit to the landlord is therefore additional security for the performance of the tenant's covenants.

The validity of such a requirement is doubtful. Insistence upon it in the case of a sub-letting justifiably at a loss has been held an unreasonable refusal of consent (*Balfour v Kensington Gardens Mansions Ltd* (1932) 49 T.L.R. 29). On an assignment, the question whether it is reasonable to require a direct covenant from the assignee is still open for consideration (*ibid, per* Macnaghten J, at 31). The suggestion that such an assignee's covenant would constitute a fine in contravention of the statutory implied proviso did not receive majority support in the Court of Appeal (*Waite v Jennings* [1906] 2 K.B. 11). It is doubted whether a landlord can ever demand a direct covenant where the lease is silent on the point.

A direct covenant by an assignee of a new tenancy is not **7–12** effective to extend his liability under the covenants in the lease (Landlord and Tenant (Covenants) Act 1995, s.25). His responsibility can be made to continue during the ownership of the next assignee, but no longer, under an authorised guarantee agreement.

Licences can be granted conditionally (*e.g.* on completing specified works). Once the condition has been fulfilled the licence takes effect as if originally granted unconditionally (*Mitten v Fagg* (1978) 247 E.G. 901). However, a licence obtained by fraud can later be set aside on that ground (*Sanctuary Housing Association v Baker* [1988] 1 E.G.L.R. 42).

Licences commonly state expressly that they relate only to the one occasion to which they refer, and that the prohibition in the lease remains otherwise in full force and effect. This seems to be unnecessary (Law of Property Act 1925, s.143).

5 Assignor to obtain consent

It is for the assignor, or the lessee, to obtain any licence that the **7–13** lease requires for the contemplated dealing (*Davis v Nisbett* (1861) 10 C.B. (NS) 752). He is not bound to take legal proceedings to obtain it (*Lehmann v McArthur* (1868) 3 Ch. App. 496).

In a contract subject to the National Conditions of Sale (20th ed), the vendor undertook to use his best endeavours to obtain the licence and pay the fee for it (cond. 11(5)). The purchaser agreed to supply any information and references reasonably required of him. The sale was subject to the licence being obtained, and if it was not, the vendor could rescind the contract. The deposit was then repayable, but without interest, costs or other compensation or payment (cond. 10(2)). The vendor was under no obligation to allow the purchaser to approach a reluctant landlord directly (*Lipmans Wallpaper Ltd v Mason & Hodghton Ltd* [1969] 1 Ch. 20).

The provisions concerned with obtaining the landlord's consent to an assignment or sub-letting in the Standard Conditions of Sale (4th edition) (SCS) differ from those in the Standard Commercial Property Conditions (2nd edition) (SCPC), which are expressly intended to be more appropriate for sales of business premises (cond. 8.3). Both provide that the seller, or tenant intending to grant a sub-lease, should apply for consent at his own expense. The buyer, or intending sub-tenant, is to provide information and references. The SCPC go on to oblige the buyer, where the landlord requires, to covenant directly with the landlord to observe the lease covenants and to execute the licence. The consent must be in the form required by the lease. This overcomes the difficulty exposed in *Aubergine Enterprises Ltd v Lakewood International Ltd* [2002] 1 W.L.R. 2149, where a verbal consent was held to satisfy the contractual conditions even though the lease required written consent.

7–14   The conditions differ in the consequences they prescribe if no licence is granted before completion. Under the SCPC, the date for completion of the contract is postponed until five working days after the seller gives written notice that the licence had been granted, with a final date of four months after the original completion date. After that final date either party may rescind the contract unless consent has been given or the court has declared that consent has been unreasonably withheld (conds 10.35, 10.36). If the SCS apply to the contract, either party has the right to rescind provided he has complied with his obligations in connection with obtaining the consent. He may rescind if consent has not been given, or has been given subject to a condition to which he reasonably objects, by three working days before completion (cond. 8.3.3).

Even if the landlord unreasonably withholds consent, so that the tenant is entitled to assign without further reference to him, there is still a contractual right to rescind (*Bickel v Courtenay Investments (Nominees) Ltd* [1984] 1 All E.R. 657).

6 Unreasonable withholding

(a) Application for consent

7–15   The tenant is obliged to ask for the landlord's consent, however unreasonable it would be of him to withhold it (*Eastern Telegraph Co v Dent* [1899] 1 Q.B. 835). The landlord must then be given a reasonable time to consider the request (*Wilson v Fynn* [1948] 2 All E.R. 40). He is entitled to be given details of the proposed transaction, *e.g.* the precise use to which the assignee will put the premises (*Isow's Restaurants Ltd v Greenhaven (Piccadilly) Properties Ltd* [1970] E.G.D. 826), and to refuse consent in their absence.

(b) What is reasonable
   Whether a landlord's action in withholding consent to assign or underlet is reasonable is normally to be judged for the circumstances of each case. However, in certain circumstances, conditions which are agreed and specified in the lease may be deemed to be reasonable (see below). The same tests are to be applied whether construing an express term of the lease or the statutory proviso. The parties cannot validly declare in the lease that a particular reason for refusal shall be deemed reasonable, *e.g.* the landlord offering to accept a surrender (*Re Smith's Lease, Smith v Richards* [1951] 1 All E.R. 346).
   Matters to be taken into account are not confined to those affecting both parties to the lease (*Viscount Tredegar v Harwood* [1929] A.C. 72). The landlord is entitled to take into account his own property interests, and estate management considerations affecting more than merely the demised premises. The landlord's reasons must normally be connected with the use and occupation of the demised premises (*Swanson v Forton* [1949] Ch. 143). If he reasonably takes the view that the proposal will damage his interests, even though the contrary view might also be reasonable, his refusal of consent is not unreasonable.

(c) Examples: reasonable
   The following circumstances have been held to justify the refusal of consent to assign or underlet: **7–16**

   (i)   unsatisfactory references (*Shanly v Ward* (1913) 29 T.L.R. 714);
   (ii) reasonable objection to the proposed use of the premises, which contravened the tenant's user covenant (*Packing Centre v Poland Street Estate* (1961) 178 E.G. 189);
   (iii) the separate occupation of the premises assigned from other premises, with which it was previously jointly occupied, where that was likely to be detrimental (*Premier Confectionery (London) Co Ltd v London Commercial Sale Rooms Ltd* [1933] Ch. 904);
   (iv) proposed underletting at a substantial premium and low rent, making it doubtful whether the landlord could effectively recover arrears of rent from the sub-tenant (Law of Distress Amendment Act 1908, s.6), and reducing the sale and mortgage value of the landlord's reversion (*Re*

Town Investments Ltd Underlease, McLaughlin v Town Investments Ltd [1954] Ch. 301);

(v) proposed underletting at under market value, even though at a profit rental, prejudicing the value of the landlord's other property in the same building by providing low evidence of market rent (*Duckworth v Witting (Liverpool) Ltd* [1970] E.G.D. 17 (*cc*));

(vi) breach of repairing covenant, but only where it is serious (*Goldstein v Sanders* [1915] 1 Ch. 549);

7–17 (vii) the premises might be allowed to deteriorate (*Re Town Investments Ltd Underlease, McLaughlin v Town Investments Ltd* [1954] Ch. 301);

(viii) the result of the assignment would be that the assignee would have the protection of the Landlord and Tenant Act 1954, Pt II (*Re Cooper's Lease, Cowan v Beaumont Property Trusts Ltd* (1968) 19 P. & C.R. 541);

(ix) a residential part of the premises would become subject to the Rent Act. The ground can be reasonable even if it would not have applied when the lease was granted (*West Layton Ltd v Ford* [1979] Q.B. 593). However, it does not automatically apply, and might not, *e.g.* if there was no other way in which that part of the premises could be satisfactorily exploited (*Leeward Securities Ltd v Lilyheath Properties Ltd* (1983) 271 E.G. 279). With the differences in the protection given to residential tenants by the Rent Act 1977 and the Housing Act 1988, it is not clear whether it would be a reasonable ground that part of the premises would become subject to an assured tenancy.

(d) Examples: unreasonable

7–18 The following are examples of circumstances in which the refusal of consent has been held unreasonable:

(i) landlord wanting possession for himself (*Re Smith's Lease, Smith v Richards* [1951] 1 All E.R. 346);

(ii) unreasonable delay in granting licence (*Lewis & Allenby (1909) Ltd v Pegge* [1914] 1 Ch. 782);

(iii) unreasonable refusal of consent by the landlord's head landlord (*Vienit Ltd v W Williams & Son (Bread Street) Ltd* [1958] 1 W.L.R. 1267);

(iv) proposed assignee owed large sums to parent company repayment of which would render it insolvent, but the subsidiary was trading profitably and the parent's only reasonable interest was to support it (*Re Greater London*

Properties Ltd's Lease, Taylor Bros (Grocers) Ltd v Covent Garden Properties Co Ltd [1959] 1 W.L.R. 503);

(v) policy to refuse all requests for consent, to satisfy applicants on the landlord's waiting list (*Oriel Property Trust v Kidd* (1949) 154 E.G. 500);

(vi) breach of covenant not to make alterations, where the **7–19** breaches would easily be remediable at the end of the term (*Cosh v Fraser* (1964) 108 S.J. 116);

(vii) want of repair in breach of covenant, where it was not serious (*Farr v Ginnings* (1928) 44 T.L.R. 249);

(viii) assignee's intention to use premises in breach of covenant, where that was not the inevitable result of the assignment (*Killick v Second Covent Garden Property Co Ltd* [1973] 1 W.L.R. 658);

(ix) landlord seeking an advantage for himself that he would not otherwise have had, *e.g.* removing part of the premises from the scope of the Rent Act (*Bromley Park Garden Estates Ltd v Moss* [1982] 1 W.L.R. 1019), requiring a rent deposit to be paid by a sub-tenant to be deposited in the joint names of the landlord and the tenant (*Mount Eden Land Ltd v Straudley Investments Ltd* (1996) 74 P. & C.R. 306);

(x) a requirement that the tenant pay the landlord's costs of granting the licence where the lease imposes no such obligation on the tenant (*Goldman v Abbott* [1989] 2 E.G.L.R. 78). Even if the tenant is liable for the landlord's costs, a demand for a solicitor's undertaking to pay them may be unreasonable if it is not limited to a reasonable sum (*Dong Bang Minerva (UK) Ltd v Davina Ltd* [1995] 1 E.G.L.R. 41).

(e) Onus of proof
The onus of proof is on the landlord in a dispute concerning his **7–20** statutory duties. It is for the landlord to show:

(i) that he served notice of his decision within a reasonable time;

(ii) that if he withheld consent, it was reasonable to do so;

(iii) that if he gave a conditional consent, the condition was reasonable; and

(iv) that if he gave consent, it was given within a reasonable time (Landlord and Tenant Act 1988, s.1(6)).

7 Conditions deemed reasonable

(a) Landlord's duty modified

7–21   Exceptionally, in the case of a new tenancy (as defined by the Landlord and Tenant (Covenants) Act 1995) demising commercial or industrial property, the parties can agree and specify in the lease what is to be considered reasonable. It can specify circumstances in which the landlord may withhold his consent to assign all or part of the premises and conditions subject to which the landlord may grant consent. Withholding consent or imposing conditions in accordance with such a provision is deemed to be reasonable. The duty of a landlord who is bound to grant consent when it is reasonable, or to do so without unreasonable conditions, is modified accordingly (Landlord and Tenant (Covenants) Act 1995, s.22).

The terms agreed between the landlord and tenant under a new tenancy to modify the landlord's duty to consent to an assignment need not be contained in the lease itself. They may validly make an agreement at any time before the tenant applies for the landlord's consent.

(b) Types of condition

7–22   There is a limit on the type of condition which can validly be imposed and presumed reasonable. The presumption of reasonableness can be applied to any agreed condition which will apply automatically and can be judged objectively. However, if it requires anything to be determined by the landlord, or someone else, there are restrictions. Either, the person making the determination must be required to act reasonably; that could be tested by litigation. Or, the tenant must have an unrestricted right to have the determination reviewed by an independent third party, identifiable from the agreement, whose view will be conclusive.

Examples of the different types of condition can be given, to illustrate where one of the two qualifications—reasonableness or reference to a third party—will be required:

(i)   Any tenant who assigns must enter into an authorised guarantee agreement (which effectively extends his liability until the proposed assignee further assigns, but no further). This is automatic: no qualification required;

(ii)   Consent will be withheld unless the proposed assignee is a company with a specified minimum issued paid-up share capital. Compliance with the condition can be judged objectively: no qualification required;

(iii)   Consent will only be granted to an assignment to a limited company if suitable guarantors are provided. Without more, the issue of suitability would be determined by the landlord: reasonableness or third party determination must be specified;

(iv) Consent would only be given to an assignment to a person intending to carry on a trade judged as suitable by the landlord's managing agent. The managing agent must be required to be reasonable, or the tenant must have the chance to refer the matter to an independent third party.

8 Remedies for unreasonable withholding

If a landlord has a duty to give consent when it is reasonable but does not, the tenant has a number of possible alternative remedies.   **7–23**

(a) Proceed without consent
   If the tenant asks for consent and the landlord does not give it when he should have done, the tenant can proceed to complete that transaction, whether an assignment (*Treloar v Bigge* (1874) L.R. 9 Exch. 151) or sub-letting (*Lewis & Allenby (1909) Ltd v Pegge* [1914] 1 Ch. 782) without further reference to the landlord and without placing the lease in jeopardy. The simplicity of this course is attractive; but it will often be impracticable for an assignment because the tenant has to persuade the assignee to take a lease which, if it were to prove that the landlord had acted reasonably, would be subject to forfeiture.

(b) Declaration
   A tenant who considers that a refusal of consent, or a condition   **7–24**
proposed to be attached to it, is unreasonable may apply to the High Court, or to the county court (Landlord and Tenant Act 1954, s.53(1)), for declarations that the consent has been unreasonably withheld, and that the dealing may proceed without it. The claimant must use the Pt 8 procedure (CPR, Pt 56 PD, para. 56.2). There is no limit on the county court jurisdiction in such cases. A successful applicant should be awarded costs (*Young v Ashley Gardens Properties Ltd* [1903] 2 Ch. 112).
   The assignee can apply for a declaration, without joining the assignor as a party (*Theodorou v Bloom* [1964] 1 W.L.R. 1152).

(c) Damages
   A landlord who is in breach of his statutory duty to give consent when it is reasonable to do so, or indeed any of the associated duties, commits the tort of breach of statutory duty (Landlord and

Tenant Act 1988, s.4) and is liable to pay damages. Damages will be assessed on normal principles, and it will therefore be necessary to prove loss. Exemplary damages may be addressed in an appropriate case (*Design Properties Ltd v Thurloe Properties Ltd* (2004) *The Times*, March 2).

The fact that this is a tortious wrong and not a breach of contract is important. An action need not be confined to those between whom there is privity of contract: a subtenant could, *e.g.* claim damages from a head landlord.

Chapter 8

Letting to Partnerships

There are now two forms of partnership to which business prem-   **8–01**
ises are likely to be let: limited liability partnerships and the traditional unlimited partnership. The results are different, so it is
important to be clear which form of partnership is concerned.

1 Limited liability partnerships

A limited liability partnership is a body corporate with legal per-   **8–02**
sonality, the members of which have limited liability. It is registered by the Registrar of Companies. This type of partnership
has unlimited capacity (Limited Liability Partnerships Act 2000,
s.1), and it can therefore freely take, hold and grant leases. There
is no need for title to be vested in all or any of the partners,
although, depending on the credit rating of a partnership taking
a lease, the landlord may wish partners to stand as guarantors for
the partnership, in the same way as directors of a limited
company may be asked to do. When a limited liability partnership applies to be registered at the Land Registry as proprietor of
land, whether as landlord or tenant, the application must state
the partnership's registered number (Land Registration Rules
2003, r.181(4)).
   Every member of a limited liability partnership is an agent of
the partnership. Each can therefore negotiate on behalf of the
partnership and contract to bind it. There is one exception. The
partnership is not bound if the partner does not have authority to
bind the partnership and the person dealing with him either knows
that or does not believe that he is a partner (Limited Liability
Partnerships Act 2000, s.6).
   A limited liability partnership can have a corporate seal, although
it need not do so. A document may be executed by a partnership as

a deed if signed for that purpose by two members (Limited Liability Partnership Regulations 2001, applying and adapting Companies Act 1985, ss.36, 36A, 350).

2 Unlimited partnerships: identity of tenant

8–03   An unlimited partnership is not a body corporate and cannot own property of its own account; partnership property belongs to the partners. All partnership property should where possible be vested in all the partners. In the case of a lease, they will be joint tenants holding in trust for themselves in their partnership shares (Partnership Act 1890, s.20). The legal estate created by the lease cannot, however, be vested in more than four partners at the same time (Law of Property Act 1925, s.34(2)). This limitation raises the question of what to do when there are more than four partners. Different methods are adopted, although the results are not dissimilar.

First, up to four partners can be chosen to hold the lease on behalf of them all. The usual objection to this is that the landlord considers that his position is stronger if he has the direct covenant of all the partners. This is not necessarily so, because all partners are jointly liable for partnership debts (Partnership Act 1890, s.9), and goods belonging to the titular tenant's partners are not exempt from distress (Law of Distress Amendment Act 1908, s.4(2)(a)). On the other hand, if all the partners are parties to the tenancy, the landlord has no need to prove the existence of the partnership and the fact that the premises are partnership property, and he can make the partners' obligations joint and several.

All the partners can be made parties to the lease either by naming them all as tenants, or by naming four of them as tenants and the rest as guarantors. In both cases, the landlord obtains direct covenants from all, and in fact the result is similar. It is sometimes assumed where all the parties are named as tenants that on the death of one of the first four, the term will devolve by survivorship on the four who then become first named.

8–04   This is not correct. Survivorship can only operate between those in whom the legal estate was originally vested. However, if it is necessary to obtain the landlord's consent to an assignment into the name of the surviving partners, he would be hard put to it to maintain a reasonable objection to an assignment into the name of someone whom he had already accepted as a tenant when the lease was granted, even if only in a supernumerary capacity. It should be remembered that payment by a guarantor in satisfaction of arrears of rent is not payment of rent, and is not necessarily sufficient to obtain relief from forfeiture (*London & County (A & D) Ltd v Wilfred Sportsman Ltd* [1971] Ch. 764).

It may be considered more convenient for one only of the partners to be the tenant. In the absence of contrary agreement, he would automatically hold the lease for the purposes of the partnership (Partnership Act 1890, s.20), and if at the end of the term he took a new lease, that also would be held for the firm (*Featherstonhaugh v Fenwick* (1810) 17 Ves. 298).

There are two principal disadvantages in the lease being vested in one partner only. First, on his death action must inevitably be taken to vest the lease in another partner, whereas if there are several named tenants, action is only absolutely necessary on the death of the last survivor. Secondly, the special provisions of the Landlord and Tenant Act 1954, s.41A, as to security of tenure where the lease is vested in partners, will not apply. It is a condition precedent for the operation of that section that the tenancy be vested in at least two people. If one of the partners owns the premises he cannot let them to himself alone on behalf of the partnership, nor can co-owners of premises let them to themselves as a partnership (*Rye v Rye* [1962] A.C. 496). **8–05**

The problems facing partnerships in dealing with leasehold premises are among the incentives for firms to form a service company in which the lease can be vested. An unlimited company allows an easy change of membership and adjustment of shares, in addition to greater freedom from the Companies Acts' requirements for disclosure. The landlord may also be persuaded to forgo the partners' personal guarantees if the tenant company does not have limited liability. This is not, however, advisable from the landlord's point of view, because he could only have recourse to the members of the tenant company if it went into liquidation. With direct personal covenants, his remedies are more direct and probably quicker.

3 Unlimited partnerships: changes of partners and dissolution

The tenancy's conditions concerning assignment are of particular concern to tenants who are partners. The tenants must envisage the possibility of changes in the composition of their partnership during the term of the lease, and the more easily the changes can be reflected in the ownership of the premises the better. Assignments to reflect partnership changes are nonetheless assignments of the legal estate and are subject to any restrictions, qualified or absolute, contained in the lease. Where partners take a new lease they should seek to provide that even if the usual restriction is in **8–06** the lease, it is relaxed so that it does not apply on a change of partners. Landlords will not always agree to this, because it is open to abuse. Even if the lease provides for assignment without consent only where at least one tenant is the same before and after the assignment, a complete transfer can be effected by two successive assignments. Another possible qualification, where the lease is not for a long term, is to permit assignments automatically so long as at least one of the original tenants remains.

8–07   Restrictions may be evaded by avoiding a formal assignment. A tenant can allow a partnership of which he is a member to use the premises without being in breach of his covenant against assignment, provided that his partnership deed is not itself properly interpreted as an assignment of the lease (*Gian Singh & Co v Nahar* [1965] 1 W.L.R. 412). The device of executing a declaration of trust instead of an assignment can also be used (*Gentle v Faulkner* [1900] 2 Q.B. 267). A covenant not to part with possession of the premises is wider than a covenant not to assign, although they frequently go together. A tenant who places another person in possession of the premises, even without executing an assignment, is in breach of the broader restriction. However, if the tenant sells the business and the premises, but nevertheless retains possession of the latter, there is still no breach (*Chaplin v Smith* [1926] 1 K.B. 198). Even wider again is a covenant against sharing the premises which is increasingly found. Most forms of joint occupation are likely to be in breach of such a covenant.

On a dissolution of partnership one partner can retain possession of the premises without breaking a covenant not to assign contained in the lease in favour of all the partners (*Bristol Corporation v Westcott* (1879) 12 Ch. D 461). If, however, the partners leaving execute an assignment in favour of the one who remains in possession, this is a breach of covenant if the landlord's consent is not obtained (*Langton v Henson* (1905) 92 L.T. 805).

8–08   Where one of the partners is himself the landlord, and there is no formal lease for a fixed term of years, there is a presumption that the tenancy subsists only during the period of the partnership (*Pocock v Carter* [1912] 1 Ch. 663). Although at common law this meant that the former tenant-partners' right to possession terminated immediately the partnership ended (*Benham v Gray* (1847) 5 C.B. 138), this will now normally be subject to s.24 of the Landlord and Tenant Act 1954, which continues business tenancies until a prescribed notice is served. However, the former partners' reprieve may be short-lived, as without the concurrence of all the tenants (one of whom, being the landlord, would not co-operate) there could be no renewal of the tenancy, always assuming that the circumstances were not such that s.41A (which gives a right to renew to some only of joint tenants) applied (*Jacobs v Chaudhuri* [1968] 2 Q.B. 470).

Two cases demonstrate ways to avoid obstruction by the landlord. The court can compel a joint owner to join in an application to renew, as part of its jurisdiction over trustees. It is unlikely to do so when the joint tenants hold the property only for themselves beneficially (*Harris v Black* (1983) 46 P. & C.R. 366). Again, if the landlord's interest in the partnership is only nominal, as where he has no share in the firm's capital, a notice signed only by the other partners may suffice (*Featherstone v Staples* [1986] 1 W.L.R. 861: a case interpreting the Agricultural Holdings (Notice to Quit) Act 1977 (repealed)).   **8–09**

If the partnership, as tenants, are in default, the fact that the landlord is one of the partners will not normally prevent his exercising his remedies (*Brenner v Rose* [1973] 1 W.L.R. 443).

When one tenant partner acquires the reversion in the property of which the firm holds a lease, he is under a duty to account to the partnership for any profit derived from that transaction. This obligation continues after the partnership has been dissolved while the leasehold interest remains an undistributed asset of the former partnership (*Thompson's Trustee in Bankruptcy v Heaton* [1974] 1 W.L.R. 605).

Chapter 9

Taxation

1 Introduction

It is not possible to give a comprehensive guide here to the impact   **9–01**
of taxation on letting business premises. However, it is useful to
draw attention to some specific rules.

2 Stamp duty land tax

On the grant of a lease, SDLT is charged on the net present   **9–02**
value of the rent and on the amount of any premium (but not a
reverse premium: Finance Act 2003, Sch.17A, para.18) which is
paid.

(a) Rent
    The net present value of the rent is calculated by applying this
formula (Finance Act 2003, Sch.5, para.3):

$$v = \sum_{i-1}^{n} \frac{r_i}{(1 + T)^i}$$

where:

v is the net present value;
r_i is the rent payable in year i;
i is the first, second, third, etc. year of the term;
n is the term of the lease;
T is the temporal discount rate, initially set at 3.5 per cent.

The rent reserved by the lease, including any VAT payable in   **9–03**
respect of it, is the rent to be taken into account. An amount which
is uncertain is taxed on a reasonable estimate. If a sum is payable

contingently, it is assumed that the result of the contingency is that it is payable (Finance Act 2003, s.51, Sch.4, para.2).

There is no tax on any service charge, but if a single rent includes payment for services, there is no apportionment. However, if there is a separate payment for services, there is a provision to stop an exaggerated amount being attributed to the non-taxable obligation. For tax purposes, there can be an apportionment on a just and reasonable basis. A tenant's obligation to repair, insure or pay the landlord's management costs attracts no tax (Finance Act 2003, Sch.17A, paras 6, 10).

The effect of a rent review after the fifth year of the term is generally ignored, unless the resulting increase is regarded as abnormal in which case SDLT may then be charged as if a new lease had been granted. When SDLT is assessed at the outset of the lease, the rent for later years is assumed to be equal to the highest sum that has to be paid during the first five years for a consecutive 12 month period. However, if the lease provides for a rent review during the first five years, tax is charged on a reasonable estimate of the outcome (Finance Act 2003, Sch.17A, paras 7, 8).

(b) Reliefs

9–04   No SDLT is payable on the grant of a lease of business premises in the following cases:

(i)   the letting is a tenancy at will. The same applies to the grant of a licence (Finance Act 2003, s.48(2)(b), (c)(i));

(ii)   the property is wholly within a disadvantaged area, designated by regulations (Finance Act 2003, Sch.6, para.4);

(iii)   the lease is granted as part of a sale and leaseback transaction, where the sale consideration consisted of money or the release of debt (Finance Act 2003, Sch.7, para.2);

(iv)   the tenant is a charity intending the use the property or the income from it for its charitable purposes (Finance Act, Sch.8, para.1);

(v)   the landlord and the tenant are companies within the same group (Finance Act 2003, Sch.7, para 1);

(vi)   the lease is granted in the course of the reconstruction or acquisition of a company, subject to compliance with detailed conditions (Finance Act 2003, Sch.7, paras 7, 8).

3 Value added tax

9–05   The basic rule is that for VAT purposes, the grant of a lease of land or a completed commercial building is an exempt supply (Value

Added Tax Act 1994, Sch.9, Pt II, Group 1). VAT is therefore not charged.

However, the landlord can elect to waive the exemption from VAT in respect of a building (Value Added Tax Act 1994, s.51, Sch.10, para.2). This means that VAT is payable on the rent and premium charged under a lease, but an election has the attraction that the landlord can set input tax against the output tax. But a head lease and a sub-lease of the same property are distinct for this purpose. Even if VAT is chargeable on the head rent, the sub-lease is exempt until the tenant makes an election (*Royal and Sun Alliance Group plc v Customs and Excise Commissioners* [2003] 1 W.L.R. 1387).

4 Income and corporation tax

(a) New lease

Income tax under Schedule A, and corporation tax computed   **9–06** on income tax principles, is charged on rent payable under a lease of business premises. The landlord may be able to offset expenses. For the tenant, the rent paid will generally be an allowable expense before tax is charged.

Special provisions apply to the taxation of a premium paid for a lease for no more than 50 years. In assessing the length of the lease, terms which make it likely that it will end prematurely or will be extended may be taken into account (Income and Corporation Taxes Act 1988, ss.34, 38). On the grant of the lease, the landlord is treated as receiving additional rent equal to:

$$P - \frac{(P \times Y)}{50}$$

where:

P is the premium

Y is the number of complete 12 month periods (other than the first).

The effect of this is to charge tax on part of the premium. For   **9–07** each year of the term, after the first, the amount of the premium taxed is reduced by two per cent. So, if the lease is granted for one year, the whole premium is taxed. If the lease term is two years, 98 per cent of the premium is taxed; if the term is 50 years, two per cent of it is taxed.

A premium charged for a sub-lease is taxed in the same way, but the intermediate landlord may set off against his receipt any amount he had to pay to the head landlord (Income and Corporation Taxes Act 1988, s.37).

(b) Varying user covenant

A landlord who agrees to vary a tenant's user covenant in a lease in consideration of an increase in the rent is liable to tax on the additional rent. If the consideration is paid as a lump sum, it is treated as a premium: if the lease is a short one, partly chargeable as income as explained above, or reopening the capital gains computation on the grant of the lease (Taxation of Chargeable Gains Act 1992, Sch.8, para.3(2)).

Part II

Renewing Business Tenancies

Citations
*In this part, unless otherwise stated, statutory references are to the Landlord and Tenant Act 1954 as it applies after amendment (*inter alia*) by the Law of Property Act 1969 and the Regulatory Reform (Business Tenancies) (England and Wales) Order 2003.*

Forms
The numbered forms for use in the course of statutory renewal procedure are prescribed by the Landlord and Tenant Act 1954, Part II (Notices) Regulations 2004 (SI 2004/1005).

Chapter 10

The Right to Renew

1 Introduction

The security of tenure given to business tenants by Pt II of the   **10–01**
1954 Act is in the form of an automatic right to renew their tenancies (which in this context always includes leases) at a full market
rent. The right is brought into operation on or after the contractual expiry date by the service, then or in advance, of a statutory
notice. Until then, the current tenancy is automatically and
indefinitely extended. The right to renew a tenancy can be enforced
by an application to the court, which either the landlord or the
tenant may make. If the tenant applies, the landlord can oppose
renewal on a few specified grounds. Ways to end a tenancy without
renewal are also laid down. The landlord can apply to for an order
terminating the lease on one of the grounds which allow him to
oppose renewal and the tenant. This Part of the 1954 Act binds the
Crown (s.56(1)).

If a tenancy to which the right to renew does not apply is
brought to an end by the landlord giving notice to quit, the
effective operation of that notice is not prejudiced by the tenancy
subsequently becoming one to which the right would otherwise
apply (s.24(3)(b)).

To determine whether a tenant has a right to renew, three
aspects of the current tenancy must be examined: the nature of it,
the use to which the premises are put and the occupation of the
premises. If the question whether the tenancy falls within the scope
of the 1954 Act is put in issue in county court proceedings in which
the tenant claims a new tenancy, it is not appropriate for the landlord simultaneously to start High Court proceedings for a declaration on the same point (*Royal Bank of Scotland Ltd v Citrusdal
Investments Ltd* [1971] 1 W.L.R. 1469).

2 Amendments in 2004

10–02 A series of changes to Pt II of the Landlord and Tenant Act 1954 were introduced on June 1, 2004 by the Regulatory Reform (Business Tenancies) (England and Wales) Order 2003. They are incorporated into the text which follows. For the convenience of those familiar with the previous form of the legislation, the main provisions are summarised below.

(i)   The right to renew may be excluded by agreement. The landlord must serve a prescribed form of notice and the tenant must make a declaration acknowledging it.

(ii)   A company and its controlling shareholder are effectively treated as the same person, for ownership and occupation of the premises, carrying on business there are making improvements.

(iii)   A landlord's notice to end a tenancy which states that he is not opposed to the grant of a new tenancy must set out his proposals for the new tenancy.

(iv)   When the landlord gives notice to terminate a tenancy, the tenant is no longer required to give a counter-notice.

(v)   The parties may agree to extend the time for an application to court, so long as they agree before the time for applying—whether or not extended—has expired.

(vi)   Both the landlord and the tenant may make an application to the court that a tenancy be renewed. In addition, the landlord may apply for an order that the current tenancy be ended without renewal.

(vii)   Either the landlord or the tenant may apply to the court to fix an interim rent. If the lease of the whole premises is to be renewed and the landlord does not oppose, the amount of the interim rent is the same as the rent under the new lease.

(viii) An order for a new tenancy may be for a term of up to 15 years.

3 The tenancy

10–03 The Act says it applies to 'any tenancy' (s.23(1)), but this is deceptive. A mere licence is, by those very words, excluded (*Shell-Mex and BP Ltd v Manchester Garages Ltd* [1971] 1 W.L.R. 612). Describing a document as a licence is not conclusive if the true nature of an arrangement between the parties is a tenancy (*Addiscombe Garden Estates v Crabbe* [1958] 1 Q.B. 513). The court will look at the substance, and has, *e.g.* found that what the parties arranged to look like a management agreement was in fact a tenancy (*Wang v Wei* (1975) 119 S.J. 492).

A true tenancy at will is not covered (*Wheeler v Mercer* [1957] A.C. 416). Certain short tenancies are outside the Act's scope and there are some express exceptions. It is also possible to obtain the court's approval to arrangements excluding the right to renew.

(a) Licences

The distinction between a licence and a tenancy has been much litigated. The following principles extracted from the authorities by McNair J., in *Finbow v Air Ministry* [1963] 1 W.L.R. 697 at 706, are a guide:

10–04

> (1) that the agreement must be construed as a whole and that the relationship is determined by law and not by the label which the parties put on it, though the label is a factor to be taken into account in determining the true relationship;... (2) that the grant of exclusive possession, if not conclusive against the view that there is a mere licence as distinct from a tenancy, is at any rate a consideration of the first importance;... (3) that in all cases where an occupier has been held to be a licensee 'there has been something in the circumstances, such as a family arrangement, an act of friendship or generosity, or such like, to negative any intention to create a tenancy. In such circumstances it would be obviously unjust to saddle the owner with a tenancy, with all the momentous consequences that that entails nowadays, when there was no intention to create a tenancy at all' (*Facchini v Bryson* [1952] 1 T.L.R. 1386 at 1389, *per* Denning L.J.).

The draftsman seeking to prepare a licence which will not attract the right to renew should exclude all indicia of a tenancy, such as references to rent, landlord and tenant, the term, forfeiture and re-entry.

(b) Tenancies at will

Manfield & Sons Ltd v Botchin [1970] 2 Q.B. 612, established that the express grant of a tenancy at will is outside the Act's scope, provided that the parties genuinely regarded it as a tenancy at will. In that case, the circumstances were that the tenant wanted to occupy a shop, even temporarily, and the landlord had redevelopment plans but was experiencing difficulties in obtaining planning consent. As it turned out, the tenant remained in occupation for over four years. The draftsman of a tenancy at will must ensure

10–05

that it is indeed terminable at will by either party, and avoid such inconsistent provisions as a proviso for re-entry on forfeiture.

The exclusion of tenancies at will was confirmed in *Hagee (London) Ltd v A B Erikson and Larson (a firm)* [1976] Q.B. 209, where Scarman L.J. added (at 217): 'Parties cannot impose upon an agreement, by a choice of label, a nature or character which on its proper construction it does not possess'.

One reason why a landlord seeking an arrangement that will not have the Act's protection may prefer a tenancy at will to a licence, is that the remedy of distress is available for arrears of rent under a tenancy at will, but cannot be used in respect of payments due under a licence (*Moreton v Woods* (1869) L.R. 4 Q.B. 293; *Interoven Stove Co Ltd v Hibbard and Painter and Shepherd* [1936] 1 All E.R. 263).

(c) Short tenancies

10–06   There is no right to renew a tenancy granted for a term certain of up to six months which contains no provision for renewing it or extending it beyond six months from the date it began (s.43(3)). This exclusion does not apply where there is an established business. If the tenant and any predecessor in business have together been in occupation for more than twelve months, the Act's provisions apply normally. Occupation by different government departments in succession counts as the same business continuing (s.56(3)).

This in effect allows two consecutive tenancies to be granted for periods totalling twelve months, provided that the first tenancy contains no provision for the grant of the second. It should, however, be noted that the reference to occupation by the tenant's predecessors in business is not solely restricted to tenant occupiers. Prior occupation by the freeholder who subsequently disposes of his business to the tenant can prevent this exception from having effect, as can an earlier occupation by the tenant as freeholder.

(d) Service tenancies

Service tenancies do not attract the right to renew (s.43(2)). A service tenancy is one granted to the tenant as a holder of an office, appointment or employment, which ends when the office, etc. terminates or a specific time afterwards, or then becomes terminable. This exclusion only applies to a tenancy which is in writing and says why it was granted. The court will enquire into the genuineness of an alleged service agreement (*Teasdale v Walker* [1958] 1 W.L.R. 1076).

(e) Tenancies limited in the public interest
   Where a new tenancy is granted by the court for a period limited   **10–07**
in accordance with a ministerial certificate that on a certain date
the use and occupation of the premises should change in the public
interest, there is no right to renew that new tenancy (s.57(3)(b)).

(f) Extended and purchased new leases
   There is no right to renew an extended tenancy granted under
the Leasehold Reform Act 1967 (1967 Act, s.16(1)). Also, after that
50 year term expires, there can be no renewal under the 1954 Act
of any sub-tenancy directly or indirectly derived out of it. The
same thing applies to purchased new leases of flats under the statutory provisions, and subleases granted out of them (Leasehold
Reform, Housing and Urban Development Act 1993, s.59(2)).

4 Use of the premises

To have the right to renew his tenancy, a tenant must occupy the   **10–08**
premises 'for the purposes of a business' which he carries on, or for
those other purposes (s.23(1)). The definition of this term and the
exceptions to the broad principle are dealt with below. A business
carried on in breach of a prohibition in the tenancy against business use, applying to the whole of the premises, does not attract the
right to renew unless either the tenant's immediate landlord or his
predecessor in title consented to the breach or the immediate landlord (but not a predecessor in title) acquiesced in it (s.23(4)).
Consent implies a positive act of approval, or at least acceptance,
but acquiescence is a passive failure to do anything about a known
breach of covenant (*Bell v Alfred Franks & Bartlett Co Ltd* [1980]
1 W.L.R. 340). A prohibition against using the premises for a
specified business, or for any but a specified one, does not count as
a prohibition for this purpose. On the other hand, it does include
a prohibition against using the premises for one or more of the
classes of trade or professional use.
   The Act says 'business' includes 'a trade, profession or employment and includes any activity carried on by a body of persons,
whether corporate or unincorporate' (s.23(2)). There is thus a distinction between, on the one hand, tenants who are individuals,
and on the other, tenants consisting of bodies of persons and corporations. Only for the latter is the definition extended to 'any
activity'.
   For tenants who are bodies of persons, the definition of business has been interpreted very widely. It has extended, for instance,
to the activities of a members' tennis club (*Addiscombe Garden*

Estates Ltd v Crabbe [1958] 1 Q.B. 513), a National Health Service hospital (*Hills (Patents) Ltd v University College Hospital Board of Governors* [1956] 1 Q.B. 90), a church community centre (*Parkes v Westminster Roman Catholic Diocese Trustee* (1978) 36 P. & C.R. 22) and a local authority park (*Wandsworth London Borough Council v Singh* (1991) 62 P. & C.R. 219).

The provision of residential accommodation can, in the right circumstances, be a business for this purpose (*Lee-Verhulst (Investments) Ltd v Harwood Trust* [1973] Q.B. 204), given a sufficient degree of management and provision of services; mere passive letting is not sufficient (*Trans-Britannia Properties Ltd v Darby Properties Ltd* [1986] 1 E.G.L.R. 151: in that case of lock-up garages). The activities of government departments are expressly included (s.56(3)).

10–09 It may be difficult to distinguish between what is, and what is not, a business for this purpose. Passive storage of cartons and samples in a lock-up garage is use for business purposes (*Bell v Alfred Franks & Bartlett Co Ltd* [1980] 1 W.L.R. 340). But dumping builders' spoil on converting two shops into one is not (*Hillil Property & Investment Co Ltd v Naraine Pharmacy Ltd* (1980) 39 P. & C.R. 67).

An individual tenant must probably be carrying on his business with a view to profit. This test excluded a one hour a week Sunday school (*Abernethie v A M & J Kleiman Ltd* [1970] 1 Q.B. 10). In that case, Widgery L.J. said (at 20), 'what a man does with his spare time in his home is most unlikely to qualify for the description 'business' unless it has some direct commercial involvement in it, whether it be a hobby or a recreation or the performance of a social duty'. The lack of profit was a ground for holding that an individual tenant who sublet did not carry on a business (*Lewis v Weldcrest Ltd* [1978] 1 W.L.R. 1107).

Where premises are used for both business and residential purposes, the amount of business use is also relevant. Minimal business use will not give protection by the Act (*Royal Life Saving Society v Page* [1978] 1 W.L.R. 1329).

(a) Agricultural property

10–10 The 1954 Act does not apply to an agricultural holding (s.43(1)(a)), defined as 'the aggregate of the land (whether agricultural land or not) comprised in a contract of tenancy which is a contract for an agricultural tenancy, not being a contract under which the said land is let to the tenant during his continuance in any office, appointment or employment held under the landlord' (Agricultural Holdings Act 1986, s.1). This exclusion from the 1954 Act's scope extends to those short grazing and mowing tenancies which do not enjoy the protection given to other tenancies of agricultural holdings and to tenancies approved by the Secretary of State for the same purpose.

Similarly, the 1954 Act does not apply to a farm business tenancy (s.43(1)(aa); Agricultural Tenancies Act 1995, Sch, para.10).

The letting of open land used for a business that is not strictly agriculture can come within the protection of the 1954 Act, e.g. gallops for racehorses (*Bracey v Read* [1963] Ch. 88) and a field used for giving riding lessons (*Wetherall v Smith* [1980] 1 W.L.R. 1290). Raising game birds is not agriculture for the purposes of the 1986 Act (*Earl Normanton v Giles* [1980] 1 W.L.R. 28), but it is thought that fish farming is.

(b) Mining leases

Tenancies created by mining leases do not carry the right to renew (s.43(1)(b)). A mining lease is one granted for mining or connected purposes. Mining purposes are defined as sinking and searching for, winning, working, getting, making merchantable, smelting or otherwise converting or working for the purposes of any manufacture, carrying away and disposing of mines and material, in or under land, and the erection of buildings, and the execution of engineering and other works suitable for those purposes (Landlord and Tenant Act 1927, s.25). There is no right to renew a tenancy for sand and gravel working (*O'Callaghan v Elliott* [1966] 1 Q.B. 601).

(c) Part residential use

The 1954 Act right to renew can apply to tenancies of premises let for joint business and residential use. Provided that regular reasonably substantial use for business purposes is one of the purposes for which the tenant occupies the premises, a separate and concurrent residential use does not stop the 1954 Act from applying (*Cheryl Investments Ltd v Saldanha* [1978] 1 W.L.R. 1329). A tenancy within the 1954 Act cannot be a regulated tenancy (Rent Act 1977, s.24(3)) or an assured tenancy (Housing Act 1988, Sch.1, para 4).

5 Occupation of the premises

For a tenant of business premises to be entitled to renew his tenancy, he must himself occupy those premises (s.23(1)). A particular rule applies to a tenant under a tenancy for a term of years certain: he must be in occupation when, apart from the Act, the   **10–11** tenancy would come to end by effluxion of time (s.27(1A)). However, a fixed term tenancy which is continued by the Act does not end simply because the tenant ceases to occupy the premises (s.27(2)). This 2004 amendment may overrule the previous rule that the tenant must continue to occupy the premises throughout the proceedings to enforce that right (*Domer v Gulf Oil (Great Britain) Ltd* (1975) 119 S.J. 392).

Whether the tenant is in occupation is a question of fact (*Pulleng v Curran* (1982) 44 P. & C.R. 58). Occupation for this purpose carries a connotation of some physical use of the property (*Graysim Holdings Ltd v P&O Properties Ltd* [1996] A.C. 329).

The right to renew does not enure in favour of tenants who have totally sub-let. But where the subletting is of part only of the demised premises, so that part is used for the tenant's business and part for the sub-tenant's, the position is less clear. The implications of it will be dealt with in conjunction with the topics affected. The tenant's right to renew does not extend to the sub-let parts (*Narcissi v Wolfe* [1960] 1 Ch. 10), but the landlord may oblige him to take a new lease of the whole if he wishes to have one of the part he occupies.

10–12   The fact that the premises must be occupied means that there is no right to renew a lease only of a shared right of way (*Land Reclamation Co Ltd v Basildon District Council* [1979] 1 W.L.R. 767). It is not decided whether the 1954 Act can apply to a lease of an exclusive right of way. However, a tenant who puts it out of his own power to occupy, for instance by giving an exclusive licence to occupy to a third party, cannot be in occupation (*Hancock & Willis v GMS Syndicate Ltd* (1983) 265 E.G. 473).

The requirement of occupation has been generously construed in certain circumstances. A tenant can occupy as an agent or manager (*Cafeteria (Keighley) Ltd v Harrison* (1956) 168 E.G. 668). One company can manage another's business (*Ross Auto Wash Ltd v Herbert* (1978) 250 E.G. 971).

A company may continue in occupation, even if it has ceased to trade there, if the facts so warrant (*I & H Caplan Ltd v Caplan (No.2)* [1963] 1 W.L.R. 1247). Occupation can be intermittent (*Bell v Alfred Franks & Bartlett Co Ltd* [1980] 1 W.L.R. 340: premises used sometimes, but not always, for storage). These reasons have been suggested as illustrations of why a tenant might allow a shop to 'lie fallow': 'death, illness, bankruptcy, or simply that the business is not paying its way' (*Pulleng v Curran* (1982) 44 P. & C.R. 58 at 68 *per* Sir George Baker). Even where fire has made the premises uninhabitable, a tenant remains in occupation for this purpose if he continues to exert and claim his right to occupy (*Morrisons Holdings Ltd v Manders Property (Wolverhampton) Ltd* [1976] 1 W.L.R. 533). What is needed is a 'thread of continuity'. This was lost, *e.g.* when gaming club premises were left empty for four years and the licence was transferred elsewhere (*Aspinall Finance Ltd v Viscount Chelsea* [1989] 1 E.G.L.R. 103).

(a) Trust beneficiaries

Business premises let to trustees but occupied by all or any of **10–13** the trust's beneficiaries for their own business are treated as occupied by the tenant (s.41). They must be true beneficiaries, not merely the trustees' managers (*Methodist Secondary Schools Trust Deed Trustees v O'Leary* [1993] 1 E.G.L.R. 105).

(b) Partnerships

Where business premises are let to partners for the partnership business, the intention is that the right to renew shall accrue to the partners for the time being (s.41A). The special rights of partners apply when:

(i) at some time during the existence of the tenancy a business was carried on upon the premises in partnership by all the then joint tenants, with or without others, and the tenancy was partnership property; and

(ii) the tenancy is currently held by two or more joint tenants, not all of whom carry on the business there, and the other tenants do not occupy any part of the premises as tenants for the purposes of some other business.

In such a case the right to renew passes to those of the tenants who are carrying on the business, and the new tenancy may be granted jointly to them and any other partners in that business.

(c) Group companies

Where the tenant is a company, the occupation of the premises by another company in the same group is sufficient for the tenant to enjoy the right to renew (s.42(2)). A company is in the same group as another in one of three cases: first, one is a subsidiary of the other; secondly, they are both subsidiaries of the third company; or thirdly, a person owns a controlling interest in both companies, which, had he been a company, would have made them his subsidiaries. The rules in the Companies Act 1985, s.736, determine whether a company is a subsidiary of another. In outline, they require either that the parent is a member of the subsidiary and controls the composition of its board of directors, or that the parent holds more than half in nominal value of the subsidiary's equity share capital. A company is a subsidiary of any company of which its immediate parent is a subsidiary.

(d) Controlling shareholders

10–14 The position of a company and of a controlling shareholder in that company are effectively equated. Where the tenant is a company, the tenancy comes within the Act if someone with a controlling interest in it occupies the premises or carries on business there; likewise, when the person who has the controlling interest is the tenant, the tenancy qualifies if the company is the one to occupy or carry on business (s.23(1A)). A person has a 'controlling interest' in a company if, had he also been a company, it would have been his subsidiary (s.46; Companies Act 1985, s.736).

(e) Limited liability partnerships

The position of limited liability partnerships is effectively equated with that of limited companies. A partnership can be a subsidiary of company and vice versa, and the consequences are as set out above for companies (paragraph *(c)*). (The relevant provisions of the Companies Act 1985 are adapted and applied by the Limited Liability Partnerships Regulations 2001). Presumably also, a partner whose votes controlled a partnership would be in the position of a controlling shareholder (paragraph *(d)*), although that would normally be contrary to the principle of partnership.

6 Forgoing the right to renew

10–15 Obviously even though the 1954 Act extends indefinitely the tenancies to which it applies, until the renewal procedure is activated, it must be possible for a tenant who wishes to give up the property to bring the tenancy to an end. On the other hand, the legislation is so framed to try to ensure that tenants do not surrender their rights under pressure from landlords.

(a) Contracting out

It is only possible to contract out of the statutory right to renew a business tenancy if prescribed formalities are observed. No application to court is needed to approve an agreement to contract out, nor indeed is one possible. Otherwise, an agreement to exclude renewal, to end a tenancy if the tenant applies to renew or to impose a penalty in that event, is void (s.38(1)).

10–16 To ensure the validity of an agreement contracting out of the right to renew, there is a preliminary procedure (s.38A(1), (3); Regulatory Reform (Business Tenancies) England and Wales) Order 2003, Schs 1, 2). The prospective landlord must serve the prospective tenant with the prescribed form of notice that ss.24 to 28 of the 1954 Act are not to apply, or a notice in substantially the same form. The notice contains a warning to the tenant explaining the significance of contracting out of his statutory rights. It must be served on the tenant before he takes the tenancy, or enters into a preliminary agreement to do so. There are also additional requirements, depending when notice is served on the tenant:

(i)   Notice served at least 14 days before the deadline for service: the tenant, or someone whom he authorises, must make a declaration before taking the tenancy or contracting to do so. The declaration, which need not be a statutory declaration, must be in the prescribed form, or substantially in that form. The declaration acknowledges the intention to exclude the statutory renewal rights, the service of the notice and the fact that the tenant has read warning on the notice.

(ii) Notice served less than 14 days of the deadline for service: **10–17** the tenant, or someone whom he authorises, must make a statutory declaration before taking the tenancy or contracting to do so. The statutory declaration must be in the prescribed form, or substantially in that form. It acknowledges the intention to exclude the statutory renewal rights, the service of the notice and the fact that the tenant has read the warning on the notice.

In either case, the facts have to be apparent on the face of the lease or tenancy agreement. It must either refer to the agreement, notice and declaration or statutory declaration, or have a reference to them endorsed on it.

CONTRACTING OUT PROCEDURE: SUMMARY

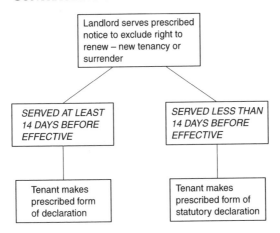

(b) Agreements with privileged landlords

10–18   There are special provisions, which validate agreements to exclude the right to renew, made with certain landlords, without the need to comply with the general requirements.

In cases where the landlord is a government department (but not the Crown Estate Commissioners), or the landlord's interest is held for one, or is a statutory undertaker, certain written agreements are valid (ss.57(8), 58(2), (3)). A statutory undertaker means a person authorised by statute to carry on any railway, light railway, tramway, road transport, water transport, canal, inland navigation, dock, harbour, pier or lighthouse undertaking, or any undertaking for the supply of electricity, gas, hydraulic power, British Telecommunications, an operator of certain airports, a public gas supplier or transporter, the National Rivers Authority, a water undertaker, a sewage undertaker and a company licensed to provide air traffic services (s.69(1); Town and Country Planning Act 1990, s.262; British Telecommunications Act 1981, Sch.3, para.10(h); Airports Act 1986, ss.57, 58, Sch.2, para.1(1); Gas Act 1986, Sch.7, para.2(1); Water Act 1989, Sch.25, para.1(1), (2)(vi); Gas Act 1995, Sch.4, para.2(1); Transport Act 2000, Sch.5, para.1).

10–19   With a government department the permitted agreement is that, on a Minister or Board in charge of a department certifying the use or occupation of the premises should cease or change for reasons of national security, the tenancy should be terminable by notice to quit containing a copy of the certificate and that thereafter there should be no right to renew. With a statutory undertaker the permitted agreement is that, on a Minister or a Board in charge of a department certifying that all or part of the premises is urgently required for carrying out repairs (to that or other property) necessary for the proper operation of the landlord's undertaking, the tenancy should be terminable by notice to quit containing a copy of the certificate and that thereafter there should be no right to renew.

(c) Surrender

The landlord and tenant under an existing tenancy which confers a right of renewal can agree that it should be surrendered, which will necessarily defeat the right to renew. These provision appear to apply to an agreement to surrender made before the tenancy was granted; the wording is not wholly appropriate for that, but there is a requirement (in the alternative) that a reference 'be contained in' the lease or tenancy agreement.

10–20   The agreement to surrender may be on specified terms, and may operate in specified circumstances or on a stated date. However, the agreement is void unless certain formalities are observed (s.38A(2), (4); Regulatory Reform (Business Tenancies) (England and Wales) Order 2003, Schs 3, 4). The prospective landlord must serve the prospective tenant with the prescribed form of notice that ss.24 to 28 of the 1954 Act are not to apply. The notice consists of a warning to the tenant explaining the significance of a surrender. It must be served on the tenant before he surrenders the tenancy, or enters into a preliminary agreement to do so. There are also additional requirements, depending when notice is served on the tenant:

(i) Notice served at least 14 days before the deadline for service: the tenant, or someone whom he authorises, must make a declaration before surrendering the tenancy or contracting to do so. The declaration, which need not be a statutory declaration, must be in the prescribed form, or substantially in that form. The declaration acknowledges the intention to surrender the tenancy, the service of the notice and the fact that the tenant has read warning on the notice.

(ii) Notice served less than 14 days of the deadline for service: the tenant, or someone whom he authorises, must make a statutory declaration before surrendering the tenancy or contracting to do so. The statutory declaration must be in the prescribed form, or substantially in that form. It acknowledges the intention to exclude the statutory renewal rights, the service of the notice and the fact that the tenant has read warning on the notice.

In either case, the facts have to be apparent on the face of the lease or tenancy agreement. It must either refer to the notice and declaration or statutory declaration, or have a reference to them endorsed on it.

(d) Notice to quit

A tenant who has a tenancy which can be ended by serving **10–21** notice to quit can, subject to one condition, relinquish his right to renew by serving notice (s.24(2)(a)). In the case of a tenancy granted for a term of years certain which is being continues by the Act, the tenant can bring it to an end at any time by giving at least three months' notice, which need not be more than an informal letter (*Provident Mutual Life Assurance Association v Greater London Employers' Association Ltd* [1996] 1 E.G.L.R. 106). There is then an appropriate apportionment of rent (s.27(2), (3)). In both cases the notice is only valid if the tenant has been in occupation in right of the tenancy for at least a month.

10–22   *(e) Avoidance measures*

Some devices to avoid the 1954 Act's right to renew which have been used in the past, but are believed to be untested by litigation, still seem to be available to parties who agree to use them. Three examples may be given. They all involve granting a lease for longer than the intended term, applying special terms to the additional term and giving the tenant an option to surrender at the end of the true term. To ensure the validity of the option, the formalities set out above (under *Surrender*) should be observed.

In the first case, the rent reserved for the additional period could be an astronomical figure. This now seems undesirable, because it would attract more stamp duty land tax than should have been payable. Further, a decision which considered an analogous device affecting an assured tenancy casts doubt on its efficacy (*Bankway Properties Ltd v Penfold-Dunsford* [2001] 1 W.L.R. 1369). Secondly, a sub-lease could be granted back to the landlord for the additional period; this also might involve paying additional stamp duty land tax. Thirdly, the tenant could covenant not to carry on any business at the premises, nor permit any to be carried on there, during the additional period.

The Act's provisions cannot be evaded by granting a reversionary lease to a third party when the tenancy ends. That reversionary lease would take effect subject to any renewal of the original tenancy (s.65(3)).

7 The landlord's position

10–23   A landlord is entitled to oppose his tenant's claim to renew his tenancy on a limited number of specified grounds. However, he does not have to wait for the tenant to take action. The landlord can take the initiative to clarify the position, whether his preference is for the grant of a new tenancy or that the tenant give possession of the premises.

The renewal procedure is usually started by the landlord serving notice to end the current lease and to state whether or not he would oppose the grant of a new tenancy. The alternative is for the tenant formally to request a new tenancy. After that, the landlord's possible courses of action depend whether or not he wishes to grant a new tenancy.

10–24   If the landlord is content to grant a new tenancy, he can negotiate with the tenant. In default of agreement on the terms of the new tenancy, the tenant may initiate court proceedings. The alternative for a landlord who wishes to precipitate matters is to initiate the proceedings (s.24(1)), although the court cannot order the tenant to take a new tenancy against his will (s.29(5)).

On the other hand, a landlord who opposes the grant of a new tenancy also has a choice of ways to proceed. He can wait to see whether the tenant brings proceedings to claim a new tenancy—because if he does not there can be no valid claim—and if he does, the landlord can oppose it. Alternatively, the landlord can himself bring proceedings to claim an order that the current tenancy end without the grant of a new tenancy (s.29(2)). The possible grounds to support that claim are the same as those for opposing the grant of a new tenancy (s.29(4)).

8 Right to renew excluded

(a) Forfeiture
The statutory right to renew does not prejudice the operation of the law of forfeiture, including the termination of a tenancy by reason of the forfeiture of a superior tenancy (s.24(2)).   **10–25**

(b) Public purposes
In certain cases the right to renew is excluded because the public interest so requires. They have in common that a certificate of the public requirement is given by a Minister or Board in charge of a public department. There is no form of appeal against such a certificate. Except in the last case mentioned below, if these powers are exercised, the tenant will be entitled to compensation, in the same way as a tenant whose landlord successfully opposes an application to renew on grounds not involving the tenant's default (s.59).

The right to renew can be excluded if it is requisite for the purposes of a public body landlord that the use and occupation of all or part of the premises should be changed (s.57(1)). That does not mean that the alternative use must be essential, merely 'required by circumstances' (R. v Secretary of State for the Environment Ex p. Powis [1981] 1 W.L.R. 584). This applies where any interest in the premises superior to the tenant's belongs to or is held for the purposes of a government department (but not the Crown Estate Commissioners), or is held by one of the authorities listed below. The certificate must say that the change is requisite for the purposes of the government department concerned. The authorities are (Leasehold Reform Act 1967, ss.28, 38(2)):

(i)   local authorities, *i.e.* county, county borough (in Wales),   **10–26**
        London borough, and district councils, the Common
        Council of the City of London, any drainage board, any

joint board or joint committee if all constituent authorities are local authorities, any authority constituting a
local authority within the meaning of the Local Loans
Act 1875, any combined police authority within the
meaning of the Police Act 1964 (except the Receiver for
the Metropolitan Police), a joint authority under Pt IV of
the Local Government Act 1985, the Broads Authority;
(ii) statutory undertakers;
(iii) development corporations and the Commission for the
New Towns;
(iv) health and special health authorities under the National
Health Service Act 1977 (Health Authorities Act 1995);
(v) universities, university colleges and colleges of universities;
(vi) bodies corporate carrying on any nationalised industry,
or part of an industry or undertaking;
(vii) any harbour authority within the meaning of the Har-
bours Act 1964 in respect of its functions as such;
(viii) the National Trust (in which case the certificate is given by
the Secretary of State for the Environment);
(ix) a service authority of visiting forces (Visiting Forces and
International Headquarters (Application of Law) Order
1965);
(x) a housing action trust (Housing Act 1988, Pt III).

The ministerial certificate is not to be given unless the tenant
has had twenty-one days' notice that the question is being considered, and inviting representations, which must be considered
before the certificate is given. A certificate can be given even where
the local authority landlord has agreed to treat the tenant as a
yearly tenant, to exclude the premises from a compulsory purchase
order (*R. v Minister of Transport Ex p. Beech-Allen* (1963) 16 P. &
C.R. 145).

10–27 National security is another ground on which a certificate may
be given, where the landlord is a government department, or that
interest is held for the purposes of such a department (s.58(1)).

Finally, the Department of Trade and Industry may certify that
a change of use or occupation is necessary or expedient in respect
of premises situated in a development area or an intermediate area
(Local Employment Act 1972, s.1) of which either the department
or the English Industrial Estates Corporation is landlord (s.60(1)).
The National Assembly Wales may similarly certify in respect of
property owned by the Welsh Development Agency for the purpose of providing employment appropriate to the needs of the area
(s.60A(1); Welsh Development Agency Act 1975, s.11).

Chapter 11

Position until Renewal

If neither landlord nor tenant takes any statutory steps to bring to an end a tenancy of business premises to which the 1954 Act applies, the tenancy continues in force, even though it was originally granted for a term of years certain (s.24(1)). The result is not the creation of a statutory tenancy, as under the Rent Act, but a prolongation of the contractual tenancy. All the contractual provisions continue to apply, save those inconsistent with the statutory prolongation of the tenancy. Despite the statutory prolongation of the contractual term, there are conflicting decisions as to whether references in the lease to the term granted by it automatically apply during the statutory extension. Even an original tenant under a lease which is not a new tenancy, who assigned before the term date, does not remain responsible for paying the rent during the statutory extension (*City of London Corporation v Fell* [1994] 1 A.C. 458).

11–01

It is as well for the lease expressly to make the position clear. In giving a contractual definition to the expression 'the term', the draftsman must take care. He must avoid the result that the lease means that it was granted for a period which includes the statutory extension. That can make the contractual term never ending, because the landlord never has a statutory right to end it. He can only serve notice to take effect on or after the date on which the contractual term ends (s.25(4)), and a contractual term defined to include the statutory extension cannot end until a notice is served. An impasse therefore results.

If the tenancy is a sub-lease, the interest of the immediate landlord may determine, in which case the reversion to the prolonged tenancy is vested in the next landlord up the chain to the freeholder (s.65(2)). If the tenancy is continued beyond when a reversionary lease has been granted to come into effect, the reversionary tenancy takes effect subject to the continued tenancy (s.65(3)).

11–02

A tenant who does not wish to renew may bring a fixed term lease which has been extended to an end by serving on the landlord at least three months' written notice ending on any day, but it does not end simply because he quits (s.27(2)).

1 On service of statutory notice

11–03   The service of a statutory notice, dealt with in the next chapter, brings the contractual tenancy to an end on a date that it specifies (ss.25(1), 26(5)). It may be extended in two ways in the course of the renewal procedure.

First, if an application is made to the court, the tenancy is extended until three months after the date when the application is finally disposed of (s.64). That date, from which the three months run, is the expiry of the time for appealing, or further appealing, unless the application is withdrawn or an appeal abandoned, in which case it is the date of the withdrawal or abandonment. Where the Court of Appeal refuses leave to appeal to the House of Lords, the date is at the end of the month allowed for registering a petition to the Appeals Committee for leave to appeal (*Austin Reed Ltd v Royal Insurance Co Ltd (No. 2)* [1956] 1 W.L.R. 1339).

This extension does not prevent the tenant ending the lease by serving three months' notice ending on a quarter day (s.27; *Long Acre Securities Ltd v Electro Acoustic Industries Ltd* [1990] 1 E.G.L.R. 91).

Secondly, the tenant in whose favour the court makes an order for the grant of a new tenancy may apply to the court within 14 days for the order to be revoked (s.36(2)). This gives the tenant the option to decline to take a new lease on unacceptable terms. The original contractual tenancy is then extended for such period as the parties may agree, or the court determines, to be necessary to give the landlord a reasonable opportunity to relet or otherwise dispose of the premises.

If the landlord and tenant agree in writing on the grant of a new tenancy, the current tenancy terminates on the date specified in the agreement (s.28). This covers the common case where a new lease, in favour of the sitting tenant, is executed. The new tenancy commonly starts on the day after the previous one would have expired by effluxion of time. Neither party can insist on this; it is a matter of bargain between them.

2 Interim rent

In the absence of an application to fix an interim rent, the rent   **11–04**
under the former tenancy continues unaltered until the new
tenancy comes into effect (*Re No 88 High Road, Kilburn, Meakers
Ltd v DAW Consolidated Properties Ltd* [1959] 1 W.L.R. 279). Once
the landlord has given notice terminating the tenancy or the tenant
has requested a new tenancy, either party may apply to the court
to determine the interim rent which the tenant should pay while the
current tenancy continues (s.24A). That interim rent may be either
more or less than the amount reserved under the current tenancy.
The court's power is discretionary (*Bloomfield v Ashwright Ltd*
(1984) 47 P. & C.R. 78), but no refusal to exercise the discretion has
been reported. It should be noted that once an interim rent is fixed,
it effectively becomes the contractual rent (s.24A(2)). Should one
be fixed which is lower than the rent reserved by the lease, what the
tenant has to pay is reduced. The landlord needs to take valuation
advice before applying.
   As will be seen, the landlord involved in the renewal procedure,
termed 'the competent landlord', may differ from the tenant's
immediate landlord. In such a case, presumably no application to
fix an interim rent will be made, because the competent landlord
would have to make the application, but the revised interim rent
would enure to the benefit of the immediate landlord.

(a) Application
   An interim rent may be higher or lower than the rent under the   **11–05**
current tenancy. For that reason, either the landlord or the tenant
can apply to the court for an amount to be determined (s.24A(1)).
However, there may only be one application at any one time; a
party cannot apply if the other has done so and that application
has not been withdrawn.
   An application to fix an interim rent may be made at any time,
but no later than six months after the end of the tenancy in question (s.24A(3)).
   If the reversion is assigned when an application for an interim
rent is pending, the benefit can be assigned to the new landlord
(*Bloomfield v Ashwright Ltd* (1984) 47 P. & C.R. 78). Presumably,
this also applies to the benefit of an application by the tenant when
the lease is assigned.
   There can only be one application to fix an interim rent at any
one time, so once one of the parties to the lease has applied the
other cannot unless the first application is withdrawn (s.24A(2)).

(b) Commencement

11–06   The date from which the interim rent runs varies depending whether it was the landlord who served notice to end the current tenancy or it was the tenant who requested a new tenancy. If the landlord served notice, the interim rent starts on the earliest termination date which the notice could have specified. If the tenant made a request, the interim rent runs from the earliest from which the request could have specified for the start of the new tenancy (s.24B). The reason for starting the interim rent on the earliest date which could have been specified, rather than the date actually given, is to prevent a party manipulating the position to his advantage. If a later date could be adopted the old rent could be artificially extended when it was significantly either above or below the current market figure.

(c) Amount: whole premises, landlord not opposed

In the case of a straightforward renewal, the amount of the interim rent is the rent which is payable under the new lease when the term starts (s.24C(2)). There is then no need to make any separate assessment of the amount of the interim rent.

This applies if the following conditions are satisfied (s.24C(1)):

(i)   the tenant occupied the whole premises when the landlord gave notice to end the tenancy or the tenant requested a new tenancy;

(ii)   either the landlord's notice stated that he would not oppose the grant of a new tenancy or the landlord gave no counter-notice to the tenant's request stating that he would oppose an application for a new tenancy;

(iii)   the landlord grants the tenant a new tenancy of the whole premises, whether or not as a result of a court order.

There are exceptions to this simple rule. The interim rent is the rent which would have been fixed for a new tenancy granted on the start date of the interim rent, if that is substantially different. Where the terms of the old and new tenancies differ and make a substantial difference to the rent, there is a separate calculation. The interim rent is fixed as if a new tenancy were granted for the actual term of the new tenancy, but having regard to the terms of the current tenancy and the rent payable under any sub-tenancy (s.24C(3)–(8)).

(d) Amount: other cases

11–07   Where the previous section does not apply, the interim rent is determined in accordance with the principles to be taken into account in fixing the rent under the renewed lease (in outline, the open market rent, disregarding any goodwill element), but on the basis that the whole of the premises are being let on a new tenancy from year to year. This will generally result in a lower rent than would finally be payable under the renewed tenancy, because the security of tenure enjoyed under a yearly tenancy is less than under a term of years certain. The court is also directed to have regard to the rent payable under the current tenancy and under any sub-tenancy. Apart from the reference to sub-tenancies, this is the same formula as applied to fixing all interim rents before the Act was amended in 2004. Accordingly, earlier decisions must be taken into account.

There have been conflicting interpretations of the requirement to take account of the rent under the current tenancy. It probably means that the current rent is to be considered as a cushion for the tenant, reducing the rise in rent there might otherwise have been (*English Exporters (London) Ltd v Eldonwall Ltd* [1973] Ch. 415; *Fawke v Viscount Chelsea* [1980] Q.B. 441).   **11-08**

In rare cases, it is possible for a differential interim rent to be ordered, *e.g.* a rent at one rate until repairs are executed and thereafter at a higher figure (*Fawke v Viscount Chelsea*, above).

It is understood that interim rents fixed by negotiation are commonly ten to fifteen per cent less than the agreed current market rent (*e.g. Janes (Gowns) Ltd v Harlow Development Corporation* (1980) 253 E.G. 799). But in one reported case the deduction was as much as fifty per cent (*Charles Follett Ltd v Cabtell Investments Ltd* [1987] 2 E.G.L.R. 88), and in another the interim rent had been agreed at a figure lower than the current rent (*O'May v City of London Real Property Co Ltd* [1983] 2 A.C. 726).

3 Sureties

The form of security given to business tenants—an extension of the original lease, rather than grafting on a separate statutory tenancy as under the Rent Act—may be vital in its effect on the position of a surety who joined in the original lease to guarantee the tenant's performance of his obligations. As the original term does not expire until a statutory notice takes effect, the surety's obligation may also continue if the tenant's liability continues. This is, however, a matter of construction of the particular covenant. The presumption seems to be against continuing liability. In one case, there was no such extension (*Junction Estates Ltd v Cope* (1974) 27 P. & C.R. 482). A sub-tenant's direct covenant with the head landlord—which is analogous to a surety's covenant—was construed in the opposite way, continuing the liability during the statutory extension (*GMS Syndicate Ltd v Gary Elliott Ltd* [1982] Ch. 1).

Chapter 12

Procedure for Renewal

1 Prescribed forms

There are two ways in which the statutory renewal procedure may **12–01**
be triggered. Either the landlord may serve notice to terminate the
current tenancy, or the tenant may serve a formal request for a new
tenancy. The notice or request must be in the prescribed form
(ss.25(1), 26(3), 66(1)–(3)).

The landlord's notice is the commoner course because landlords generally anticipate a higher rent when the tenancy is
renewed, and therefore want it to start at the earliest possible
moment. From this point of view, it is not usually in the tenant's
interest to serve a request for a new tenancy but there can be other
reasons. A landlord may delay serving notice because his plans for
the future of the property are uncertain, and the tenant may want
to achieve greater security of tenure before making capital com-
mitments in his business.

Where a mortgagee of the landlord's interest is in possession, or
a receiver of the rents and profits has been appointed by him or by
the court the mortgagee is substituted for the landlord in the 1954
Act procedure (s.67).

For convenience, here is a list of the prescribed forms. **12–02**

Form 1: Landlord's Notice Ending a Business Tenancy with
Proposals for a New One.

Form 2: Landlords Notice a Business Tenancy and Reasons for
Refusing a New One.

Form 3: Tenant's request for a New Business Tenancy.

Form 4: Landlord's request for Information about Occupation **12–03**
and Sub-tenancies.

Form 5: Tenant's request for Information from Landlord or
Landlord's Mortgagee about Landlord's Interest.

Form 6: Landlord's Withdrawal of Notice Terminating Tenancy.

Form 7: Landlord's Notice Ending a Business Tenancy (with Reasons for Refusing a New Tenancy) where the Leasehold Reform Act 1967 May Apply.

12–04   *Form 8*: Landlord's Notice Ending a Business Tenancy on Public Interest Grounds.

Form 9: Notice Ending a Business Tenancy where a Change is Required at a Future Date and the Landlord Opposes a New Tenancy.

Form 10: Notice Ending a Business Tenancy where a Change is Required at a Future Date and the Landlord Does Not Oppose a New Tenancy.

Form 11: Notice Ending a Business Tenancy on Grounds of National Security and Without the Option to Renew.

12–05   *Form 12*: Notice Ending a Business Tenancy where the Property is Required for Regeneration.

Form 13: Notice Ending a Business Tenancy on Public Interest Grounds where the Leasehold Reform Act 1967 May Apply.

Form 14: Notice Ending a Business Tenancy on Public Interest Grounds where a Change is Required at a Future Date and where the Leasehold Reform Act 1967 May Apply.

12–06   *Form 15*: Notice Ending a Business Tenancy where the Property is Required for Regeneration and the Leasehold Reform Act 1967 May Apply.

Form 16: Notice Ending a Business Tenancy of Welsh Development Agency Premises where the Property is Required for Employment Purposes.

Form 17: Notice Ending a Business Tenancy of Welsh Development Agency Premises where the Property is Required for Employment Purposes and the Leasehold Reform Act 1967 May Apply.

2 The competent landlord

12–07   The competent landlord within the meaning of the Act is the land-lord with whom the tenant must conduct the renewal procedure (s.44, Sch.6). It is extremely important to ascertain his identity, as he is not necessarily the tenant's immediate landlord, and when it comes to proceedings an application to substitute another person for the respondent landlord may, if made outside the time limit for launching the proceedings, be fatal to the tenant's chances (*Beardmore Motors Ltd v Birch Bros (Properties) Ltd* [1959] Ch. 298). The identity of the competent landlord can change during the course of the statutory procedure.

The competent landlord's interest, which can be equitable

(*Shelley v United Artists Corporation* [1990] 1 E.G.L.R. 103), must be in reversion to the relevant tenancy, and:

(a)   in fee simple; or
(b)   a tenancy not expiring by effluxion of time within 14 months and in respect of which no notice has been served to end it within that period. Extensions to allow for court proceedings, or on the revocation of an order for the grant of a new tenancy, are ignored.

If the immediate landlord's interest does not comply with these conditions, then the next most immediate landlord whose interest does comply is the competent landlord.

The effect of these provisions where the tenant is in possession **12–08** under a sub-tenancy varies. If the subletting is of the whole of the property comprised in the head lease, the immediate landlord is only the competent landlord if the head lease has over 14 months to run. As the immediate landlord is not himself in possession for the purpose of a business carried on by him, his tenancy is not one to which the Act applies, and so it will expire by effluxion of time or pursuant to an ordinary notice to quit. The position is the same if the property comprised in the head lease has been sub-let in parts, but is all sub-let and none is retained by the head tenant.

On the other hand, if the immediate landlord is in possession for business purposes of part of what was let to him, and has sub-let the remainder, the head lease still constitutes a tenancy to which the Act applies. It does not come to an end in respect of any part of the property by effluxion of time alone: the statutory procedure must be used. Accordingly, the immediate landlord is the competent landlord of the sub-tenant unless, or until, statutory notice is served on him bringing the head lease to an end within 14 months.

The reversion may have been divided, so that more than one person owns the relevant interest in different parts of the property. In that case, all the relevant owners collectively constitute the landlord (s.44(1A)).

3 Information

(a) Duty to provide information
The parties may not be in possession of all the information **12–09** which they need to claim or resist the right to renew. For this reason there are statutory rights to require information which apply at any time after the renewal procedure has started (s.40).

There is, however, a limit to how early it applies, and this is judged by reference to when the tenancy would expire ignoring the Act's provisions. There must not be more than two years to go before the tenancy would expire by effluxion of time or could be brought to an end by notice to quite given by the landlord (s.40(6)).

The information must be sought by serving a prescribed form of notice (Form 4, served by the landlord; Form 5, served by the tenant) and given within a month of service. The nature of it varies depending who initiates the renewal procedure.

(b) Information from tenant

A landlord, who may not be the immediate landlord, who has served notice to end a tenancy require the tenant to give him information. The information is (s.40(1), (2)):

(a)   whether the tenant occupies all or part of the premises for a business he carries on;

(b)   whether there is any immediate sub-tenancy and if so: what relating to what premises; its term or how it is terminable; the rent payable; who is the sub-tenant; whether (so far as he knows) the sub-tenant is in occupation, otherwise his address; whether an agreement relating to the sub-tenancy excludes renewal; whether statutory notice has been given to end the tenancy, the tenant has made a request to renew and his landlord have given a counter-notice, with details;

(c)   (so far as he knows) the name and address of any other reversioner.

(c) Information from the landlord

12–10   A tenant who has served a request for a new tenancy may require the landlord, or his mortgagee in possession, to give him information. The information is (s.40(3), (4)):

(a)   whether he owns, or is mortgagee of, the fee simple;

(b)   if not (so far as he knows): the name and address of the immediate landlord; the term of the his, or the mortgagee's, tenancy and the earliest date on which it could be ended by notice to quit; whether statutory notice has been given to end the superior tenancy, the tenant has made a request to renew and his landlord have given a counter-notice, with details;

(c)   (so far as he knows) the name and address of any other reversioner;

(d)   whether there is a mortgagee in possession of his interest, with (so far he knows) the name and address of any that there is.

(d) Transferred interests
The recipient of a notice to supply information who transfers his interest in the premises ceases to be under a duty to supply information if he complies with required formalities. He must give written notice of the transfer, with the name and address of the transferee, to the person to whom the information should be given. On a transfer of part of the premises, this applies to information relating to that part (s.40A(1)).

The position following a transfer of his interest in the premises **12–11** by the person who served notice requiring information does not remove the duty to give the information. But to whom it must be given depends whether the recipient of the notice is given written notice of the transfer with the transferee's name and address. If he is, the information must be given to the transferee. If not, it may be given either to the transferor or to the transferee (s.40A(2), (3)).

(e) Default
Not supplying information in breach of the obligation imposed by the Act is a breach of statutory duty. If civil proceedings are brought, the court can order compliance and make an award of damages.

A landlord who takes a step which represents him as competent landlord, *e.g.* serving a counter-notice, has a duty to tell the tenant if he ceases to be competent landlord: he must correct what has become a misrepresentation (*Shelley v United Artists Corporation* [1990] 1 E.G.L.R. 103).

4 Notice by the landlord

(a) Person serving the notice
The notice may be signed on the landlord's behalf by his agent: **12–12** the prescribed form expressly makes provision for that. Where there are joint landlords, one of them alone may give the notice, at least if there is no breach of trust (*Leckhampton Dairies Ltd v Artus Whitfield Ltd* (1986) 130 S.J. 225).

(b) Person to be served
The landlord's notice must be served on 'the tenant' (s.25(1)). In context, this means the tenant entitled to claim a new lease. Where the landlord's direct tenant is in occupation of the whole of the premises for business purposes this causes no problem. However, if

the premises have been sublet, the person on whom the competent landlord should serve notice varies depending on the circumstances. If the whole premises are sublet and the subtenants are in occupation for business purposes, notice is served on the subtenants.

When the premises have been partly sublet, and the immediate tenant still occupies part for business purposes, the landlord has a choice. If he wants to grant a new tenancy of the whole premises to his immediate tenant, he serves notice on him only. The landlord must then opt to include the whole of the original premises in the new tenancy (s.32(2)). That new tenancy will be subject to the subletting of part. In such a case the landlord's intention, to grant a new tenancy of the whole premises, will be frustrated if the immediate tenant decides not to ask for a new tenancy, but to quit. The landlord's alternative course is to serve notice direct on any subtenant. The renewal will then in each case relate only to the property comprised in the current subtenancy.

When notice is served on a subtenant, the time for service of it depends on the date of termination of that subtenancy, not on when the head tenancy ends.

(c) Form of notice

12–13   The landlord's notice to terminate a business tenancy must be in the prescribed form (s.25(1)). Which form is appropriate depends on the landlord's intentions. If he does not intend to resist renewal, Form 1 is normally the one to use. If he opposes renewal, he will normally need to use Form 2, or if leasehold enfranchisement might apply, Form 7. There is a series of other forms of notice for special cases.

Use of the printed form is advisable, because the extensive notes are part of the form as prescribed. A notice in a form not 'materially' different from the prescribed form is valid (*Sun Alliance and London Assurance Co Ltd v Hayman* [1975] 1 W.L.R. 177).

There are three statutory requirements as to the form of notice, depending on the circumstances which apply. A careful user of the correct prescribed form can hardly fail to comply as, not unnaturally, it makes suitable provision.

12–14   First, the landlord's notice must state whether he would oppose an application to the court for a new tenancy, and if so on which statutory grounds (s.25(6), (7)). The form enables the user to refer to the statutory wording, set out in the notes, by using the paragraph letter. Consent made conditional on something which is not related to the statutory grounds for opposition, *e.g.* finding a suitable guarantor, invalidates the notice (*Barclays Bank Ltd v Ascott* [1961] 1 W.L.R. 717).

If the landlord states that he is not opposed to the grant of a new tenancy, the second requirement applies. The notice must then set out the landlord's proposals the new tenancy: the property to be demised, the rent to be paid and the other terms. Without these details, the notice is ineffective (s.25(8)). This information is the equivalent of the new tenancy proposals that a tenant is bound to include in a statutory request for a new tenancy. It allows the parties to negotiate realistically. The other terms of a proposed tenancy can often be summarised by saying that they will be the same as the current tenancy, or by limiting details to the changes proposed.

The third requirement relates to premises which are a house let on a long tenancy at a low rent and the tenant is not a company or other artificial person. The notice must give information about enfranchisement or claiming an extended lease (Leasehold Reform Act 1967, Sch.3, para.10). There is a different prescribed form, Form 7. It must say that if the tenant has the right to claim under the 1967 Act, notice can only be given within two months after the service of the landlord's notice to terminate the tenancy, that thereupon the landlord's notice will not operate and that if the tenant does give notice, whether the landlord can apply under s.17 or s.18 of the 1967 Act (which gives the landlord rights for redevelopment and residential purposes) and whether he will do so. The landlord must also name and give addresses for anyone he knows or believes to have interests superior to the tenant's or their agents.

To be valid, the landlord's notice must relate to the whole of the **12–15** premises comprised in the lease (*Kaiser Engineers & Construction Inc v E R Squibb & Sons Ltd* [1971] E.G.D. 553) unless the lease itself makes it clear that it is to be interpreted as separate lettings of different parts and the notice refers to the whole of one of those parts (*Moss v Mobil Oil Co Ltd* [1988] 1 E.G.L.R. 71). The general rule applies even if the reversion has been severed so that there are different landlords for different parts of the property demised by a single lease (*Dodson Bull Carpet Co Ltd v City of London Corporation* [1975] 1 W.L.R. 781).

A single notice may be used to end more than one tenancy, if the parties to each are the same and all can validly be ended on the same day (*Tropis Shipping Co Ltd v Ibex Property Corporation Ltd* [1967] E.G.D. 433). However, if the owners of more than one property joined together to grant a single lease, they cannot act separately to end the tenancy in so far as it relates to their property (*M&P Enterprises (London) Ltd v Norfolk Square Hotels Ltd* [1994] 1 E.G.L.R. 129).

In the exceptional cases where there is no right to renew, or a **12–16** limited one, on the grounds of national interest, there are different prescribed forms of notice. When notice is given on the grounds of public interest, Form 8 must be used (enfranchisement cases: Form 13). Where the ground for giving notice is the fact that a change of use or occupation will be required at a future date on the grounds of public interest, Form 9 is appropriate where the landlord opposes renewal (enfranchisement cases: Form 14); when the landlord does not oppose renewal, he should use Form 10 (enfranchisement cases: Form 15). When national security is the reason, Form 11 is used. Notice given to allow for regeneration must be on Form 12 (enfranchisement cases: Form 16). In all these cases a ministerial or similar certificate has to be given, and a copy of it must be set out in the schedule to the notice. Where a change of use or of occupier is required to provide employment, the appropriate notice for Welsh Development Agency premises is Form 16 (enfranchisement cases: Form 17).

There is normally no need to have a separate notice in non-statutory form to bring to an end a tenancy not expiring by effluxion of time (*Commercial Properties Ltd v Wood* [1968] 1 Q.B. 15). The same has been held to apply when the landlord exercises an option to determine granted by the lease (*Scholl Manufacturing Co Ltd v Clifton (Slim-Line) Ltd* [1967] Ch. 41). An ordinary, non-statutory, notice exercising the option is effective only to convert the tenancy into one extended indefinitely by s.24.

A landlord whose own interest is leasehold must forthwith send a copy of the notice he serves on the tenant to his own landlord (Sch.6, para.7).

(d) Which form of notice: summary

12–17 This is a guide to the form of notice which the landlord should use to give in the different circumstances which may apply.

Do special circumstances apply?	Does the landlord oppose renewal?	Can the Leasehold Reform Act 1967 apply?	Use Form No.
No ⇨	No	→ → →	1
	Yes ⇨	No Yes	2 7
Yes ↳ ↳ s.57 (immediate)	Yes	No Yes	8 13
↳ s.57 (future)	No	No	10
↳	Yes	No Yes	9 14
↳ s.58	Yes	→ → →	11
↳ s.60	Yes	No Yes	12 15
↳ s.60A	Yes	No Yes	16 17

(e) Irregularities

Certain irregularities in completing forms have been overlooked   **12–18**
by the courts, although obviously careful completion of the forms
is preferable. An undated notice has been held valid (*Falcon Pipes
Ltd v Stanhope Gate Property Co Ltd* (1967) 117 N.L.J. 1345), as
has an unsigned one when it was sent with a covering letter and an
addressed return envelope (*Stidolph v American School in London
Educational Trust* (1969) 113 S.J. 689). In another case, however,
where the validity of an unsigned notice was challenged and a
fresh one served, the first notice was held to be abandoned (*Nasim
v Wilson* (1975) 119 S.J. 611). A notice which omitted the year of
termination of the tenancy has even been held effective, because
the ambiguity could be resolved by referring to the notes on
the back (*Sunrose Ltd v Gould* [1962] 1 W.L.R. 20). Even using the
wrong form was accepted, when the error was apparent and the
tenant treated the notice as effective (*Keepers etc. of the Free
Grammar School of John Lyon v Mayhew* [1997] 1 E.G.L.R. 88).

On the other hand, an inaccuracy in the landlord's name and
address invalidated a notice (*Morrow v Nadeem* [1986] 1 W.L.R.
1381). Accordingly, a notice naming only one of two joint landlords is bad (*Pearson v Alyo* [1990] 1 E.G.L.R. 114). A notice which
did not make clear what property was affected—it referred to
offices, but not to storage and car parking which had also been
let—was invalid (*Herongrove Ltd v Wates City of London
Properties plc* [1988] 1 E.G.L.R. 82).

A landlord who realises that he has served an ineffective notice
may tell the tenant and validly serve a second one (*Smith v Draper*
[1990] 2 E.G.L.R. 69).

(f) Dates of service and expiry

The landlord's notice must be served between 12 and six months   **12–19**
before the date it specifies for the termination of the current
tenancy (s.25(2)). In cases where, in the absence of the statutory
provisions, the contractual tenancy would have needed more than
six months' notice to quit to bring it to an end, the earliest date for
the service of the landlord's statutory notice becomes the beginning of the period six months longer than the contractually
required notice, reckoned back from the date specified for the
tenancy's end (s.25(3)(b)). For example, where the tenancy
expressly requires nine months' notice to terminate it, the landlord's statutory notice may be served up to 15 months before the
date it gives the tenancy to end on.

The notice cannot bring the tenancy to an end earlier than it
would have ended under the common law had the Act not been in
force. Accordingly, the date specified can be on or after the date

that a tenancy for a fixed term expires by effluxion of time, or on or after the date that any other tenancy could have been terminated by notice given on the day the statutory notice is given (s.25(3)(a), (4)). Provided that these limits are observed, the statutory notice may expire on any day, not necessarily a rent day or a day when the tenancy is renewed.

12–20   Notice cannot be given after the tenant has served a request for a new tenancy (s.26(4)). This means that a landlord who delays serving his notice, intending to do so at the last possible moment, may find himself pre-empted. If the tenant serves a request taking effect as far ahead as possible, the contractual rent will run on until the date the request takes effect. The possible financial disadvantage of this from the landlord's point of view can be countered in the original drafting of the lease. If a rent review clause operates on the day following the original term date, the rent which the tenant's request allows to continue can be adjusted under that clause. That may, depending on the terms of the clause, yield a higher rent than the court would order as an interim rent.

Where the whole premises are sub-let, it is possible to arrive at the position that the subtenancy is terminated by the head landlord, acting as 'competent landlord', on a date earlier than he terminates the head tenancy (*Lewis v MTC (Cars) Ltd* [1975] 1 W.L.R. 457).

A landlord's notice cannot be given during the currency of a claim to purchase the freehold or for an extended lease (Leasehold Reform Act 1967, Sch.3, para.2). It ceases to have effect if a claim is made after it has been served, but a new notice can be served if that claim is not effective. In the new notice, the date of termination must be the date for termination given in the original notice or three months after the second notice is given, whichever is later.

(g) Mode of service
12–21   The provisions of s.23 of the Landlord and Tenant Act 1927 are incorporated for the service of notices under the 1954 Act (s.66(4)). The possible methods of service are:

(i)   personal service;
(ii)   leaving it at the addressee's last known place of abode in England and Wales (this includes a person's business address: *Price v West London Investment Building Society* [1964] 1 W.L.R. 616);
(iii) sending it addressed to him there by registered or recorded delivery post (Recorded Delivery Service Act 1962, s.1). A notice is served on the date it is posted (*Beanby Estates Ltd v Egg Stores (Stamford Hill) Ltd*

[2003] 1 W.L.R. 2064), whether or not it is received and even if it is returned undelivered (*Commercial Union Life Assurance Co Ltd v Moustafa* [1999] 2 E.G.L.R. 44);

(iv) in the case of a local or public authority or a statutory or public utility company, sending it addressed to the secretary or other proper officer at the principal office by registered or recorded delivery post.

These modes of service are not exhaustive. If the notice is received by the addressee, that is good service (*Stylo Shoes Ltd v Prices Tailors Ltd* [1960] Ch. 396). Other methods, such as the use of a document exchange, are therefore acceptable provided the notice actually arrives. In one case, a landlord who was unsure of the identity of the current lessee sent a notice addressed to several companies. As it in fact came to the tenant's notice, it was held valid (*Keith Bayley Rogers & Co v Cubes* (1975) 31 P. & C.R. 412).

Where the tenant is a limited company or a limited liability   **12–22** partnership, service may be effected by leaving the notice at its registered office, or sending it there by post (Companies Act 1985, s.725(1); Limited Liability Partnership Regulations 2001). The type of post is not, in this case, specified. A local authority may also be served at an office that it designates for receiving such notices (Local Government Act 1972, s.231(1)).

Apparently, a landlord's notice may be validly served on the tenant's solicitors, even though they have no express authority to accept it (*Nasim v Wilson* (1975) 119 S.J. 611).

(h) Withdrawal of landlord's notice
During the two months following service of the landlord's notice on the tenant, the notice can be withdrawn, if during that period the competent landlord changes (Sch.6, para.6). To withdraw it, the new competent landlord must serve on the tenant notice in Form 12.

5 Request by the tenant

(a) When appropriate
The tenant can only request a new tenancy when his current one was granted for a term of years certain exceeding one year, or a term of years certain and thereafter from year to year (s.26(1)). The extension of the current tenancy under the 1954 Act does not affect the position; if the original tenancy was such that it did not entitle the tenant to make a request to renew he does not gain that right merely because of the statutory extension. A request cannot

be made after the landlord has given notice terminating the tenancy (s.26(4)), nor during the currency of a claim to purchase the freehold or for an extended lease (Leasehold Reform Act 1967, Sch.3, para.1). A request served by a tenant who is not entitled to make one is invalid and does not terminate the tenancy (*Watkins v Emslie* (1981) 132 N.L.J. 295). But the tenant need not genuinely wish to have a new tenancy when he makes the request (*Sun Life Assurance plc v Thales Tracs Ltd* [2001] 1 W.L.R. 1562).

(b) Form of request

12–23   The tenant's request must be made on the prescribed form (s.26(3)). This is prescribed Form 3. It must set out the tenant's proposals for the new tenancy. If the proposals are for a tenancy on the same terms as the current one, the assumption is that that means a term of similar duration (*Sidney Bolsom Investment Trust Ltd v E Karmios & Co (London) Ltd* [1956] 1 Q.B. 529).

(c) Dates of service and expiry

The request must be made between 12 and six months before the date specified for the current tenancy to end (s.26(1)). This date must be on or after the date on which the tenancy would expire by effluxion of time, or could have, ignoring the provisions of the Act, been brought to an end by the tenant giving notice to quit (s.26(2)). Strict observance of these time limits can be waived, *e.g.* by a landlord who takes steps in the renewal procedure, even if he did not know the request was served early (*Bristol Cars Ltd v RKH Hotels Ltd* (1979) 38 P. & C.R. 411). Unlike the case of the landlord's notice, there is no variation if the contractual terms of the tenancy require long notice.

The tenant is only entitled to serve a single request for a new tenancy. If he serves one which becomes abortive because he does not apply to the court in time, he cannot abandon it and serve another (*Polyviou v Seeley* [1980] 1 W.L.R. 55). The original request takes effect to end the tenancy on the date it stated.

(d) Mode of service

12–24   The tenant's request may be served by any of the means allowed for a landlord's notice. In addition, it may be served on any agent of the landlord duly authorised in that behalf (s.66(4); Landlord and Tenant Act 1927, s.23).

(e) Action by landlord

Within two months after the tenant's request is made, the landlord may give notice that he would oppose any application to the court for the grant of a new tenancy (s.26(6)). The notice must specify on which of the statutory grounds of opposition the landlord will rely. There is no prescribed form for this notice.

Where the landlord's own interest is leasehold, he must forthwith upon receiving the tenant's request send a copy of it to his own immediate landlord (Sch. 6, para.7).

6 Application to court

(a) Application by either party
The 2004 changes to the Act for the first time allowed the land-   **12–25**
lord, as well as the tenant, to apply for a new tenancy. But they cannot jointly apply, and if an application by one has already been served the other cannot make a claim (s.24(2A)). Whichever application is made first is the one which proceeds. The same applies to an application to fix an interim rent (s.24A(2)). Similarly, the landlord may only make a claim to end the current tenancy without renewal if neither he nor the tenant has started proceedings for a new tenancy (s.29(3)).

A court application by the landlord cannot result in a new tenancy being foisted on the tenant against his will. The court must dismiss a renewal application by the landlord if the tenant informs the court that he does not want a new tenancy (s.29(5)). Even if an order is made, the tenant has 14 days within which he may apply to the court to revoke it (s.36(2)).

Court decisions relating to cases before the 2004 changes applied necessarily concern the tenants' applications to renew. Most of these rulings would appear to continue to apply, whichever party makes the application.

(b) Time limits
A court application to renew a tenancy made after the landlord   **12–26**
served notice to end the current tenancy cannot, necessarily, be made before the notice is served. There is no other limit on how early the claim can be made, whether by the tenant or the landlord. However, if the renewal process is started by a tenant's request, there is an earliest date before which no action can be taken. This is designed to give time for the landlord to make clear whether he opposes the request, and if so on what grounds. The application cannot be made earlier than two months after the request was made (precisely two months is acceptable: *E J Riley Instruments v Eurostile Holdings Ltd* [1985] 1 W.L.R. 1139) or earlier if the landlord has given a counter-notice (s.29A(3)).

There is a final time limit for bringing proceedings, whether by the tenant or by the landlord. The application must be made no later than the date specified in the landlord's notice (*i.e.* for the current tenancy to end) or in the tenant's request (*i.e.* for the new tenancy to begin). Those time limits may, however, be extended by written agreement between the parties, provided that the agreement is entered into before the time for making the application has expired (ss.29A (1), (2), 29B). There can be more than one extension agreement. The first must be made before the date given in the notice or request, and any later agreement must be made before the previous one expires.

12–27   Before the 2004 changes to the Act, tenants frequently made court applications to safeguard their right to renew, although no further steps were taken because the matter was resolved by negotiation. This was done even though the time limit for proceedings could be waived by the parties (*Kammins Ballroom Co Ltd v Zenith Investments (Torquay) Ltd* [1971] A.C. 850). Spelling out the right to extend the time limit by agreement, and making the arrangements statutory, should give the parties more confidence to do so pending a negotiated settlement and remove the need for abortive applications.

There is a separate final time limit for making an application to fix an interim rent. It cannot be made more than six months after the current tenancy has ended (s.24A(3)).

Where the time limit for making any application expires on a day when the court office is closed, it may be made on the next working day (*Pritam Kuar v S Russell & Sons Ltd* [1973] Q.B. 336).

(c) Applicant

12–28   Both or all joint tenants or joint landlords must join in an application. The court has a discretionary power to order one joint owner, as a trustee, to join in to protect the trust property. The power is not likely to be used when joint owners hold the premises in trust for themselves beneficially (*Harris v Black* (1983) 127 S.J. 224).

A tenant's executor can make the application, but must first obtain probate (*Re Crowhurst Park, Sims-Hilditch v Simmons* [1974] 1 W.L.R. 583).

(d) Property

A single court application can relate to a number of properties let under separate leases, where the parties are the same, and acting in the same capacities, and the statutory notice procedure has been completed for each property (*Curtis v Calgary Investments Ltd* (1984) 47 P. & C.R. 13). Issues relating to individual properties can be argued separately, and the court may order separate trials if appropriate.

(e) Jurisdiction
    The claim must normally be started in the county court for the **12–29** district in which the premises are situated. Exceptionally, it may be started in the High Court if the claimant files a certificate stating his reasons for doing so, verified by a statement of truth. Appropriate grounds are complicated disputes of fact or points of law of general importance; the value of the property or the amount of any financial claim will not of themselves normally justify starting a claim in the High Court. A claim which should have been started in the county court but was started in the High Court will normally be either struck out or transferred by the court on its own initiative, and the High Court costs will be disallowed (CPR, r.56.2, CPR Practice Direction Pt 56, para.2).

(f) Evidence
    Evidence on which the parties intend to rely in court proceedings must be filed and served in advance. Unless served within time limits, it can only be relied upon with the permission of the court (CPR, r.56.3(10)–(13)).
    A number of case, decided before the introduction of the Civil Procedure Rules, examined the extent which the court would order discovery (now, disclosure). It will only be ordered in very special cases where the facts justify it (*Wine Shippers (London) Ltd v Bath House Syndicate Ltd* [1960] 1 W.L.R. 989). It was refused where the tenant wanted to challenge the landlord's intention to occupy the premises (*John Miller (Shipping) Ltd v Port of London Authority (Practice Note)* [1959] 1 W.L.R. 910). But a tenant was ordered to produce accounts, where the issue was its financial ability to perform the lease covenants (*Re St Martin's Theatre, Bright Enterprises Ltd v Lord Willoughby de Broke* [1959] 1 W.L.R. 872).

(g) Preliminary issues
    Issues raised by the landlord's opposition to the new tenancy **12–30** are the first to be determined by the court, and they can be taken as preliminary issues (*Dutch Oven Ltd v Egham Estate and Investment Co Ltd* [1968] 1 W.L.R. 1483). So, there may be a trial as a preliminary issue of the question whether the premises are occupied for the purpose of a business (*Gurton v Parrott* [1991] 1 E.G.L.R. 98), or the question whether the landlord intends to occupy the premises for his own business (*London Hilton Jewellers Ltd v Hilton International Hotels Ltd* [1990] 1 E.G.L.R. 112).

(h) Registration
    It is considered that the tenant's application to the court should be registered as a pending land action, in the Land Registry or the

Land Charges Department as appropriate. This conclusion is based on a decision that a forfeiture action is registrable because its aim is to end a legal estate (*Selim Ltd v Bickenhall Engineering Ltd* [1981] 1 W.L.R. 1318). An application under the Landlord and Tenant Act 1954 is, in effect, an action to create a new legal estate.

(i) Withdrawal

12–31   The right to withdraw some proceedings in relation to the right to renew a lease is restricted. As the claim may be made by either the landlord or the tenant, but only by one of them at a time, it is necessary to ensure that the landlord cannot prejudice the tenant by starting proceedings and then abandoning them so that the court has no opportunity to adjudicate. Accordingly, the landlord needs the tenant's consent if he is to withdraw proceedings which he has started seeking either an order for a new tenancy or an order to end the current tenancy without renewal (ss.24(2C), 29(6)). A copy of the tenant's consent must be attached to the notice of discontinuance which the landlord files (CPR, r.38.3(3)).

No similar restriction is placed on the tenant. This is because his proceedings will be to renew the tenancy and if he abandons them there will be no renewal. Although this may not be the outcome which the landlord is seeking, he cannot oblige the tenant take a new lease; the court must dismiss the application if the tenant informs the court that he does not want one (s.29(5)).

(j) Result

12–32   Unless one of the statutory grounds for refusal is established, the court must make an order for the grant of a new tenancy (s.29(1)).

If a new tenancy is granted, the tenant has 14 days within which to apply for the order to be revoked, presumably in case he changes his mind on learning what the terms of the new tenancy are going to be (s.36(2)). Unless he does so apply, or both parties agree not to proceed, the landlord is bound to grant, and the tenant to take, a new lease (s.36(1)). The tenant must execute a counterpart or duplicate if the landlord requires it.

If the landlord successfully establishes one of the statutory grounds of opposition to the tenant's claim to renew, the application must be dismissed (s.31). There is a further possibility if the landlord's opposition is based on one of the following three grounds: an offer of alternative accommodation, a claim to let a whole property more profitably than in parts, or an intention to demolish or reconstruct. Even if the ground is not established, the landlord may seek to show that the court would have been satisfied had the operative date of the landlord's original notice, or the tenant's request for a new tenancy, been up to a year later. If this is established, the court must make a declaration stating the grounds on which it would have been satisfied and on what date. No order for a new tenancy is made. The tenant then has 14 days to apply to the court for an order substituting the date in the declaration for the date in the landlord's notice or the tenant's request. The notice or request then has effect as if that had been the date originally specified, and the current tenancy comes to an end on that substituted date.

(k) Costs

Costs of an application are in the discretion of the court (*Decca Navigator Co Ltd v Greater London Council* [1974] 1 W.L.R. 748).

A landlord who gave notice that it would oppose the grant of a new tenancy on the ground of its intention to occupy the premises, and then withdrew its opposition after the tenant had commenced proceedings, was ordered to pay costs (*Demag Industrial Equipment Ltd v Canada Dry (UK) Ltd* [1969] 1 W.L.R. 985). So was a tenant who exercised his right to have the order for a new tenancy revoked (*Re No.88 High Road, Kilburn, Meakers Ltd v DAW Consolidated Properties Ltd* [1959] 1 W.L.R. 279).

7 Renewing subtenancies

It is when the tenancy to be renewed is a sub-tenancy that the designation of the competent landlord becomes important. As has been mentioned, the identity of the competent landlord can change during the renewal procedure, and it is vital that each step is conducted by the tenant with the current competent landlord, even where the change is immediately prior to the hearing of the application to the court (*René Claro (Haute Coiffure) Ltd v Hallé Concerts Society* [1969] 1 W.L.R. 909).

Special provisions apply to sub-tenancy cases to cover the fact that the implementation of the tenant's renewal rights may affect the rights of more than one of those with interests superior to his, and to take account of the effects of a change in superior landlords (Sch.6). Where the new tenancy to be granted to the tenant is longer than the reversion enjoyed by his immediate landlord (and even by any superior landlord with a leasehold reversion), the court can order the grant of one or more reversionary tenancies necessary to make up the full period.

The competent landlord has power to bind any mesne landlord, *i.e.* a person whose interest is intermediate between the

12–33

tenant and the competent landlord. This applies to any notice he gives to terminate the tenancy in possession, and any agreement he makes with the tenant as to the grant, duration or terms of a new tenancy. He has power to give effect to such an agreement. An instrument made in exercise of this power takes effect as if the mesne landlord were a party to it. If, however, the competent landlord acts without the mesne landlord's consent, he is liable to pay compensation for any loss arising as a consequence of what he does. The mesne landlord's consent may not unreasonably be withheld, but it may be conditional. The court decides whether consent is unreasonably withheld or conditions unreasonably imposed. The tenant does not need to enquire whether the mesne landlord's consent has been given, as its absence does not invalidate the agreement.

12–34   On the other hand, the competent landlord has no power to bind anyone with an interest superior to his. If the new tenancy is to extend for longer than the remainder of his lease, no agreement with the tenant is effective unless every superior landlord who will in due course be the tenant's immediate landlord at any time during the period concerned is also a party to it. In this case, the tenant needs to enquire into the length of the interests of all involved, to ensure that all necessary parties have been joined in the agreement.

At If the competent landlord's interest is one that will or could be brought to an end within sixteen months of the date when he gives notice to terminate the tenancy, or receives a tenant's request for a new tenancy, he must forthwith send a copy of the notice or request to his immediate landlord, and the copies must be passed all the way up the line of landlords. If the competent landlord changes within two months of the giving of a notice to terminate a tenancy, the new competent landlord can withdraw the notice within that two months by serving on the tenant a notice on Form 6.

8 Landlord's interest in mortgage

12–35   Where the landlord's interest is in mortgage, a lease executed pursuant to an order of the court for renewal is deemed to be one authorised by the Law of Property Act 1925, s.99, which confers powers of leasing on mortgagors (s.36(4)). Moreover, any restriction or exclusion of these powers, which is almost universal practice in mortgages now, is ineffective. So the mortgagee's consent is never required. This provision does not, however, cover new leases granted by agreement.

9 Summary

(a) Tenant wishes to renew

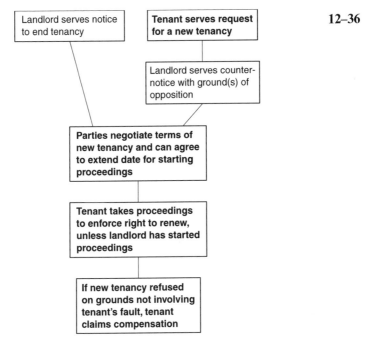

12–36

(b) Tenant does not wish to renew

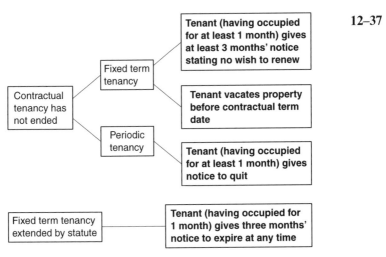

12–37

(c) Landlord opposes renewal

12–38

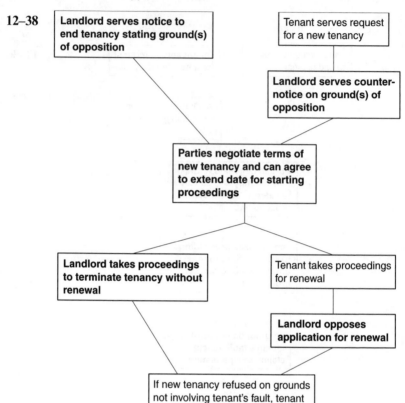

(d) Landlord does not oppose renewal

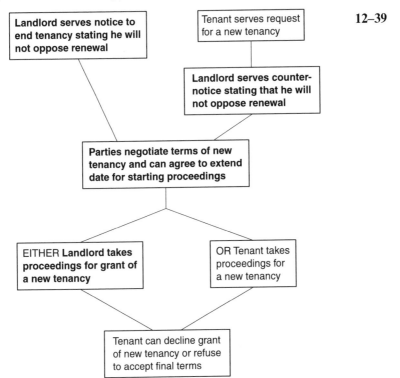

12–39

10 **Alternative to proceedings**

An alternative dispute resolution procedure has been developed   **12–40**
to offer an alternative to taking court proceedings in cases where
the landlord does not oppose renewal of a business tenancy.
'Professional Arbitration on Court Terms' (PACT) was launched
in 1997 jointly by the Law Society and the Royal Institution of
Chartered Surveyors. It may be that it will need some adaptation
in the light of the 2004 changes to the legislation.

The scheme envisages this procedure:

(i)   The tenant applies to the court for a new tenancy. This
       establishes that the right to apply has not been lost
       because the time limit had expired. An extension can now
       be agreed (s.29B). Formerly, only the tenant could apply
       to the court; either party may now apply (s.24(1)).

(ii)   Any ground of opposition to renewal is dealt with by the court.

(iii) The parties seek a consent order, recording the terms on which they agree and referring outstanding matters to a third party under the scheme.

(iv)   Unresolved matters are then referred to a third party, acting either as an arbitrator or an independent expert. The third party may be appointed by agreement or by the Law Society or the R.I.C.S.

Chapter 13

Terms of the New Lease

1 Agreement

Some or all of the terms of the new tenancy may be agreed **13–01** between the landlord and the tenant (ss.33–35). To be effective in excluding the jurisdiction of the court to determine those terms the agreement must be in writing (s.69(2)). Also, the agreement must be made for the purpose of a court application (*Derby & Co Ltd v ITC Pensions Trust Ltd* [1977] 2 All E.R. 890), *i.e.* to eliminate certain points of contention on which the court would otherwise have to adjudicate. The parties' negotiation of the terms of a new lease, which they often conduct separately from, but in parallel to, an application to the court, does not yield an agreement for this purpose while still subject to contract.

It is possible for a formal offer of new terms, which on acceptance will be binding, to be made in the pleadings of an application for a new lease (*Lovely & Orchard Services Ltd v Daejan Investments (Grove Hall) Ltd* (1977) 121 S.J. 711).

2 Property

Normally, the property comprised in the new tenancy is that part **13–02** of the property included in the current tenancy which is occupied by the applicant tenant or by a person employed by him for the purpose of the business which brings the tenancy within the 1954 Act (ss.23(3), 32). Landlord's fixtures are included (*Poster v Slough Estates Ltd* [1969] 1 Ch. 495). The whole of the property currently let may well be included, but if it is not, the extent of what is to be in the new tenancy may be agreed in writing between the landlord and the tenant. In default, the court designates it, by reference to the circumstances at the date of the order.

13–03   The landlord may require the whole of the property comprised in the current tenancy to be included in the new one, notwithstanding that some of it is sub-let. He cannot, however, insist that some sub-let portions are included while others are not.

Where the tenant agrees to accept a new tenancy of part only of the property comprised in the current tenancy, so that the landlord can carry out works on the remainder, the new tenancy is confined to the part he accepts.

Appurtenant rights included in the current tenancy are included in the new one, unless excluded by written agreement between landlord and tenant, or by order of the court. The tenant has no right to insist that a benefit that he has been enjoying, but not as of right, be included in the new lease (*G Orlik (Meat Products) Ltd v Hastings & Thanet Building Society* (1974) 29 P. & C.R. 126).

3 Term

13–04   Unless the landlord and tenant agree in writing on the term of the new tenancy, the court is empowered to grant such term, up to a maximum of 15 years, as it considers reasonable in all the circumstances (s.33). The new tenancy starts when the current one comes to an end under the Act's provisions. The parties can agree on a different commencement date. That agreed date, *e.g.* the day immediately following the expiry of the original contractual term, can be incorporated into a court order by consent (*Bradshaw v Pawley* [1980] 1 W.L.R. 10). The Court of Appeal has recommended that, to achieve certainty, a term should be defined as a period from a fixed date (*Warwick & Warwick (Philately) Ltd v Shell (UK) Ltd* (1981) 42 P. & C.R. 136).

The court's discretion in fixing the length of the new tenancy is very wide, but certain guidance emerges from the cases. The new term will not generally be longer than the one previously enjoyed by the same tenant except possibly where he has been in continuous possession for a long time. In practice the new term will often be the same length as the current one. Where a property is ripe for redevelopment, a short term is generally appropriate, even though the landlord has no immediate plans enabling him successfully to resist the tenant's application for a new tenancy (*London & Provincial Millinery Stores Ltd v Barclays Bank Ltd* [1962] 1 W.L.R. 510). The period of extension under s.24 before the grant of the new lease already enjoyed by the tenant is a material factor (*ibid*), and so is the landlord's narrowly missing the five year ownership period which would have allowed him to obtain possession (*Upsons Ltd v E Robins Ltd* [1956] 1 Q.B. 131).

A break clause (*i.e.* an option to determine) can be ordered by **13–05** the court (*McCombie v Grand Junction Co Ltd* [1962] 1 W.L.R. 581). This power will be exercised to facilitate development that is reasonably likely, even though not immediately in prospect (*Adams v Green* (1978) 247 E.G. 49) or to allow comprehensive redevelopment of the area in a form yet to be decided (*National Car Parks Ltd v Paternoster Construction Ltd* [1990] E.G.L.R. 99). The clause may be ordered in a form which prevents the landlord serving notice for an initial fixed period, to give the tenant some security (*J H Edwards & Sons Ltd v Central London Commercial Estates Ltd; Eastern Bazaar Ltd v Central London Commercial Estates Ltd* (1983) 271 E.G. 697). If the existing lease has a break clause, the new one will normally also do so, although it is not automatic (*Leslie & Goodwin Investments Ltd v Prudential Assurance Co Ltd* [1987] 2 E.G.L.R. 95).

Among factors militating against including a break clause in a new lease can be that it will only be for a short time until the tenant's retirements and the tenant has installed equipment which it would be costly to move (*Becker v Hill Street Properties Ltd* [1990] 2 E.G.L.R. 78).

Where a ministerial certificate has been given that the use or occupation of premises must in the national interest be changed by a certain date, the term cannot extend beyond then (s.57(3)(b)). There is no right to renew when that further term expires.

The term may be made subject to termination on notice in **13–06** certain cases in the national interest. The first applies where the interest of the competent landlord is vested in or held for the purposes of any government department, or is held by any of the specified public bodies (Leasehold Reform Act 1967, s.38(2)). The Minister or Board in charge of any government department may certify that it is necessary in the public interest that, if the landlord so applies, the court shall determine that the tenancy be terminable by the landlord on six months' notice (s.57(5)). In such a case, the court is obliged to include that term. The tenant must be given notice that a certificate is being sought, and at least 21 days must be allowed for representations.

The other cases deal with premises required for reasons of national security. The Minister or Board in charge of any government department may certify that it is in the public interest that the new tenancy includes certain terms, in which case the court must, if the landlord so applies, include them (s.58(4)). These terms make the tenancy subject to a specified length of notice and include the form of the agreement to exclude the right to renew which the Act specially validates for national security purposes.

4 Rent

13–07   *(a) Agreement*
   The rent payable under the new lease is to be agreed in writing
between landlord and tenant, or in default determined by the court
(s.34). Where the reversion has been divided, the apportionment of
the rent between the different parts is similarly to be agreed or
determined (s.35(1)).

(b) Reviews
   The court may order the inclusion of a rent revision clause
(s.34(3)). Whether this will be an upward only review or an upward
and downward review will depend on the circumstances and the
evidence given. The question has been much litigated, but it seems
unlikely that earlier decisions will proffer binding precedents.
Upward and downward reviews were ordered in: *Janes (Gowns)
Ltd v Harlow Development Corporation* (1980) 253 E.G. 799; *Boots
the Chemists Ltd v Pinkland Ltd* [1992] 2 E.G.L.R. 96 (*cc*); *Amerjee
v Barrowfen Properties Ltd* [1993] 2 E.G.L.R. 133 (*cc*); *Forbuoys plc
v Newport Borough Council* [1994] 1 E.G.L.R. 138 (*cc*). That form
of review was refused in *Blythewood Plant Hire Ltd v Spiers Ltd*
[1992] 2 E.G.L.R. 103.
   The court also has power to order a differential rent, *i.e.* a rent
at one level until a certain date or the happening of a specified
event, and then at a different level (*Fawke v Viscount Chelsea* [1980]
Q.B. 411). However, that is only likely in exceptional circumstances
and there is no reported decision where it has been done.

(c) Amount
13–08   The Act lays down a formula by which the rent is to be fixed.
The court determines it on the basis of what could reasonably be
expected on a letting of the premises in the open market by a
willing lessor on the terms of the tenancy (other than rent). A
'willing lessor' is a hypothetical landlord, not affected by any personal attributes of the actual landlord (*F R Evans (Leeds) Ltd v
English Electric Co Ltd* (1977) 36 P. & C.R. 185). The statutory
formula does not specify, as many rent review clauses do, that the
new rent must assume a letting to a 'willing tenant'. Presumably,
the tenant's willingness is taken for granted because it is he who
makes the application to the court.
   If the result of the introduction of the Landlord and Tenant
(Covenants) Act 1995 is that a two-tier market develops, with
different levels of market rent for old and new tenancies, the rent
payable under a renewed lease which is a new tenancy should
reflect the market level for that type of letting.

Certain matters affecting the amount of the rent have to be disregarded:

(i)   the fact that the premises have been occupied by the tenant or his predecessors in title. This allows the condition of the premises, resulting from the tenant's non-observance of repairing covenants, to be ignored (*Family Management v Gray* (1980) 253 E.G. 369);

(ii)   any goodwill attached to the premises by reason of the carrying on there of the tenant's business, whether by him or by any predecessor in that business;

(iii) the effect of any relevant improvement;

(iv) any value attributable to a licence to sell intoxicating liquor where the benefit of the licence belongs to the tenant.

The rent must be fixed after the other terms of the tenancy are decided (*Cardshops Ltd v Davies* [1971] 1 W.L.R. 591). Those other terms may affect the rent. The date at which the level of the new rent is to be judged is the date of the hearing, but taking into account foreseeable trends between then and the date it is likely to take effect (*Lovely & Orchard Services Ltd v Daejan Investments (Grove Hall) Ltd* (1977) 121 S.J. 711).

(d) Improvements   **13–09**

For the effect on rent of an improvement to be disregarded in fixing the rent, that improvement must have been carried out by the tenant, otherwise than in pursuance of an obligation to his immediate landlord. Work done at a time when the lease had not been granted, when the prospective tenant was only a licensee under an agreement for lease, does not count because it was not done by the tenant in that capacity (*Euston Centre Properties Ltd v H & J Wilson Ltd* (1981) 262 E.G. 1079).

There are also conditions as to the time when the improvement was carried out which must be satisfied. It must have been done during the current tenancy, or within 21 years prior to the application for a new tenancy. In the latter case, the premises (or at least the part affected by the improvement) must at all times since the improvement was made have been let on business tenancies, with the tenant remaining in possession at the end of each of them (had the tenant quit at the end of the term, he might have qualified for compensation under the Landlord and Tenant Act 1927). Where the improvement in question is a fixture, the 21 years does not begin to run until the tenant loses the right to remove the fixture from the freehold. That right is not lost until one lease comes to an end without a new one being granted to the tenant in possession (*New Zealand Property Corporation v H M & S Ltd* [1982] Q.B. 1145).

(e) Evidence

13–10   The normal evidence of what is the market rent is the amount reserved on recent lettings of similar properties in the area ('comparables').

Evidence of the profitability of the tenant's business is normally irrelevant (*W J Barton Ltd v Long Acre Securities Ltd* [1982] 1 W.L.R. 398). In the exceptional case of a hotel, it was allowed (*Harewood Hotels Ltd v Harris* [1958] 1 W.L.R. 108). It has been suggested that profit could also be relevant in the case of a petrol filling station, a theatre and a racecourse. Normally, the fact that the premises command a higher rent than the tenant's business can afford will not be a reason for reducing it (*Giannoukakis v Saltfleet Ltd* [1988] 1 E.G.L.R. 73).

If the premises could be used for a more profitable purpose, the more valuable use must be considered (*e.g.* club premises which could have been used as offices: *Aldwych Club Ltd v Copthall Property Co Ltd* (1962) 185 E.G. 219). But where a clause is included in the new lease restricting the use, the lower rent appropriate to that use should be reserved (*Gorleston Golf Club v Links Estate (Gorleston)* [1959] C.L.Y. 1830 (*cc*)). The existence of a protected residential sub-tenancy of part of the premises may serve to reduce their open market value (*Oscroft v Benabo* [1967] 1 W.L.R. 1087).

The rent paid under the current lease is not a factor in fixing the new rent unless (as only occurs exceptionally) it constitutes definite evidence of the market rent. This means that on a renewal no account is taken of the fact that the previous rent was concessionary.

5 Other terms

The other terms of the tenancy are as agreed in writing between the landlord and the tenant, or determined by the court (s.35). The

13–11   court is to have regard to the terms of the current tenancy and all relevant circumstances. This seemingly wide power does not extend to enlarging the holding (*G Orlik (Meat Products) Ltd v Hastings & Thanet Building Society* (1974) 29 P. & C.R. 126), nor to inserting an option to buy the freehold (*Kirkwood v Johnson* (1979) 38 P. & C.R. 392).

(a) Variations
The new lease will generally follow the current one, but variations can be ordered. The court starts from the existing terms, and the onus is on the party proposing a change to show that it is fair and reasonable (*O'May v City of London Real Property Co Ltd* [1983] 2 A.C. 726). In *Gold v Brighton Corporation* [1956] 1 W.L.R. 1291, the permitted use of the premises was varied to accord with the tenant's actual business. A landlord's attempt to substitute an absolute covenant against assignment and underletting for a qualified one, was rejected because it imperilled the tenant's goodwill (*Cardshops Ltd v Davies* [1971] 1 W.L.R. 591). Another landlord failed to substitute a provision that the tenant contribute a proportion of the cost of major repairs for a fixed service charge, because the tenant was not adequately compensated and the provision was inappropriate for a short lease (*O'May v City of London Real Property Co Ltd*, above).

A possible ground for variation of the lease terms, as yet **13–12** untested, occurs where new statutes change the effect of provisions, depending when the lease was granted. One party or the other may argue that the lease wording should be altered in order to keep the status quo, or in order to maintain balance between landlord and tenant. Two recent examples may be given.

The extent of the liability of the original tenant and later assignees under a new tenancy was radically changed by the Landlord and Tenant (Covenants) Act 1995. In one case, a landlord argued for including in the new lease a requirement that an assigning tenant should have to enter into an authorised guarantee agreement. The court accepted this, but only subject to including the modification 'where reasonable' (*Wallis Fashion Group Ltd v CGU Life Assurance Ltd* [2000] 2 E.G.L.R. 49).

Again, a tenant's covenant in a lease of retail premises to open for business during trading hours specified by the landlord, now allows the landlord to require Sunday opening. In a lease granted before August 26, 1994, for trades previously prohibited on Sundays, the same covenant did not have that effect, even since the 1994 Act came into force (Sunday Trading Act 1994, 5.3).

(b) Official requirements
Where the landlord is the Department of Trade and Industry **13–13** or the English Industrial Estates Corporation, and the premises are in a development or intermediate area (Local Employment Act 1972, s.1), the Department may certify that it is necessary or expedient that the tenancy include a term prohibiting or restricting the tenant from assigning the tenancy or subletting, charging or parting with possession of the premises or any part of them, or

changing their use (s.60(2)). The National Assembly for Wales can issue a similar certificate where the landlord is the Welsh Development Agency (s.60A(2); Welsh Development Agency Act 1975, s.11). In such a case, the court must include the term so certified in the new tenancy.

(c) Costs

No term that the tenant pay the landlord's costs of the grant should be included in the new lease. This applies even if there was such a term in the current lease (*Cairnplace Ltd v CBL (Property Investment) Co Ltd* [1984] 1 W.L.R. 696).

6 Sureties

13–14   A court can only indirectly order the tenant to provide a surety for the new lease. The fact that the current lease incorporates a guarantee of the tenant's covenants does not automatically entitle the landlord to demand that the same shall apply to the new tenancy. He must demonstrate that it would be reasonable. There is no provision for a surety who has no property interest in the premises to be made a party to proceedings under the 1954 Act, and the court cannot make an order for a new tenancy that is directly binding on a surety.

What the landlord must do is to argue for the inclusion of a term that the tenant provide one or more sureties, who are reasonably acceptable to the landlord, within a period of, say, six months from the grant of the lease (*Cairnplace Ltd v CBL (Property Investments) Co Ltd* [1984] 1 W.L.R. 696). A landlord cannot oppose a tenant's application for a new tenancy solely on the ground that no sufficient surety is offered (*Barclays Bank Ltd v Ascott* [1961] 1 W.L.R. 717).

Chapter 14

Opposition to Renewal

1 Ways to oppose renewal

The renewal procedure now offers two ways for the landlord to **14–01** oppose the tenant who wishes to renew his tenancy. Either the landlord can defend the tenant's application to the court seeking renewal or he can himself apply for an order to end the current tenancy without renewal. In either case there is the same choice of statutory grounds available on which the landlord can rely.

These grounds are dealt with individually below. Each is separate and distinct; to oppose the grant of a new tenancy, the landlord must specify the correct ground (*Nursey v P Currie (Dartford) Ltd* [1959] 1 W.L.R. 273). The landlord cannot rely on a ground not specified in his notice or counter-notice, but it may be appropriate for him to give evidence of the facts which would have established it. The judge may take them into account in considering whether to exercise his discretion to refuse renewal on another ground (*Hutchinson v Lamberth* (1983) 270 E.G. 545).

In addition to the statutory grounds of opposition, it is open to the landlord to show that the tenant does not qualify for the right to renew, *e.g.* the tenant does not occupy the premises at least partly for the purposes of a business. Again, in some circumstances it will be possible for the landlord to resist the grant of a new tenancy on the ground that the use to which the tenant would put the property would be illegal (*Turner & Bell v Searles (Stanford-le-Hope) Ltd* (1977) 33 P. & C.R. 208).

2 Landlord's court application

Once the statutory procedure had been started, either by the land- **14–02** lord serving notice to end the current tenancy or by the tenant serving a request for a new tenancy, the landlord can seek an early determination that the tenant is not entitled to renew by applying to court to end the current tenancy without a renewal (s.29(2)).

The application must normally be made before the date given in the landlord's notice (for the current tenancy to end) or the tenant's request (for the new tenancy to start). That time limit can be extended by written agreement between the parties which they reach before the current limit has expired (ss.29A(1), (2), 29B). The landlord cannot apply if an application to renew the tenancy has already been made to the court. But once he has made an application for termination without renewal, the landlord can only withdraw it with the tenant's consent (s.29(3), (6)).

If the landlord satisfies the court on any of the statutory grounds of opposition, it makes an order to end the current tenancy. It finishes three months after the final disposal of the application, or, if later, on the date in the landlord's notice or tenant's request (ss.29(4)(a), 64). If the landlord does not successfully establish a ground of opposition, the court makes an order for the grant of a new tenancy and for the termination of the current one immediately before the commencement of the new one (s.29(4)(b)).

3 Repairing default

14-03   The first ground of opposition is that the state of repair of the property, resulting from the tenant's failure to comply with repairing and maintenance obligations in his current tenancy, is such that he should not be granted a new tenancy (s.30(1)(a)). Whether that degree of disrepair has been reached is a matter for the judge (*Lyons v Central Commercial Properties London Ltd* [1958] 1 W.L.R. 869); he can properly take into account the amount which the tenant has spent on repairs (*Hazel v Akhtar* [2002] 2 P. & C.R. 17).

4 Rent arrears

14-04   The tenant's persistent delay in paying rent is the second ground of opposition (s.30(1)(b)). The arrears need not be substantial or for a long period (*Horowitz v Farrand* [1956] C.L.Y. 4843 (*cc*)), nor need they stretch over the whole of the period of the lease (*Hopcutt v Carver* (1969) 209 E.G. 1069). It is a question of degree on which the judge must exercise his discretion. Two contrasting examples may be given: the landlord's opposition was successful when every instalment of rent, except the first and last, had been late and the landlord had twice taken possession proceedings (*Rawashdeh v Lane* [1988] 2 E.G.L.R. 109); but a new lease was ordered for a tenant who had been in arrear with eleven consecutive rent instalments, the judge being satisfied that there would be no repetition (*Hurstfell Ltd v Leicester Square Property Co Ltd* [1988] 2 E.G.L.R. 105).

5 Other breaches

Other substantial breaches of the tenant's obligations under the current tenancy, or any other reason connected with his use or management of the premises is the third ground (s.30(1)(c)). This gives the judge a very wide discretion. When the renewal is opposed on this ground, and also on the previous two—repairing defaults and rent arrears—the judge is entitled to take into account the conduct of the tenant as a whole in relation to his obligations under the tenancy (*Eichner v Midland Bank Executor & Trustee Co Ltd* [1970] 1 W.L.R. 1120).

14-05

6 Alternative accommodation

The landlord who offers and is willing to provide or secure alternative accommodation for the tenant establishes the fourth ground of opposition to renewal (s.30(1)(d)). The offer can be made at any time before the landlord files his answer to the tenant's claim (*M Chaplin Ltd v Regent Capital Holdings Ltd* [1994] 1 E.G.L.R. 249 (*cc*)). The alternative accommodation must be available on terms that are reasonable having regard to the provisions of the current tenancy and to all other relevant circumstances. It must be suitable, and available at a time suitable for the tenant's requirements, including the need to preserve goodwill. The nature and class of his business, and the situation and extent of the property (or the part of it actually occupied by the tenant) and the facilities it affords, are all taken into account.

14-06

7 Uneconomic subletting

Where the current tenancy is a sub-tenancy and was originally created as such, there is a purely financial ground of opposition open to the competent landlord if he is a superior landlord, and not the immediate landlord (s.30(1)(e)). If by letting the tenant's premises together with the rest of the property in the head lease as

14-07

a single unit more rent could reasonably be expected than by letting the individual units separately, the judge may refuse the grant of a new lease. This situation might arise in circumstances where the sub-letting required the grant of mutual rights between the separated parts of the property of such a nature as to reduce the convenience of occupation of those smaller units, and so reduce their letting value.

8 Demolition or reconstruction

14-08 The application to renew will be dismissed if the landlord successfully shows that he intends to demolish or reconstruct the premises, or a substantial part of them, on the termination of the current tenancy, and could not reasonably do so without obtaining possession (s.30(1)(f)). The same applies to an intention to carry out substantial work of construction on the premises, or part of them. If the part on which the work is to be carried out can be severed from the remainder, or the tenant can provide facilities for the work to be done, a new tenancy of some or all of the property may still be granted.

The questions which this ground of opposition can raise have been conveniently summarised as including: 'whether the landlord's intention is genuine; whether the work to be carried out constitutes substantial work of construction; whether the landlords could or could not reasonably do the work without obtaining possession of the holding' (*Romulus Trading Co Ltd v Henry Smith's Charity Trustees (No.2)* [1991] 1 E.G.L.R. 95 at 96 *per* Neill L.J.).

(a) Landlord's intention

The landlord must show that he has the intention required by the subsection. He must have that intention at the date of the hearing of the tenant's application (*Betty's Cafés Ltd v Phillips Furnishing Stores Ltd* [1959] A.C. 20), and if he does it is irrelevant that the intention was not formed until after proceedings were served (*Spook Erection Ltd v British Railways Board* [1988] 1 E.G.L.R. 76). It follows that it is the competent landlord at the date of the hearing that must have the intention (*Marks v British Waterways Board* [1963] 1 W.L.R. 1008). The landlord's original notice determining the tenancy, or his notice in reply to the tenant's request for a new tenancy, must specify the intention as his ground of opposition. It does not matter that the identity of the competent landlord changes between giving the notice and the hearing day, nor does it matter that the landlord who gave the notice had no such intention.

Intention means more than 'contemplating' (*Reohorn v Barry*   **14–09**
Corporation [1956] 1 W.L.R. 845). It includes the ability to carry
out the work. This in turn includes the landlord's legal ability, by
obtaining planning permission, and financial ability. A reasonable
prospect of the necessary finance—which is a question of fact—is
enough (*DAF Motoring Centre (Gosport) Ltd v Hutfield &*
Wheeler Ltd (1982) 263 E.G. 976). The court will also consider
whether the circumstances seem to show the intention to be
genuine. A decision to redevelop a relatively new property would,
e.g. raise doubts.

Where the landlord is a corporation, the intention must be
shown to be a corporate intention. In particular circumstances, it
has been held that the intention of three influential directors was
enough without formal board approval (*H L Bolton Engineering*
Co Ltd v T J Graham & Sons Ltd [1957] 1 Q.B. 159), but a resolution is preferable (*Espresso Coffee Machine Co Ltd v Guardian*
Assurance Co Ltd [1959] 1 W.L.R. 250). If the board does not have
sufficient powers, a resolution of the company in general meeting
is needed (*A & W Birch Ltd v P B (Sloane) Ltd and Cadogan*
Settled Estates Co (1956) 106 L.J. 204 (*cc*)). In the case of a local
authority, a resolution is not necessary to establish intention, if
there is other evidence (*Poppett's (Caterers) Ltd v Maidenhead*
Borough Council [1971] 1 W.L.R. 69). An intention to arrange for
work to be done suffices, *e.g.*, by the landlords entering into an
agreement with a third party for a building lease obliging the new
lessees to do the work (*Gilmour Caterers Ltd v Governors of St*
Bartholomew's Hospital [1956] 1 Q.B. 387).

(b) The work
It will be a question of fact in any case whether the proposals   **14–10**
constitute demolition, reconstruction or substantial work of construction. To judge whether it qualifies, the work should be looked
at as a whole (*Ivorygrove Ltd v Global Grange Ltd* [2003] 1 W.L.R.
2090). The Court of Appeal has said that 'reconstruction' postu-
lates all or some of the existing structure being demolished—
although 'structure' is not necessarily confined to outside or other
load-bearing walls (*Romulus Trading Co Ltd v Trustees of Henry*
Smith's Charity (1989) 60 P. & C.R. 62); indeed, where only the
internal shell of a building was let, the destruction of that shell
sufficed (*Pumperninks of Piccadilly Ltd v Land Securities Ltd*
[2002] Ch. 332)—whereas 'construction' covers new or additional
work (*Cook v Mott* (1961) 178 E.G. 637). A mere change in the
identity of the premises is not enough (*Percy E Cadle & Co Ltd v*
Jacmarch Properties Ltd [1957] 1 Q.B. 323). Demolition of a
wooden garage and a brick wall was sufficient for the subsection

where that was all that was standing on the property (*Housleys Ltd v Bloomer-Holt Ltd* [1966] 1 W.L.R. 1244). Resurfacing hard standing might be enough for a substantial work of construction but resurfacing a field (dumping soil, replacing top soil and planting a few trees) was not (*Botterill v Bedfordshire County Council* [1985] 1 E.G.L.R. 82). It does not matter that the motive for demolition is to relet as part of an agricultural holding (*Craddock v Hampshire County Council* [1958] 1 W.L.R. 202).

Whether work is 'substantial' involves viewing the project as a whole. For that purpose work can be taken into consideration which is not constructional, but is subsidiary to work which qualifies (*Barth v Pritchard* [1990] 1 E.G.L.R. 109).

(c) The premises

14–11   The tenant can still obtain a new tenancy if he can show, in either of two ways, that it is not necessary for the landlord to have possession of the whole for the work that he has in mind (s.31A).

'Possession' for this purpose means legal not physical possession. So a landlord cannot successfully oppose the grant of a new tenancy if it would contain a reservation entitling him to enter to carry out the works (*Heath v Drown* [1973] A.C. 498), except possibly if the work will deprive the tenant of facilities to carry on the trade permitted by the tenancy (*Leathwoods Ltd v Total Oil (Great Britain) Ltd* (1984) 270 E.G. 1083). If the terms of the reservation are wide enough, it can authorise the landlord totally to demolish and rebuild (*Price v Esso Petroleum Co Ltd* (1980) 255 E.G. 243).

The tenant can agree that his new lease shall include terms giving the landlord access and other facilities needed for the work. He must show that these will reasonably allow the landlord to carry out the work without obtaining possession, and also that the work will not interfere to a substantial extent or for a substantial time with the tenant's business on the premises. A 'substantial time' for this purpose is a question of fact and degree: closing a shop for a fortnight was not (*Cerex Jewels Ltd v Peachey Property Corporation plc* (1986) 52 P. & C.R. 127), closing a café for 12 months was (*Blackburn v Hussain* [1988] 1 E.G.L.R. 77). The onus of proof is on the landlord (*Mirza v Nicola* [1990] 2 E.G.L.R. 73). It is not sufficient that the tenant will continue to trade from other premises (*Redfern v Reeves* (1978) 37 P. & C.R. 364).

14–12   The alternative course for the tenant is to agree to accept a tenancy of an economically separable part of the property. A part is economically separate for this purpose only if, when the work is completed, the rent then reasonably obtainable on letting the parts separately would not be substantially less than that obtainable on letting the whole as a single unit. The tenant must also show that with possession of what would not be relet to him the landlord could carry out the work, or must again agree to give access and facilities allowing the work to be done without substantially affecting his business. The tenant cannot, however, insist that the landlord change his plans to confine the redevelopment to a smaller area, even if feasible (*Decca Navigator Co Ltd v Greater London Council* [1974] 1 W.L.R. 748).

9 Own occupation

The landlord can successfully oppose the tenant's application if he **14–13** proves his intention to occupy the premises himself (either personally or through an agent: *Skeet v Powell-Sheddon* [1988] 2 E.G.L.R. 112) when the current tenancy comes to an end, either wholly or partly for a business carried on by him there, or as his residence (s.30(1)(g)).

The term 'business' is widely interpreted here (*e.g.* including a community centre run in connection with an adjoining church: *Parkes v Westminster Roman Catholic Diocese Trustee* (1978) 36 P. & C.R. 22). This ground is distinct from the intention to demolish or reconstruct. A landlord who wanted to demolish premises served notice, opposing the grant of a new tenancy on the ground of his intention to occupy the premises, and failed because he had specified the wrong ground of opposition (*Nursey v P Currie (Dartford) Ltd* [1959] 1 W.L.R. 273).

The landlord's intention to carry on business on the premises in partnership with someone else suffices (*Re Crowhurst Park, Sims-Hilditch v Simmons* [1974] 1 W.L.R. 583). Similarly, a landlord successfully maintained this ground of opposition when the business to be carried on was in fact the business of a company which he controlled (*Harvey Textiles Ltd v Hillel* (1978) 249 E.G. 1063).

The landlord can be successful if he shows the necessary intention to occupy a substantial part of the property within a reasonable time after the end of the tenancy, rather than all of it immediately (*Method Development Ltd v Jones* [1971] 1 W.L.R. 168). This is subject to the important restriction that the landlord cannot rely on this ground if his interest (or one merged in it which was his interest) was purchased or created within five years ending with the termination of the current tenancy, and throughout that period the property has been let on one or a number of tenancies protected by the 1954 Act (s.30(2)).

As is the case of the previous ground of opposition, the land- **14–14** lord's intention has to be proved. It must be an honest, present and real intention, and exist at the date of the hearing (*JW Thornton*

Ltd v Blacks Leisure Group plc [1986] E.G.L.R. 61). It is the intention of the person who is then the landlord (*A D Wimbush & Son Ltd v Franmills Properties Ltd* [1961] Ch. 419). Here also, the feasibility of carrying out the intention must be established, *e.g.* by showing the necessary planning permission (*Gregson v Cyril Lord Ltd* [1963] 1 W.L.R. 41). But the wisdom of the intention, and the viability of the proposed business, is not an issue (*Cox v Binfield* [1989] E.G.L.R. 97). If there is doubt about the landlord's intention, he cannot necessarily resolve that doubt merely by giving an undertaking to use the premises in a particular way (*Lightcliffe and District Cricket and Lawn Tennis Club v Walton* (1977) 245 E.G. 393).

There are a number of ways in which the occupation for the landlord's own business is less than strictly interpreted, and these need to be examined. The five year ownership rule also requires consideration.

(a) Corporate bodies

Where the landlord is a company, and that company is a member of a group of companies, occupation for its own use by any member of the group suffices to sustain the landlord's opposition to renewal (s.42(3)). Companies are in the same group for this purpose if one is a subsidiary of the other or both are subsidiaries of a third, but not otherwise (s.42(1)). 'Subsidiary' has the meaning assigned to it by the Companies Act 1985, s.736. The main provisions of the definition are that the parent holds more than half in nominal value of the subsidiary's share capital, or is a member of the subsidiary and controls the composition of its board of directors, or that the subsidiary is a subsidiary of another subsidiary of the parent. This brings in the 'grandchild' situation: where *A* Ltd controls *B* Ltd which in turn controls *C* Ltd, *A* Ltd can obtain possession of premises of which it is landlord, for *C* Ltd to use for its (*C* Ltd's) business.

14–15   A company's intention to occupy its property can be established by evidence of the intention of a company official, if the decision is within his authority and is not inconsistent with his superiors' intention (*Manchester Garages Ltd v Petrofina (UK) Ltd* (1974) 233 E.G. 509).

Where a company is controlled not by another company, but by an individual, that individual can as landlord obtain possession so that the company can carry on its business in the premises (s.30(3)). The landlord has a controlling interest where either he holds more than half the company's equity share capital (disregarding nominee and fiduciary holdings) or he is a member of the company and can alone appoint or remove the holders of at least a majority of the directorships. Definitions are imported from the Companies Act, for 'company', 'share' and 'equity share capital'. It should be noted that it is the landlord who must be the individual in this situation. If a family company owned the property and its majority shareholder wanted to carry on business personally there, the company would not be able to oppose a renewal on this ground.

The position of limited liability partnerships is effectively **14–16** equated with that of limited companies. A partnership can be a subsidiary of company and vice versa, and the consequences are as set out above for companies. The relevant provisions of the Companies Act 1985 are adapted and applied by the Limited Liability Partnerships Regulations 2001.

There have been cases where this ground of opposition has been successful, even when the business was not strictly to be carried on by the landlord. In one case, a non-profit making company in liquidation showed that the premises would be occupied by a new company established by royal charter to take over its activities (*Willis v Association of Universities of the British Commonwealth* [1965] 1 Q.B. 140).

Use as a residence in this section presumably has the usual meaning of living accommodation, so that a company cannot take advantage of that provision.

(b) Trustees

Where the landlord's interest is held on trust, the intention of **14–17** all or any of the beneficiaries to occupy the premises for their business establishes the ground of opposition (s.41(2)). The beneficiary must be going to occupy in that capacity (*Meyer v Riddick* (1990) 60 P. & C.R. 50). It is not enough that the trustee's tenant happens also to be a beneficiary (*Frish Ltd v Barclays Bank Ltd* [1955] 2 Q.B. 541). Nor does a beneficiary's intention to occupy suffice if he only has the right to occupy by taking an assignment of another beneficiary's interest (*Carshalton Beeches Bowling Club Ltd v Cameron* (1978) 249 E.G. 1279).

The landlord's notice giving this ground of opposition to the tenant claiming a new tenancy could be validly given by the trustee in whom the property is vested (*Sevenarts Ltd v Busvine* [1968] 1 W.L.R. 1929).

(c) Five-year rule

The requirement, mentioned above, that the landlord must have owned his interest for five years to establish this ground of opposition applies only where the landlord purchased or his interest was created subject to an existing tenancy. It has no application if the landlord himself granted the tenancy (*Northcote Laundry Ltd v Frederick Donnelly Ltd* [1968] 1 W.L.R. 562).

The landlord's interest in the property dates from its first purchase or creation. It can include a period as freeholder and a period as leaseholder (*VCS Car Park Management Ltd v Regional Railways North East Ltd* [2001] Ch. 121) and interests under a succession of leases (*Artemiou v Procopiou* [1966] 1 Q.B. 878). 'Purchase' is used here in its popular sense (*H L Bolton Engineering Co Ltd v T J Graham & Sons Ltd* [1957] 1 Q.B. 159). Where the landlord's interest is leasehold, the five years date from the date of the execution of the lease, not the date that the term commenced (*Northcote Laundry Ltd v Frederick Donnelly Ltd* [1968] 1 W.L.R. 562)—although if the lease were executed before it became effective the reverse would presumably be the case—nor the date of registration by HM Land Registry (*Denny Thorn & Co Ltd v George Harker & Co Ltd* (1957) 108 L.J. 348). The five years start to run if the landlord is granted a reversionary lease (*A D Wimbush & Sons Ltd v Franmills Properties Ltd* [1961] Ch. 419).

Even though the five-year rule may preclude the court from denying the tenant a new tenancy, it may influence the judge in reducing the length of the term granted (*Upsons Ltd v E Robins Ltd* [1956] 1 Q.B. 131).

10 Procedure on successful opposition

14–18   Where the landlord's opposition succeeds, the court cannot make an order for a new tenancy (s.31). There is a compromise position in certain cases: where the landlord's opposition is on the grounds of alternative accommodation, uneconomic subletting and/or demolition and reconstruction. If the court would have been satisfied on the grounds of opposition had the date for the termination of the tenancy been up to a year later, it must make a declaration to that effect without an order for a new tenancy. Within 14 days, the tenant can require the court to make an order that that later date be substituted in the landlord's notice or tenant's request, which then takes effect accordingly. If the tenant takes no action, the current tenancy terminates on the date originally specified.

The tenant may be entitled to compensation where his application is refused, see the next Chapter.

Chapter 15

Compensation

1 Compensation for non-renewal

(a) When payable: general

There are three cases in which the landlord is liable to compensate the tenant because the current tenancy is not renewed on one of the grounds from which the landlord benefits. Where the reversion is divided, the appropriate proportion of the compensation is payable by the landlord of each part (s.37(3A)). The relevant grounds are: uneconomic subletting (s.30(1)(e)); demolition or reconstruction (s.30(1)(f)); landlord's own occupation (s.30(1)(g)). The cases for compensation are (s.37(1A)–(1C)):

15–01

(i)   When the tenant applies to renew, the court is precluded, by any of the relevant grounds but by no other, from ordering the grant of a new tenancy;

(ii)   The court is similarly precluded when the landlord applies for order that the tenant is not entitled to renew;

(iii) The landlord's notice, or his counter-notice to the tenant's request, states that he opposes the grant of a new tenancy on any of the relevant grounds but no other. In addition, in this case, there must either be no application by the tenant to renew or by the landlord to end the current tenancy without renewal, or if an application was made it must have been withdrawn.

(b) When payable: public purposes

The tenant has a right to compensation when, although his tenancy is one to which the 1954 Act applies, he is deprived of his right to renew through no fault of his own. Accordingly, where the landlord successfully opposes the application for a new tenancy on the grounds of uneconomic subletting, demolition

15–02

and reconstruction or own occupation, compensation is payable, and for this purpose the tenant can require the court to certify the reason why his application failed (s.37(1), (4)). Although opposition on the ground of alternative accommodation involves no fault on the tenant's part, there is no compensation for the obvious reason that with the provision of other suitable accommodation the tenant suffers no loss. Where the only grounds of opposition stated in the landlord's notice terminating the tenancy, or his notice replying to the tenant's request for a new tenancy, is one or more of those three entitling the tenant to compensation, he can claim the compensation even though he makes no application to the court.

Where the right to renew is excluded on the grounds of public interest or national security, or a certificate on those grounds prevents a renewal beyond a specified date, compensation is similarly payable (s.59). This compensation extends to cases of certificates given for the purposes of the Local Employment Act 1972, and for providing appropriate employment in Wales (ss.60, 60A). To this, there are certain exceptions relating to property in Wales. No compensation is payable (s.59(1A), (1B)):

(i)   to a tenant who became tenant after the Welsh Development Agency or the Development Board for Rural Wales acquired its interest, by virtue of which the certificate was given;

(ii)   where the premises were formerly the property of the Welsh Industrial Estates Corporation and were transferred to the Agency;

(iii)   where the premises were held by a Minister for the purposes of the Local Employment Act 1972 and were transferred to the Agency;

(iv)   where industrial premises were transferred by the Agency to the Board, having been acquired by the Agency as in (iii) or when no tenancy subsisted.

15–03   Compensation becomes due from the landlord to the tenant in all these cases when the tenant actually quits the premises he occupies.

In a limited class of cases, the right to compensation (but not that related to public interest or national security) can be excluded by agreement (ss.38(2), (3), 59(2)). This is where the premises the tenant occupies have not been occupied by someone carrying on the business there for the whole of the five years ending with the date on which the tenant is obliged to quit. Even if there has been continuous occupation for five years, the right to compensation can be excluded if there was a change of occupier during that period unless each occupier was successor to the business of his predecessor. A provision excluding compensation is not infrequently found in leases for terms longer than five years, inserted by the landlord in case circumstances may render it effective, *e.g.* on premature termination or a late change in both the tenant and the business carried on there.

(c) Amount

The compensation that the tenant receives is geared to the rateable value of the premises that he actually occupies for his business on the date the landlord serves notice to end the tenancy (s.37(2), (3); Local Government, Planning and Land Act 1980, Sch.33, para. 4; *Edicron Ltd v William Whiteley Ltd* (1983) 127 S.J. 257 (reversed on appeal on other grounds)). The rates of compensation can be varied by ministerial order.

A higher rate is payable if for the 14 years ending with the date of termination of the current tenancy any part of the premises which have been occupied for business purposes, or for those and other purposes, and on any change of occupier each succeeded to his predecessor's business (*Edicron Ltd v William Whiteley Ltd* [1984] 1 W.L.R. 59). This is the actual period of occupation, not the term of the lease (*Department of the Environment v Royal Insurance plc* [1989] 1 E.G.L.R. 83). For this purpose, one government department is deemed to succeed to the business of another (s.56(3)).

The rates of compensation are: **15–04**

	Occupation for less than 14 years	*Occupation for 14 years or more*
Tenant of partly residential premises (see below) opting for compensation based on rateable value on March 31, 1990	Rateable value multiplied by eight	Rateable value multiplied by 16
Notice served on or after April 1, 1990 in other cases	Rateable value	Rateable value multiplied by two

The rateable value is that shown in the valuation list in force on the date of the landlord's notice terminating the tenancy, or his notice in reply to the tenant's request for a new tenancy (s.37(5)–(7)). If the rateable value has been temporarily reduced because of fire **15–05** damage, the calculation is made with that nominal sum (*Plessey Co Ltd v Eagle Pension Funds Ltd* [1990] 2 E.G.L.R. 209). If there is no separate value, a proper apportionment or aggregation must be made. Any dispute is to be referred to the Commissioners of Inland Revenue for decision by a valuation officer, whose decision is final, subject to an appeal to the Lands Tribunal. The reference to the Commissioners is made on Form A prescribed by the Landlord and Tenant (Determination of Rateable Value Procedure) Rules 1954.

Different appropriate multipliers may be prescribed for different cases (s.37(7)). When the multiplier to be applied to the rateable value changes, the rate payable is that which applies on the date the landlord's notice takes effect and the tenant vacates (*Cardshops Ltd v John Lewis Properties Ltd* [1983] Q.B. 161).

(d) Partly residential premises

For domestic premises included in a business tenancy, the abolition of general rates in April 1990 meant changes to the compensation scheme. Subject to transitional arrangements, the domestic property is excluded when determining the rateable value used to calculate the compensation. If the tenant was in occupation of any of it, he is entitled to his reasonable removal expenses, the amount to be agreed between landlord and tenant or fixed by the court (s.37(5A), (5B)).

15–06   The transitional arrangements give the tenant a choice in certain cases. He can opt for statutory compensation on the basis of the rateable value on March 31, 1990, by giving notice to the landlord during the period in which he can apply to the court for a new tenancy (Local Government and Housing Act 1989, Sch.7, paras 4, 5). This option is available if:

(i)   the tenancy was entered into before April 1, 1990, or, if later, pursuant to a contract made before that date:

(ii)   the landlord gives notice to terminate the tenancy (under s.25) or counter-notice to the tenant's request for a new tenancy (under s.26(6)) before April 1, 2000; and

(iii)   on the date of the landlord's notice or counter-notice a rateable value is shown in the valuation list for the property, or values are shown for its constituent parts or a larger value so that the value could be arrived at by apportionment or aggregation (s.37(5)(*a*), (*b*)).

(e) Taxation

Statutory compensation to a tenant refused a new tenancy is not subject to capital gains tax in the hands of the tenant (*Drummond v Brown* [1986] Ch. 52).

2 Compensation for misrepresentation

The court may order the landlord to pay compensation to the **15–07** tenant in two circumstances if satisfied that there has been misrepresentation or concealment of material facts (s.37A). The first case is where the court was induced to refuse the grant of a new tenancy or to order the termination of the current tenancy without renewal. The second case is where the tenant was induced to quit the premises before June 1, 2004 without making an application to renew his tenancy, or he made an application and withdrew it.

In either case the amount ordered to be paid is what appears sufficient to compensate the tenant for the damage or loss sustained.

3 Compulsory acquisition

In assessing the compensation payable by an authority compulsor- **15–08** ily acquiring property subject to a business tenancy, the tenant's right to renew under the 1954 Act is to be taken into account (Land Compensation Act 1973, s.47). This reverses the original provision of the 1954 Act. In assessing compensation, it must be assumed that there is no proposal for compulsory acquisition of any interest in the property. A tenant whose interest is for no more than a year, or from year to year, only receives compensation for compulsory acquisition when required to give up possession, at which time it is limited to the value (if any) of the unexpired term (Lands Clauses Consolidation Act 1845, s.121). This remains the case even if notice to treat is served on the tenant (*London Borough of Newham v Benjamin* [1968] 1 W.L.R. 694). Should compensation for the tenant under the rules governing assessment in cases of compulsory acquisition not be as much as compensation would have been under s.37 of the 1954 Act had that section applied, it is increased to the higher figure (1954 Act, s.39(2)).

Appendices

Appendix A

The Law of Property Act 1925

Effect of licences granted to lessees

143.—(1) Where a licence is granted to a lessee to do any act, the   **A–01**
licence, unless otherwise expressed, extends only—

(a)   to the permission actually given; or
(b)   to the specific breach of any provision or covenant referred to;
      or
(c)   to any other matter specifically authorised to be done;

and the licence does not prevent any proceeding for any subsequent
breach unless otherwise specified in the licence.

(2) Notwithstanding any such licence—

(a)   all rights under covenants and powers of re-entry contained in
      the lease remain in full force and are available as against any sub-
      sequent breach of covenant, condition or other matter not
      specifically authorised or waived, in the same manner as if no
      licence had been granted; and
(b)   the condition or right of entry remains in force in all respects as
      if the licence had not been granted, save in respect of the partic-
      ular matter authorised to be done.

(3) Where in any lease there is a power or condition of re-entry on the
lessee assigning, subletting or doing any other specified act without a
licence, and a licence is granted—

(a)   to any one of two or more lessees to do any act, or to deal with
      his equitable share or interest; or
(b)   to any lessee, or to any one of two or more lessees to assign or
      underlet part only of the property, or to do any act in respect of
      part only of the property;

the licence does not operate to extinguish the right of entry in case of any breach of covenant or condition by the co-lessees of the other shares or interests in the property, or by the lessee or lessees of the rest of the property (as the case may be) in respect of such shares or interests or remaining property, but the right of entry remains in force in respect of the shares, interests or property not the subject of the licence.

This subsection does not authorise the grant after the commencement of this Act of a licence to create an undivided share in a legal estate.

(4) This section applies to licences granted after the thirteenth day of August, eighteen hundred and fifty-nine.

No fine to be exacted for licence to assign

A–02   **144.** In all leases containing a covenant, a condition, or agreement against assigning, underletting, or parting with the possession, or disposing of the land or property leased without licence or consent, such covenant, condition, or agreement shall, unless the lease contains an express provision to the contrary, be deemed to be subject to a proviso to the effect that no fine or sum of money in the nature of a fine shall be payable for or in respect of such licence or consent; but this proviso does not preclude the right to require the payment of a reasonable sum in respect of any legal or other expense incurred in relation to such licence or consent.

Appendix B

The Landlord and Tenant Act 1927

PART I

COMPENSATION FOR IMPROVEMENTS AND GOODWILL ON THE
TERMINATION OF TENANCIES OF BUSINESS PREMISES

Tenant's rights to compensation for improvements

1.—(1) Subject to the provisions of this Part of this Act, a tenant of a   **B–01**
holding to which this part of this Act applies shall, if a claim for the
purpose is made in the prescribed manner and within the time limited by
section 47 of the Landlord and Tenant Act 1954 be entitled, at the termination of the tenancy, on quitting his holding, to be paid by his landlord
compensation in respect of any improvement (including the erection of
any building) on his holding made by him or his predecessors in title, not
being a trade or other fixture which the tenant is by law entitled to remove,
which at the termination of the tenancy adds to the letting value of the
holding:

Provided that the sum to be paid as compensation for any improvement shall not exceed—

(a)   the net addition to the value of the holding as a whole which
      may be determined to be the direct of the improvement; or
(b)   the reasonable cost of carrying out the improvement at the ter-
      mination of the tenancy, subject to a deduction of an amount
      equal to the cost (if any) of putting the works constituting the
      improvement into a reasonable state of repair, except so far as
      such cost is covered by the liability of the tenant under any cov-
      enant or agreement as to the repair of the premises.

(2) In determining the amount of such net addition as aforesaid,
regard shall be had to the purpose for which it is intended that the

premises shall be used after the termination of the tenancy, and if it is shown that it is intended to demolish or to make structural alterations in the premises or any part thereof or to use the premises for a different purpose, regard shall be had to the effect of such demolition, alteration or change of user on the additional value attributable to the improvement, and to the length of time likely to elapse between the termination of the tenancy and the demolition, alteration or change of user.

(3) In the absence of agreement between the parties, all questions as to the right of compensation under this section, or as to the amount thereof, shall be determined by the tribunal hereinafter mentioned, and if the tribunal determines that, on account of the intention to demolish or alter or to change the user of the premises, no compensation or a reduced amount of compensation shall be paid, the tribunal may authorise a further application for compensation to be made by the tenant if effect is not given to the intention within such time as may be fixed by the tribunal.

Limitation on tenant's right to compensation in certain cases

B–02   **2.**—(1) A tenant shall not be entitled to compensation under this Part of this Act—

(a)   in respect of any improvement made before the commencement of this Act; or

(b)   in respect of any improvement made in pursuance of a statutory obligation, or of any improvement which the tenant or his predecessors in title were under an obligation to make in pursuance of a contract entered into, whether before or after the passing of this Act, for valuable consideration, including a building lease; or

(c)   in respect of any improvement made less than three years before the termination of the tenancy; or

(d)   if within two months after the making of the claim under section 1, subsection (1), of this Act the landlord serves on the tenant notice that he is willing and able to grant to the tenant, or obtain the grant to him of, a renewal of the tenancy at such rent and for such term as, failing agreement, the tribunal may consider reasonable; and, where such a notice is so served and the tenant does not within one month from the service of the notice send to the landlord an acceptance in writing of the offer, the tenant shall be deemed to have declined the offer.

(2) Where an offer of the renewal of a tenancy by the landlord under this section is accepted by the tenant, the rent fixed by the tribunal shall be the rent which in the opinion of the tribunal a willing lessee other than the tenant would agree to give and a willing lessor would agree to accept for the premises, having regard to the terms of the lease, but irrespective

of the value attributable to the improvement in respect of which compensation would have been payable.

(3) The tribunal in determining the compensation for an improvement shall in reduction of the tenant's claim take into consideration any benefits which the tenant or his predecessors in title may have received from the landlord or his predecessors in title in consideration expressly or impliedly of the improvement.

Landlord's right to object

3.—(1) Where a tenant of a holding to which this part of this Act   **B–03**
applies proposes to make an improvement on his holding, he shall serve on his landlord notice of his intention to make such improvement, together with a specification and plan showing the proposed improvement and the part of the existing premises affected thereby, and if the landlord within three months after the service of the notice, serves on the tenant notice of objection, the tenant may, in the prescribed manner, apply to the tribunal, and the tribunal may, after ascertaining that notice of such intention has been served upon any superior landlords interested and after giving such persons an opportunity of being heard, if satisfied that the improvement—

(a)   is of such a nature as to be calculated to add to the letting value of the holding at the termination of the tenancy; and

(b)   is reasonable and suitable to the character thereof; and

(c)   will not diminish the value of any other property belonging to the same landlord, or to any superior landlord from whom the immediate landlord of the tenant directly or indirectly holds;

and after making such modifications (if any) in the specification or plan as the tribunal thinks fit, or imposing such other conditions as the tribunal may think reasonable, certify in the prescribed manner that the improvement is a proper improvement:

Provided that, if the landlord proves that he has offered to execute the improvement himself in consideration of a reasonable increase of rent, or of such increase of rent as the tribunal may determine, the tribunal shall not give a certificate under this section unless it is subsequently shown to the satisfaction of the tribunal that the landlord has failed to carry out his undertaking.

(2) In considering whether the improvement is reasonable and suitable to the character of the holding, the tribunal shall have regard to any evidence brought before it by the landlord or any superior landlord (but not any other person) that the improvement is calculated to injure the amenity or convenience of the neighbourhood.

(3) The tenant shall, at the request of any superior landlord or at the request of the tribunal, supply such copies of the plans and specifications of the proposed improvements as may be required.

(4) Where no such notice of objection as aforesaid to a proposed improvement has been served within the time allowed by this section, or where the tribunal has certified an improvement to be a proper improvement, it shall be lawful for the tenant as against the immediate and any superior landlord to execute the improvement according to the plan and specification served on the landlord, or according to such plan and specification as modified by the tribunal or by agreement between the tenant and the landlord or landlords affected, anything in any lease of the premises to the contrary notwithstanding:

Provided that nothing in this subsection shall authorise a tenant to execute an improvement in contravention of any restriction created or imposed—

(a)   for naval, military or air force purposes;
(b)   for civil aviation purposes under the powers of the Civil Aviation Act 1949;
(c)   for securing any rights of the public over the foreshore or bed of the sea.

(5) A tenant shall not be entitled to claim compensation under this Part of this Act in respect of any improvement unless he has, or his predecessors in title have, served notice of the proposal to make the improvement under this section, and (in case the landlord has served notice of objection thereto) the improvement has been certified by the tribunal to be a proper improvement and the tenant has complied with the conditions, if any, imposed by the tribunal, nor unless the improvement is completed within such time after the service on the landlord of the notice of the proposed improvement as may be agreed between the tenant and the landlord or may be fixed by the tribunal, and where proceedings have been taken before the tribunal, the tribunal may defer making any order as to costs until the expiration of the time so fixed for the completion of the improvement.

(6) Where a tenant has executed an improvement of which he has served notice in accordance with this section and with respect to which either no notice of objection has been served by the landlord or a certificate that it is a proper improvement has been obtained from the tribunal, the tenant may require the landlord to furnish to him a certificate that the improvement has been duly executed; and if the landlord refuses or fails within one month after the service of the requisition to do so, the tenant may apply to the tribunal who, if satisfied that the improvement has been duly executed, shall give a certificate to that effect.

Where the landlord furnishes such a certificate, the tenant shall be liable to pay any reasonable expenses incurred for the purpose by the landlord, and if any question arises as to the reasonableness of such expenses, it shall be determined by the tribunal.

*   *   *   *   *

Rights of mesne landlords

8.—(1) Where, in the case of any holding, there are several persons   **B–04**
standing in the relation to each other of lessor and lessee, the following
provisions shall apply:—

Any mesne landlord who has paid or is liable to pay compensation
under this Part of this Act shall, at the end of his term, be entitled
to compensation from his immediate landlord in like manner and on
the same conditions as if he had himself made the improvement in
question, except that it shall be sufficient if the claim for compensation is made at least two months before the expiration of his term;

A mesne landlord shall not be entitled to make a claim under this
section unless he has, within the time and in the manner prescribed,
served on his immediate superior landlord copies of all documents
relating to proposed improvements and claims which have been sent
to him in pursuance of this Part of this Act:

Where such copies are so served, the said superior landlord shall have,
in addition to the mesne landlord, the powers conferred by or in pursuance of this Part of this Act in like manner as if he were the immediate landlord of the occupying tenant, and shall, in the manner and
to the extent prescribed, be at liberty to appear before the tribunal
and shall be bound by the proceedings.

(2) In this section, references to a landlord shall include references to
his predecessors in title.

Restriction on contracting out

9. This Part of this Act shall apply notwithstanding any contract to   **B–05**
the contrary, being a contract made at any time after the eighth day of
February, nineteen hundred and twenty-seven:

Provided that, if on the hearing of a claim or application under this Part
of this Act it appears to the tribunal that a contract made after such date as
aforesaid, so far as it deprives any person of any right under this Part of this
Act, was made for adequate consideration, the tribunal shall in determining
the matter give effect thereto.

Right of entry

10. The landlord of a holding to which this Part of this Act applies, or
any person authorised by him, may at all reasonable times enter on the
holding or any part of it, for the purpose of executing any improvement
he has undertaken to execute and of making any inspection of the premises which may reasonably be required for the purposes of this Part of this
Act.

Right to make deductions

11.—(1) Out of any money payable to a tenant by way of compensation under this Part of this Act, the landlord shall be entitled to deduct any sum due to him from the tenant under or in respect of the tenancy.

(2) Out of any money due to the landlord from the tenant under or in respect of the tenancy, the tenant shall be entitled to deduct any sum payable to him by the landlord by way of compensation under this Part of this Act.

Application of 13 & 14 Geo. 5, c. 9, s.20

12. Section 20 of the Agricultural Holdings Act 1923 (which relates to charges in respect of money paid for compensation), as set out and modified in the First Schedule to this Act, shall apply to the case of money paid for compensation under this Part of this Act, including any proper costs, charges, or expenses incurred by a landlord in opposing any proposal by a tenant to execute an improvement, or in contesting a claim for compensation, and to money expended by a landlord in executing an improvement the notice of a proposal to execute which has been served on him by a tenant under this Part of this Act.

Power to apply and raise capital money

B–06   **13.**—(1) Capital money arising under the Settled Land Act 1925, or under the University and College Estates Act 1925, may be applied—

(a) in payment as for any improvement authorised by the Act of any money expended and costs incurred by a landlord under or in pursuance of this Part of this Act in or about the execution of any improvement;

(b) in payment of any sum due to a tenant under this Part of this Act in respect of compensation for an improvement and any costs, charges, and expenses incidental thereto;

(c) in payment of the costs, charges, and expenses of opposing any proposal by a tenant to execute an improvement.

(2) The satisfaction of a claim for such compensation as aforesaid shall be included amongst the purposes for which a tenant for life, stat-

utory owner may raise money under section 71 of the Settled Land Act 1925.

(3) Where the landlord liable to pay compensation for an improvement is a tenant for life or in a fiduciary position, he may require the sum payable as compensation and any costs, charges, and expenses incidental thereto, to be paid out of any capital money held on the same trusts as the settled land.

In this subsection 'capital money' includes any personal estate held on the same trusts as the land.

Power to sell or grant leases notwithstanding restrictions

14. Where the powers of a landlord to sell or grant leases are subject to any statutory or other restrictions, he shall, notwithstanding any such restrictions or any rule of law to the contrary, be entitled to offer to sell or grant any such reversion or lease as would under this Part of this Act relieve him from liability to pay compensation thereunder, and to convey and grant the same, and to execute any lease which he may be ordered to grant under this Part of this Act.   **B–07**

Provisions as to reversionary leases

15.—(1) Where the amount which a landlord is liable to pay as compensation for an improvement under this Part of this Act has been determined by agreement or by an award of the tribunal, and the landlord had before the passing of this Act granted or agreed to grant a reversionary lease commencing on or after the termination of the then existing tenancy, the rent payable under the reversionary lease shall, if the tribunal so directs, be increased by such amount as, failing agreement, may be determined by the tribunal having regard to the addition to the letting value of the holding attributable to the improvement:

Provided that no such increase shall be permissible unless the landlord has served or caused to be served on the reversionary lessee copies of all documents relating to the improvement when proposed which were sent to the landlord in pursuance of this Part of this Act.

(2) The reversionary lessee shall have the same right of objection to the proposed improvement and of appearing and being heard at any proceedings before the tribunal relative to the proposed improvement as if he were a superior landlord, and if the amount of compensation for the improvement is determined by the tribunal, any question as to the increase of rent under the reversionary lease shall, where practicable, be settled in the course of the same proceedings.

Landlord's right to reimbursement of increased taxes, rates or insurance premiums

B–08   **16.** Where the landlord is liable to pay any rates (including water rate) in respect of any premises comprised in a holding, or has undertaken to pay the premiums on any fire insurance policy on any such premises, and in consequence of any improvement executed by the tenant on the premises under this Act the assessment of the premises or the rate of premium on the policy is increased, the tenant shall be liable to pay to the landlord sums equal to the amount by which—

    (a)   the rates payable by the landlord are increased by reason of the increase of such assessment;

    (b)   the fire premium payable by the landlord is increased by reason of the increase in the rate of premium;

and the sums so payable by the tenant shall be deemed to be in the nature of rent and shall be recoverable as such from the tenant.

Holdings to which Part I applies

B–09   **17.**—(1) The holdings to which this Part of this Act applies are any premises held under a lease, other than a mining lease, made whether before or after the commencement of this Act, and used wholly or partly for carrying on thereat any trade or business, and not being—

    (a)   agricultural holdings within the meaning of the Agricultural Holdings Act 1986 held under leases in relation to which that Act applies, or

    (b)   holdings held under farm business tenancies within the meaning of the Agricultural Tenancies Act 1995.

(2) This Part of this Act shall not apply to any holding let to a tenant as the holder of any office, appointment or employment, from the landlord, and continuing so long as the tenant holds such office, appointment or employment, but in the case of a tenancy created after the commencement of this Act, only if the contract is in writing and expresses the purpose for which the tenancy is created.

(3) For the purposes of this section, premises shall not be deemed to be premises used for carrying on thereat a trade or business—

    (a)   by reason of their being used for the purpose of carrying on thereat any profession;

    (b)   by reason that the tenant thereof carries on the business of sub-letting the premises as residential flats, whether or not the provision of meals or any other service for the occupants of the flats is undertaken by the tenant:

Provided that, so far as this Part of this Act relates to improvements, premises regularly used for carrying on a profession shall be deemed to be premises used for carrying on a trade or business.

(4) In the case of premises used partly for purposes of a trade or business and partly for other purposes, this Part of this Act shall apply to improvements only if and so far as they are improvements in relation to the trade or business.

*   *   *   *   *

PART II

GENERAL AMENDMENTS OF THE LAW OF LANDLORD AND TENANT

Provisions as to covenants not to assign, &c without licence or consent

19.—(1) In all leases whether made before or after the commencement   **B–10**
of this Act containing a covenant condition or agreement against assigning, under-letting, charging or parting with the possession of demised premises or any part thereof without licence or consent, such covenant condition or agreement shall, notwithstanding any express provision to the contrary, be deemed to be subject—

(a)   to a proviso to the effect that such licence or consent is not to be unreasonably withheld, but this proviso does not preclude the right of the landlord to require payment of a reasonable sum in respect of any legal or other expenses incurred in connection with such licence or consent; and

(b)   (if the lease is for more than forty years, and is made in consideration wholly or partially of the erection, or the substantial improvement, addition or alteration of buildings, and the lessor is not a Government department or local public authority, or a statutory or public utility company) to a proviso to the effect that in the case of any assignment, underletting, charging or parting with the possession (whether by the holders of the lease or any under-tenant whether immediate or not) effected more than seven years before the end of the term no consent or licence shall be required, if notice in writing of the transaction is given to the lessor within six months after the transaction is effected.

(1A) Where the landlord and the tenant under a qualifying lease have   **B–11**
entered into an agreement specifying for the purposes of this subsection—

(a)   any circumstances in which the landlord may withhold his licence or consent to an assignment of the demised premises or any part of them, or

(b)   any conditions subject to which any such licence or consent may be granted,

then the landlord—

(i)   shall not be regarded as unreasonably withholding his licence or consent to any such assignment if he withholds it on the ground (and it is the case) that any such circumstances exist, and

(ii)   if he gives any such licence or consent subject to any such conditions, shall not be regarded as giving it subject to unreasonable conditions;

and section 1 of the Landlord and Tenant Act 1988 (qualified duty to consent to assignment etc) shall have effect subject to the provisions of this subsection.

(1B) Subsection (1A) of this section applies to such an agreement as is mentioned in that subsection—

(a)   whether it is contained in the lease or not, and

(b)   whether it is made at the time when the lease is granted or at any other time falling before the application for the landlord's licence or consent is made.

B–12   (1C) Subsection (1A) shall not, however, apply to any such agreement to the extent that any circumstances or conditions specified in it are framed by reference to any matter falling to be determined by the landlord or by any other person for the purposes of the agreement, unless under the terms of the agreement—

(a)   that person's power to determine that matter is required to be exercised reasonably, or

(b)   the tenant is given an unrestricted right to have any such determination reviewed by a person independent of both landlord and tenant whose identity is ascertainable by reference to the agreement,

and in the latter case the agreement provides for the determination made by any such independent person on the review to be conclusive as to the matter in question.

(1D) In its application to a qualifying lease, subsection (1)(b) of this section shall not have effect in relation to any assignment of the lease.

(1E) In subsections (1A) and (1D) of this section—

(a)   'qualifying lease' means any lease which is a new tenancy for the purposes of section 1 of the Landlord and Tenant (Covenants) Act 1995 other than a residential lease, namely a lease by which a building or part of a building is let wholly or mainly as a single private residence; and

(b)   references to assignment include parting with possession on assignment.

(2) In all leases whether made before or after the commencement of this Act containing a covenant condition or agreement against the making of improvements without licence or consent, such covenant condition or agreement shall be deemed, notwithstanding any express provision to the contrary, to be subject to a proviso that such licence or consent is not to be unreasonably withheld; but this proviso does not preclude the right to require as a condition of such licence or consent the payment of a reasonable sum in respect of any damage to or diminution in the value of the premises or any neighbouring premises belonging to the landlord, and of any legal or other expenses properly incurred in connection with such licence or consent nor, in the case of an improvement which does not add to the letting value of the holding, does it preclude the right to require as a condition of such licence or consent, where such a requirement would be reasonable, an undertaking on the part of the tenant to reinstate the premises in the condition in which they were before the improvement was executed.

(3) In all leases whether made before or after the commencement of **B–13** this Act containing a covenant condition or agreement against the alteration of the user of the demised premises, without licence or consent, such covenant condition or agreement shall, if the alteration does not involve any structural alteration of the premises, be deemed, notwithstanding any express provision to the contrary, to be subject to a proviso that no fine or sum of money in the nature of a fine, whether by way of increase of rent or otherwise, shall be payable for or in respect of such licence or consent; but this proviso does not preclude the right of the landlord to require payment of a reasonable sum in respect of any damage to or diminution in the value of the premises or any neighbouring premises belonging to him and of any legal or other expenses incurred in connection with such licence or consent.

Where a dispute as to the reasonableness of any such sum has been determined by a court of competent jurisdiction, the landlord shall be bound to grant the licence or consent on payment of the sum so determined to be reasonable.

(4) This section shall not apply to leases of agricultural holdings within the meaning of the Agricultural Holdings Act 1986, which are leases in relation to which that Act applies, or to farm business tenancies within the meaning of the Agricultural Tenancies Act 1995 and paragraph (b) of subsection (1), subsection (2) and subsection (3) of this section shall not apply to mining leases.

*   *   *   *   *

PART III

GENERAL

The tribunal

B–14   21. The tribunal for the purposes of Part I of this Act shall be the court exercising jurisdiction in accordance with the provisions of section 63 of the Landlord and Tenant Act 1954.

*   *   *   *   *

Service of notices

23.—(1) Any notice, request, demand or other instrument under this Act shall be in writing and may be served on the person on whom it is to be served either personally, or by leaving it for him at his last known place of abode in England or Wales, or by sending it through the post in a registered letter addressed to him there, or, in the case of a local or public authority or a statutory or a public utility company, to the secretary or other proper officer at the principal office of such authority or company, and in the case of a notice to a landlord, the person on whom it is to be served shall include any agent of the landlord duly authorised in that behalf.

(2) Unless or until a tenant of a holding shall have received notice that the person theretofore entitled to the rents and profits of the holding (hereinafter referred to as 'the original landlord') has ceased to be so entitled, and also notice of the name and address of the person who has become entitled to such rents and profits, any claim, notice, request, demand, or other instrument which the tenant shall serve upon or deliver to the original landlord shall be deemed to have been served upon or delivered to the landlord of such holding.

Application to Crown, Duchy, ecclesiastical and charity lands

B–15   24.—(1) This Act shall apply to land belonging to His Majesty in right of the Crown or the Duchy of Lancaster and to land belonging to the Duchy of Cornwall, and to land belonging to any Government department, and for that purpose the provisions of the Agricultural Holdings Act 1923, relating to Crown and Duchy lands, as set out and adapted in Part I of the Second Schedule to this Act, shall have effect.

(2) The provisions of the Agricultural Holdings Act 1923, with respect to the application of that Act to ecclesiastical and charity lands, as set out and adapted in Part II of the Second Schedule to this Act, shall apply for the purposes of this Act.

*   *   *   *   *

(4) Where any land is vested in the official custodian for charities in trust for any charity, the trustees of the charity and not the custodian shall be deemed to be the landlord for the purposes of this Act.

Interpretation

25.—(1) For the purposes of this Act, unless the context otherwise requires:

B–16

The expression 'tenant' means any person entitled in possession to the holding under any contract of tenancy, whether the interest of such tenant was acquired by original contract, assignment, operation of law or otherwise;

The expression 'landlord' means any person who under a lease is, as between himself and the tenant or other lessee, for the time being entitled to the rents and profits of the demised premises payable under the lease;

The expression 'predecessor in title' in relation to a tenant or landlord means any person through whom the tenant or landlord has derived title, whether by assignment, by will, by intestacy, or by operation of law;

The expression 'lease' means a lease, under-lease or other tenancy, assignment operating as a lease or under-lease, or an agreement for such lease, under-lease tenancy, or assignment;

The expression 'mining lease' means a lease for any mining purpose or purposes connected therewith, and 'mining purposes' include the sinking and searching for, winning, working, getting, making merchantable, smelting or otherwise converting or working for the purposes of any manufacture, carrying away, and disposing of mines and minerals, in or under land, and the erection of buildings, and the execution of engineering and other works suitable for those purposes;

The expression 'term of years absolute' has the same meaning as in the Law of Property Act 1925;

The expression 'statutory company' means any company constituted by or under an Act of Parliament to construct, work or carry on any tramway, hydraulic power, dock, canal or railway undertaking; and the expression 'public utility company' means any company within the meaning of the Companies (Consolidation) Act 1908, or a society registered under the Industrial and Provident Societies Act 1893 to 1913, carrying on any such undertaking;

The expression 'prescribed' means prescribed by rules of court or by a practice direction.

(2) The designation of landlord and tenant shall continue to apply to the parties until the conclusion of any proceedings taken under or in pursuance of this Act in respect of compensation.

Short title, commencement and extent

26.—(1) This Act may be cited as the Landlord and Tenant Act 1927.

* * * * *

(3) This Act shall extend to England and Wales only.

SCHEDULES

Section 12   FIRST SCHEDULE

Provisions As To Charges

B–17   (1) A landlord, on paying to the tenant the amount due to him under Part I of this Act, in respect of compensation for an improvement under that Part, or on expending after notice given in accordance with that Part such amount as may be necessary to execute an improvement, shall be entitled to obtain from the Minister of Agriculture, Fisheries, and Food (hereinafter referred to as the Minister) an order in favour of himself and the persons deriving title under him charging the holding, or any part thereof, with repayment of the amount paid or expended, including any proper costs, charges or expenses incurred by a landlord in opposing any proposal by a tenant to execute an improvement or in contesting a claim for compensation, and of all costs properly incurred by him in obtaining the charge, with such interest, and by such instalments, and with such directions for giving effect to the charge, as the Minister thinks fit.

(2) Where the landlord obtaining the charge is not an absolute owner of the holding for his own benefit, no instalment or interest shall be made payable after the time when the improvement in respect whereof compensation is paid will, in the opinion of the Minister, have become exhausted.

(3) Where the estate or interest of a landlord is determinable or liable to forfeiture by reason of his creating or suffering any charge thereon, that

estate or interest shall not be determined or forfeited by reason of his obtaining such a charge, anything in any deed, will or other instrument to the contrary thereof notwithstanding.

(4) The sum charged shall be a charge on the holding, or the part thereof charged, for the landlord's interest therein and for interests in the reversion immediately expectant on the termination of the lease; but so that, in any case, where the landlord's interest is an interest in a leasehold, the charge shall not extend beyond that leasehold interest.

(5) Any company now or hereafter incorporated by Parliament, and having power to advance money for the improvement of land, may take an assignment of any charge made under this Schedule, upon such terms and conditions as may be agreed upon between the company and the person entitled to the charge, and may assign any charge so acquired by them.

(6) Where a charge may be made under this Schedule for compensation due under an award, the tribunal making the award shall, at the request and cost of the person entitled to obtain the charge, certify the amount to be charged and the term for which the charge may properly be made, having regard to the time at which each improvement in respect of which compensation is awarded is to be deemed to be exhausted.

(7) A charge under this Schedule may be registered under section 10 of the Land Charges Act 1925, as a land charge of Class A.

SECOND SCHEDULE   **Section 24**

PART I

APPLICATION TO CROWN AND DUCHY LAND

1.—(a) With respect to any land belonging to His Majesty in right of   **B–18** the Crown, or to a Government department, for the purposes of this Act, the Commissioners of Crown Lands, or other the proper officer or body having charge of the land for the time being, or, in case there is no such officer or body, then such person as His Majesty may appoint in writing under the Royal Sign Manual, shall represent His Majesty, and shall be deemed to be the landlord.

*   *   *   *   *

2.—(a) With respect to land belonging to His Majesty in right of the Duchy of Lancaster, for the purposes of this Act, the Chancellor of the Duchy shall represent His Majesty, and shall be deemed to be the landlord.

(b) The amount of any compensation under Part I of this Act payable by the Chancellor of the Duchy shall be raised and paid as an expense incurred in improvement of land belonging to His Majesty in the right of the Duchy within section 25 of the Act of the fifty-seventh year of King George the Third, chapter ninety-seven.

3.—(a) With respect to land belonging to the Duchy of Cornwall, for the purposes of this Act, such person as the Duke of Cornwall, or the possessor for the time being of the Duchy of Cornwall appoints, shall represent the Duke of Cornwall or other the possessor aforesaid, and be deemed to be the landlord, and may do any act or thing under this Act which a landlord is authorised or required to do thereunder.

(b) Any compensation under Part I of this Act payable by the Duke of Cornwall, or other the possessor aforesaid, shall be paid, and advances therefore made, in the manner and subject to the provisions of section 8 of the Duchy of Cornwall Management Act 1863, with respect to improvements of land mentioned in that section.

PART II

APPLICATION TO ECCLESIASTICAL AND CHARITY LAND

B–19 1.—(a) Where lands are assigned or secured as the endowment of a see, the powers by this Act conferred on a landlord in respect of charging land shall not be exercised by the bishop in respect of those lands, except with the previous approval in writing of the Estates Committee of the Ecclesiastical Commissioners.

*   *   *   *   *

(c) The Ecclesiastical Commissioners may, if they think fit, on behalf of an ecclesiastical corporation, out of any money in their hands, pay to the tenant the amount of compensation due to him under Part I of this Act, and thereupon they may, instead of the corporation obtain from the minister a charge on the holding in respect thereof in favour of themselves.

2. The powers by this Act conferred on a landlord in respect of charging land shall not be exercised by trustees for ecclesiastical or charitable purposes, except with the approval in writing of the Charity Commissioners or the Board of Education, as the case may require.

Appendix C

The Landlord and Tenant Act 1954

PART II

SECURITY OF TENURE FOR BUSINESS, PROFESSIONAL AND OTHER TENANTS

Tenancies to which Part II applies

Tenancies to which Part II applies

23.—(1) Subject to the provisions of this Act, this Part of this Act   **C–01**
applies to any tenancy where the property comprised in the tenancy is or
includes premises which are occupied by the tenant and are so occupied for
the purposes of a business carried on by him or for those and other purposes.

(1A) Occupation or the carrying on of a business—

(a)   by a company in which the tenant has a controlling interest; or
(b)   where the tenant is a company, by a person with a controlling
interest in the company,

shall be treated for the purposes of this section as equivalent to occupation or, as the case may be, the carrying on of a business by the tenant.

(1B) Accordingly references (however expressed) in this Part of this
Act to the business of, or to use, occupation or enjoyment by, the tenant
shall be construed as including references to the business of, or to use,
occupation or enjoyment by, a company falling within subsection (1A)(a)
above or a person falling within subsection (1A)(b) above.

(2) In this Part of this Act the expression 'business' includes a trade,
profession or employment and includes any activity carried on by a body
of persons, whether corporate or unincorporate.

(3) In the following provisions of this Part of this Act the expression

'the holding', in relation to a tenancy to which this Part of this Act applies, means the property comprised in the tenancy, there being excluded any part thereof which is occupied neither by the tenant nor by a person employed by the tenant and so employed for the purposes of a business by reason of which the tenancy is one to which this Part of this Act applies.

(4) Where the tenant is carrying on a business, in all or any part of the property comprised in a tenancy, in breach of a prohibition (however expressed) of use for business purposes which subsists under the terms of the tenancy and extends to the whole of that property, this Part of this Act shall not apply to the tenancy unless the immediate landlord or his predecessor in title has consented to the breach or the immediate landlord has acquiesced therein.

In this subsection the reference to a prohibition of use for business purposes does not include a prohibition of use for the purposes of a specified business, or of use for purposes of any but a specified business, but save as aforesaid includes a prohibition of use for the purposes of some one or more only of the classes of business specified in the definition of that expression in subsection (2) of this section.

Continuation and renewal of tenancies

Continuation of tenancies to which Part II applies and grant of new tenancies

C–02   **24.**—(1) A tenancy to which this Part of this Act applies shall not come to an end unless terminated in accordance with the provisions of this Part of this Act; and, subject to the following provisions of this Act either the tenant or the landlord under such a tenancy may apply to the court for an order for the grant of a new tenancy—

(a)   if the landlord has given notice under section 25 of this Act to terminate the tenancy, or

(b)   if the tenant has made a request for a new tenancy in accordance with section 26 of this Act.

(2) The last foregoing subsection shall not prevent the coming to an end of a tenancy by notice to quit given by the tenant, by surrender or forfeiture, or by the forfeiture of a superior tenancy unless—

(a)   in the case of a notice to quit, the notice was given before the tenant had been in occupation in right of the tenancy for one month;

(2A) Neither the tenant nor the landlord may make an application under subsection (1) above if the other has made such an application and the application has been served.

(2B) Neither the tenant nor the landlord may make such an application if the landlord has made an application under section 29(2) of this Act and the application has been served.

(2C) The landlord may not withdraw an application under subsection (1) above unless the tenant consents to its withdrawal.

(3) Notwithstanding anything in subsection (1) of this section—

(a) where a tenancy to which this Part of this Act applies ceases to be such a tenancy, it shall not come to an end by reason only of the cesser, but if it was granted for a term of years certain and has been continued by subsection (1) of this section then (without prejudice to the termination thereof in accordance with any terms of the tenancy) it may be terminated by not less than three nor more than six months' notice in writing given by the landlord to the tenant;

(b) where, at a time when a tenancy is not one to which this Part of this Act applies, the landlord gives notice to quit, the operation of the notice shall not be affected by reason that the tenancy becomes one to which this Part of this Act applies after the giving of the notice.[1]

Applications for determination of interim rent while tenancy continues

24A.—(1) Subject to subsection (2) below, if—   **C–03**

(a) the landlord of a tenancy to which this Part of this Act applies has given notice under section 25 of this Act to terminate the tenancy; or

(b) the tenant of such a tenancy has made a request for a new tenancy in accordance with section 26 of this Act,

either of them may make an application to the court to determine a rent (an 'interim rent') which the tenant is to pay while the tenancy ('the relevant tenancy') continues by virtue of section 24 of this Act and the court may order payment of an interim rent in accordance with section 24C or 24D of this Act.

(2) Neither the tenant nor the landlord may make an application under subsection (1) above if the other has made such an application and has not withdrawn it.

(3) No application shall be entertained under subsection (1) above if it is made more than six months after the termination of the relevant tenancy.

---

[1] S.29 substituted by virtue of Law and Property Act 1969 (c.59) s.15 Sch.1.

Date from which interim rent is payable

C–04   **24B.**—(1) The interim rent determined on an application under section 24A(1) of this Act shall be payable from the appropriate date.

(2) If an application under section 24A(1) of this Act is made in a case where the landlord has given a notice under section 25 of this Act, the appropriate date is the earliest date of termination that could have been specified in the landlord's notice.

(3) If an application under section 24A(1) of this Act is made in a case where the tenant has made a request for a new tenancy under section 26 of this Act, the appropriate date is the earliest date that could have been specified in the tenant's request as the date from which the new tenancy is to begin.

Amount of interim rent where new tenancy of whole premises granted and landlord not opposed

C–05   **24C.**—(1) This section applies where—

(a)   the landlord gave a notice under section 25 of this Act at a time when the tenant was in occupation of the whole of the property comprised in the relevant tenancy for purposes such as are mentioned in section 23(1) of this Act and stated in the notice that he was not opposed to the grant of a new tenancy; or

(b)   the tenant made a request for a new tenancy under section 26 of this Act at a time when he was in occupation of the whole of that property for such purposes and the landlord did not give notice under subsection (6) of that section,

and the landlord grants a new tenancy of the whole of the property comprised in the relevant tenancy to the tenant (whether as a result of an order for the grant of a new tenancy or otherwise).

(2) Subject to the following provisions of this section, the rent payable under and at the commencement of the new tenancy shall also be the interim rent.

(3) Subsection (2) above does not apply where—

(a)   the landlord or the tenant shows to the satisfaction of the court that the interim rent under that subsection differs substantially from the relevant rent; or

(b)   the landlord or the tenant shows to the satisfaction of the court that the terms of the new tenancy differ from the terms of the relevant tenancy to such an extent that the interim rent under that subsection is substantially different from the rent which (in default of such agreement) the court would have determined under section 34 of this Act to be payable under a tenancy which commenced on the same day as the new tenancy and whose other terms were the same as the relevant tenancy.

(4) In this section 'the relevant rent' means the rent which (in default of agreement between the landlord and the tenant) the court would have determined under section 34 of this Act to be payable under the new tenancy if the new tenancy had commenced on the appropriate date (within the meaning of section 24B of this Act).

(5) The interim rent in a case where subsection (2) above does not apply by virtue only of subsection (3)(a) above is the relevant rent.

(6) The interim rent in a case where subsection (2) above does not apply by virtue only of subsection (3)(b) above, or by virtue of subsection (3)(a) and (b) above, is the rent which it is reasonable for the tenant to pay while the relevant tenancy continues by virtue of section 24 of this Act.

(7) In determining the interim rent under subsection (6) above the court shall have regard—

(a)   to the rent payable under the terms of the relevant tenancy; and
(b)   to the rent payable under any sub-tenancy of part of the property comprised in the relevant tenancy,

but otherwise subsections (1) and (2) of section 34 of this Act shall apply to the determination as they would apply to the determination of a rent under that section if a new tenancy of the whole of the property comprised in the relevant tenancy were granted to the tenant by order of the court and the duration of that new tenancy were the same as the duration of the new tenancy which is actually granted to the tenant.

(8) In this section and section 24D of this Act 'the relevant tenancy' has the same meaning as in section 24A of this Act.

Amount of interim rent in any other case

24D.—(1) The interim rent in a case where section 24C of this Act does not apply is the rent which it is reasonable for the tenant to pay while the relevant tenancy continues by virtue of section 24 of this Act.   C–06

(2) In determining the interim rent under subsection (1) above the court shall have regard—

(a)   to the rent payable under the terms of the relevant tenancy; and
(b)   to the rent payable under any sub-tenancy of part of the property comprised in the relevant tenancy,

but otherwise subsections (1) and (2) of section 34 of this Act shall apply to the determination as they would apply to the determination of a rent under that section if a new tenancy from year to year of the whole of the property comprised in the relevant tenancy were granted to the tenant by order of the court.

(3) If the court—

(a)   has made an order for the grant of a new tenancy and has ordered payment of interim rent in accordance with section 24C of this Act, but

(b)   either—

    (i)   it subsequently revokes under section 36(2) of this Act the order for the grant of a new tenancy; or

    (ii)   the landlord and tenant agree not to act on the order,

the court on the application of the landlord or the tenant shall determine a new interim rent in accordance with subsections (1) and (2) above without a further application under section 24A(1) of this Act.

Termination of tenancy by the landlord

C–07   **25.**—(1) The landlord may terminate a tenancy to which this Part of this Act applies by a notice given to the tenant in the prescribed form specifying the date at which the tenancy is to come to an end (hereinafter referred to as 'the date of termination'):

Provided that this subsection has effect subject to the provisions of section 29B(4) of this Act and the provisions of Part IV of this Act as to the interim continuation of tenancies pending the disposal of applications to the court.

(2) Subject to the provisions of the next following subsection, a notice under this section shall not have effect unless it is given not more than twelve nor less than six months before the date of termination specified therein.

(3) In the case of a tenancy which apart from this Act could have been brought to an end by notice to quit given by the landlord—

(a)   the date of termination specified in a notice under this section shall not be earlier than the earliest date on which apart from this Part of this Act the tenancy could have been brought to an end by notice to quit given by the landlord on the date of the giving of the notice under this section; and

(b)   where apart from this Part of this Act more than six months' notice to quit would have been required to bring the tenancy to an end, the last foregoing subsection shall have effect with the substitution for twelve months of a period six months longer than the length of notice to quit which would have been required as aforesaid.

(4) In the case of any other tenancy, a notice under this section shall not specify a date of termination earlier than the date on which apart from this Part of this Act the tenancy would have come to an end by effluxion of time.

*   *   *   *   *

(6) A notice under this section shall not have effect unless it states whether the landlord is opposed to the grant of a new tenancy to the tenant.

(7) A notice under this section which states that the landlord is opposed to the grant of a new tenancy to the tenant shall not have effect unless it also specifies one or more of the grounds specified in section 30(1) of this Act as the ground or grounds for his opposition.

(8) A notice under this section which states that the landlord is not opposed to the grant of a new tenancy to the tenant shall not have effect unless it sets out the landlord's proposals as to—

(a) the property to be comprised in the new tenancy (being either the whole or part of the property comprised in the current tenancy);

(b) the rent to be payable under the new tenancy; and

(c) the other terms of the new tenancy.

Tenant's request for a new tenancy

26.—(1) A tenant's request for a new tenancy may be made where the current tenancy is a tenancy granted for a term of years certain exceeding one year, whether or not continued by section 24 of this Act, or granted for a term of years certain and thereafter from year to year. **C–08**

(2) A tenant's request for a new tenancy shall be for a tenancy beginning with such date, not more than twelve nor less than six months after the making of the request, as may be specified therein:

Provided that the said date shall not be earlier than the date on which apart from this Act the current tenancy would come to an end by effluxion of time or could be brought to an end by notice to quit given by the tenant.

(3) A tenant's request for a new tenancy shall not have effect unless it is made by notice in the prescribed form given to the landlord and sets out the tenant's proposals as to the property to be comprised in the new tenancy (being either the whole or part of the property comprised in the current tenancy), as to the rent to be payable under the new tenancy and as to the other terms of the new tenancy.

(4) A tenant's request for a new tenancy shall not be made if the landlord has already given notice under the last foregoing section to terminate the current tenancy, or if the tenant has already given notice to quit or notice under the next following section; and no such notice shall be given by the landlord or the tenant after the making by the tenant of a request for a new tenancy.

(5) Where the tenant makes a request for a new tenancy in accordance with the foregoing provisions of this section, the current tenancy shall, subject to the provisions of sections 29B(4) and 36(2) of this Act and the provisions of Part IV of this Act as to the interim continuation of tenancies, terminate immediately before the date specified in the request for the beginning of the new tenancy.

(6) Within two months of the making of a tenant's request for a new tenancy the landlord may give notice to the tenant that he will oppose an application to the court for the grant of a new tenancy, and any such notice shall state on which of the grounds mentioned in section 30 of this Act the landlord will oppose the application.

Termination by tenant of tenancy for fixed term

C–09   **27.**—(1) Where the tenant under a tenancy to which this Part of this Act applies, being a tenancy granted for a term of years certain, gives to the immediate landlord, not later than three months before the date on which apart from this Act the tenancy would come to an end by effluxion of time, a notice in writing that the tenant does not desire the tenancy to be continued, section 24 of this Act shall not have effect in relation to the tenancy, unless the notice is given before the tenant has been in occupation in right of the tenancy for one month.

(1A) Section 24 of this Act shall not have effect in relation to a tenancy for a term of years certain where the tenant is not in occupation of the property comprised in the tenancy at the time when, apart from this Act, the tenancy would come to an end by effluxion of time.

(2) A tenancy granted for a term of years certain which is continuing by virtue of section 24 of this Act shall not come to an end by reason only of the tenant ceasing to occupy the property comprised in the tenancy but may be brought to an end on any day by not less than three months' notice in writing given by the tenant to the immediate landlord, whether the notice is given after the date on which apart from this Act the tenancy would have come to an end or before that date, but not before the tenant has been in occupation in right of the tenancy for one month.

(3) Where a tenancy is terminated under subsection (2) above, any rent payable in respect of a period which begins before, and ends after, the tenancy is terminated shall be apportioned, and any rent paid by the tenant in excess of the amount apportioned to the period before termination shall be recoverable by him.

Renewal of tenancies by agreement

C–10   **28.** Where the landlord and tenant agree for the grant to the tenant of a future tenancy of the holding, or of the holding with other land, on terms and from a date specified in the agreement, the current tenancy shall continue until that date but no longer, and shall not be a tenancy to which this Part of this Act applies.

Applications to court

Order by court for grant of new tenancy or termination of current tenancy

29.—(1) Subject to the provisions of this Act, on an application under **C–11**
section 24(1) of this Act, the court shall make an order for the grant of a
new tenancy and accordingly for the termination of the current tenancy
immediately before the commencement of the new tenancy.

(2) Subject to the following provisions of this Act, a landlord may
apply to the court for an order for the termination of a tenancy to which
this Part of this Act applies without the grant of a new tenancy—

(a)   if he has given notice under section 25 of this Act that he is
opposed to the grant of a new tenancy to the tenant; or
(b)   if the tenant has made a request for a new tenancy in accordance
with section 26 of this Act and the landlord has given notice
under subsection (6) of that section.

(3) The landlord may not make an application under subsection (2)
above if either the tenant or the landlord has made an application under
section 24(1) of this Act.

(4) Subject to the provisions of this Act, where the landlord makes an
application under subsection (2) above—

(a)   if he establishes, to the satisfaction of the court, any of the
grounds on which he is entitled to make the application in accordance with section 30 of this Act, the court shall make an order
for the termination of the current tenancy in accordance with
section 64 of this Act without the grant of a new tenancy; and
(b)   if not, it shall make an order for the grant of a new tenancy and
accordingly for the termination of the current tenancy immediately before the commencement of the new tenancy.

(5) The court shall dismiss an application by the landlord under section
24(1) of this Act if the tenant informs the court that he does not want a
new tenancy.

(6) The landlord may not withdraw an application under subsection (2)
above unless the tenant consents to its withdrawal.

Time limits for applications to court

29A.—(1) Subject to section 29B of this Act, the court shall not enter-   **C–12**
tain an application—

(a)   by the tenant or the landlord under section 24(1) of this Act; or
(b)   by the landlord under section 29(2) of this Act,

if it is made after the end of the statutory period.

(2) In this section and section 29B of this Act 'the statutory period' means a period ending—

 (a) where the landlord gave a notice under section 25 of this Act, on the date specified in his notice; and

 (b) where the tenant made a request for a new tenancy under section 26 of this Act, immediately before the date specified in his request.

(3) Where the tenant has made a request for a new tenancy under section 26 of this Act, the court shall not entertain an application under section 24(1) of this Act which is made before the end of the period of two months beginning with the date of the making of the request, unless the application is made after the landlord has given a notice under section 26(6) of this Act.

Agreements extending time limits

C–13 **29B.**—(1) After the landlord has given a notice under section 25 of this Act, or the tenant has made a request under section 26 of this Act, but before the end of the statutory period, the landlord and tenant may agree that an application such as is mentioned in section 29A(1) of this Act, may be made before the end of a period specified in the agreement which will expire after the end of the statutory period.

(2) The landlord and tenant may from time to time by agreement further extend the period for making such an application, but any such agreement must be made before the end of the period specified in the current agreement.

(3) Where an agreement is made under this section, the court may entertain an application such as is mentioned in section 29A(1) of this Act if it is made before the end of the period specified in the agreement.

(4) Where an agreement is made under this section, or two or more agreements are made under this section, the landlord's notice under section 25 of this Act or tenant's request under section 26 of this Act shall be treated as terminating the tenancy at the end of the period specified in the agreement or, as the case may be, at the end of the period specified in the last of those agreements.

Opposition by landlord to application for new tenancy

C–14 **30.**—(1) The grounds on which a landlord may oppose an application under section 24(1) of this Act, or make an application under section 29(2) of this Act, are such of the following grounds as may be stated in the landlord's notice under section 25 of this Act, or as the case may be, under subsection (6) of section 26 thereof, that is to say—

(a) where under the current tenancy the tenant has any obligations as respects the repair and maintenance of the holding, that the tenant ought not to be granted a new tenancy in view of the state of repair of the holding, being a state resulting from the tenant's failure to comply with the said obligations;

(b) that the tenant ought not to be granted a new tenancy in view of his persistent delay in paying rent which has become due;

(c) that the tenant ought not to be granted a new tenancy in view of other substantial breaches by him of his obligations under the current tenancy, or for any other reason connected with the tenant's use or management of the holding;

(d) that the landlord has offered and is willing to provide or secure the provision of alternative accommodation for the tenant, that the terms on which the alternative accommodation is available are reasonable having regard to the terms of the current tenancy and to all other relevant circumstances, and that the accommodation and the time at which it will be available are suitable for the tenant's requirements (including the requirement to preserve goodwill) having regard to the nature and class of his business and to the situation and extent of, and facilities afforded by, the holding:

(e) where the current tenancy was created by the sub-letting of part only of the property comprised in a superior tenancy and the landlord is the owner of an interest in reversion expectant on the termination of that superior tenancy, that the aggregate of the rents reasonably obtainable on separate lettings of the holding and the remainder of that property would be substantially less than the rent reasonably obtainable on a letting of that property as a whole, that on the termination of the current tenancy the landlord requires possession of the holding for the purpose of letting or otherwise disposing of the said property as a whole, and that in view thereof the tenant ought not to be granted a new tenancy;

(f) that on the termination of the current tenancy the landlord intends to demolish or reconstruct the premises comprised in the holding or a substantial part of those premises or to carry out substantial work of construction on the holding or part thereof and that he could not reasonably do so without obtaining possession of the holding;

(g) subject as hereinafter provided, that on the termination of the current tenancy the landlord intends to occupy the holding for the purposes, or partly for the purposes, of a business to be carried on by him therein, or as his residence.

(1A) Where the landlord has a controlling interest in a company, the reference in subsection (1)(g) above to the landlord shall be construed as a reference to the landlord or that company.

(1B) Subject to subsection (2A) below, where the landlord is a company and a person has a controlling interest in the company, the reference in subsection (1)(g) above to the landlord shall be construed as a reference to the landlord or that person.

(2) The landlord shall not be entitled to oppose an application under section 24(1) of this Act, or make an application under section 29(2) of this Act on the ground specified in paragraph (g) of the last foregoing subsection if the interest of the landlord, or an interest which has merged in that interest and but for the merger would be the interest of the landlord, was purchased or created after the beginning of the period of five years which ends with the termination of the current tenancy, and at all times since the purchase or creation thereof the holding has been comprised in a tenancy or successive tenancies of the description specified in subsection (1) of section 23 of this Act.

(2A) Subsection (1B) above shall not apply if the controlling interest was acquired after the beginning of the period of five years which ends with the termination of the current tenancy, and at all times since the acquisition of the controlling interest the holding has been comprised in a tenancy or successive tenancies of the description specified in section 23(1) of this Act.

Dismissal of application for new tenancy where landlord successfully opposes

C–15   **31.**—(1) If the landlord opposes an application under subsection (1) of section 24 of this Act on grounds on which he is entitled to oppose it in accordance with the last foregoing section and establishes any of those grounds to the satisfaction of the court, the court shall not make an order for the grant of a new tenancy.

(2) Where the landlord opposes an application under section 24(1) of this Act, or makes an application under section 29(2) of this Act, on one or more of the grounds specified in section 30(1)(d) to (f) of this Act but establishes none of those grounds, and none of the other grounds specified in section 30(1) of this Act, to the satisfaction of the court, then if the court would have been satisfied on any of the grounds specified in section 30(1)(d) to (f) of this Act if the date of termination specified in the landlord's notice or, as the case may be, the date specified in the tenant's request for a new tenancy as the date from which the new tenancy is to begin, had been such later date as the court may determine, being a date not more than one year later than the date so specified,—

(a)   the court shall make a declaration to that effect, stating of which of the said grounds the court would have been satisfied as aforesaid and specifying the date determined by the court as aforesaid, but shall not make an order for the grant of a new tenancy;

(b)   if, within fourteen days after the making of the declaration, the tenant so requires the court shall make an order substituting the said date for the date specified in the said landlord's notice or tenant's request, and thereupon that notice or request shall have effect accordingly.

Grant of new tenancy in some cases where section 30(1)(f) applies

31A.—(1) Where the landlord opposes an application under section 24(1) of this Act on the ground specified in paragraph (f) of section 30(1) of this Act, or makes an application under section 29(2) of this Act on that ground, the court shall not hold that the landlord could not reasonably carry out the demolition, reconstruction or work of construction intended without obtaining possession of the holding if—   **C–16**

    (a)   the tenant agrees to the inclusion in the terms of the new tenancy of terms giving the landlord access and other facilities for carrying out the work intended and, given that access and those facilities, the landlord could reasonably carry out the work without obtaining possession of the holding and without interfering to a substantial extent or for a substantial time with the use of the holding for the purposes of the business carried on by the tenant; or

    (b)   the tenant is willing to accept a tenancy of an economically separable part of the holding and either paragraph (a) of this section is satisfied with respect to that part or possession of the remainder of the holding would be reasonably sufficient to enable the landlord to carry out the intended work.

(2) For the purposes of subsection (1)(b) of this section a part of a holding shall be deemed to be an economically separate part if, and only if, the aggregate of the rents which, after the completion of the intended work, would be reasonably obtainable on separate lettings of that part and the remainder of the premises affected by or resulting from the work would not be substantially less than the rent which would then be reasonably obtainable on a letting of those premises as a whole.

Property to be comprised in new tenancy

32.—(1) Subject to the following provisions of this section, an order under section 29 of this Act for the grant of a new tenancy shall be an order for the grant of a new tenancy of the holding; and in the absence of agreement between the landlord and the tenant as to the property which constitutes the holding the court shall in the order designate that property by reference to the circumstances existing at the date of the order.   **C–17**

(1A) Where the court, by virtue of paragraph (b) of section 31A(1) of this Act, makes an order under section 29 of this Act for the grant of a new tenancy in a case where the tenant is willing to accept a tenancy of part of the holding, the order shall be an order for the grant of a new tenancy of that part only.

(2) The foregoing provisions of this section shall not apply in a case where the property comprised in the current tenancy includes other property besides the holding and the landlord requires any new tenancy ordered

to be granted under section 29 of this Act to be a tenancy of the whole of the property comprised in the current tenancy; but in any such case—

(a)   any order under the said section 29 for the grant of a new tenancy shall be an order for the grant of a new tenancy of the whole of the property comprised in the current tenancy, and

(b)   references in the following provisions of this Part of this Act to the holding shall be construed as references to the whole of that property.

(3) Where the current tenancy includes rights enjoyed by the tenant in connection with the holding, those rights shall be included in a tenancy order to be granted under section 29 of this Act, except as otherwise agreed between the landlord and the tenant or, in default of such agreement, determined by the court.

Duration of new tenancy

C–18   **33.**—Where on an application under this Part of this Act the court makes an order for the grant of a new tenancy, the new tenancy shall be such tenancy as may be agreed between the landlord and the tenant, or, in default of such an agreement, shall be such a tenancy as may be determined by the court to be reasonable in all the circumstances, being, if it is a tenancy for a term of years certain, a tenancy for a term not exceeding fifteen years, and shall begin on the coming to an end of the current tenancy.

Rent under new tenancy

C–19   **34.**—(1) The rent payable under a tenancy granted by order of the court under this Part of this Act shall be such as may be agreed between the landlord and the tenant or as, in default of such agreement, may be determined by the court to be that at which, having regard to the terms of the tenancy (other than those relating to rent), the holding might reasonably be expected to be let in the open market by a willing lessor, there being disregarded—

(a)   any effect on rent of the fact that the tenant has or his predecessors in title have been in occupation of the holding,

(b)   any goodwill attached to the holding by reason of the carrying on thereat of the business of the tenant (whether by him or by a predecessor of his in that business),

(c)   any effect on rent of an improvement to which this paragraph applies,

(d)   in the case of a holding comprising licensed premises, any addition to its value attributable to the licence, if it appears to the court that having regard to the terms of the current tenancy and any other relevant circumstances the benefit of the licence belongs to the tenant.

(2) Paragraph (c) of the foregoing subsection applies to any improvement carried out by a person who at the time it was carried out was the tenant, but only if it was carried out otherwise than in pursuance of an obligation to his immediate landlord, and either it was carried out during the current tenancy or the following conditions are satisfied, that is to say—

(a)   that it was completed not more than twenty-one years before the application to the court was made; and

(b)   that the holding or any part of it affected by the improvement has at all times since the completion of the improvement been comprised in tenancies of the description specified in section 23(1) of this Act; and

(c)   that at the termination of each of those tenancies the tenant did not quit.

(2A) If this Part of this Act applies by virtue of section 23(1A) of this Act, the reference in subsection (1)(d) above to the tenant shall be construed as including—

(a)   a company in which the tenant has a controlling interest, or

(b)   where the tenant is a company, a person with a controlling interest in the company.

(3) Where the rent is determined by the court the court may, if it thinks fit, further determine that the terms of the tenancy shall include such provision for varying the rent as may be specified in the determination.

(4) It is hereby declared that the matters which are to be taken into account by the court in determining the rent include any effect on rent of the operation of the provisions of the Landlord and Tenant (Covenants) Act 1995.

Other terms of new tenancy

35.—(1) The terms of a tenancy granted by order of the court under   C–20
this Part of this Act (other than terms as to the duration thereof and as to the rent payable thereunder), including, where different persons own interests which fulfil the conditions specified in section 44(1) of this Act in different parts of it, terms as to the apportionment of the rent, shall be such as may be agreed between the landlord and the tenant or as, in default of such agreement, may be determined by the court; and in determining those terms the court shall have regard to the terms of the current tenancy and to all relevant circumstances.

(2) In subsection (1) of this section the reference to all relevant circumstances includes (without prejudice to the generality of that reference) a reference to the operation of the provisions of the Landlord and Tenant (Covenants) Act 1995.

Carrying out of order for new tenancy

C–21   **36.**—(1) Where under this Part of this Act the court makes an order for the grant of a new tenancy, then, unless the order is revoked under the next following subsection or the landlord and the tenant agree not to act upon the order, the landlord shall be bound to execute or make in favour of the tenant, and the tenant shall be bound to accept, a lease or agreement for a tenancy of the holding embodying the terms agreed between the landlord and the tenant or determined by the court in accordance with the foregoing provisions of this Part of this Act; and where the landlord executes or makes such a lease or agreement the tenant shall be bound, if so required by the landlord, to execute a counterpart or duplicate thereof.

(2) If the tenant, within fourteen days after the making of an order under this Part of this Act for the grant of a new tenancy, applies to the court for the revocation of the order the court shall revoke the order; and where the order is so revoked, then, if it is so agreed between the landlord and the tenant or determined by the court, the current tenancy shall continue, beyond the date at which it would have come to an end apart from this subsection, for such period as may be so agreed or determined to be necessary to afford to the landlord a reasonable opportunity for reletting or otherwise disposing of the premises which would have been comprised in the new tenancy; and while the current tenancy continues by virtue of this subsection it shall not be a tenancy to which this Part of this Act applies.

(3) Where an order is revoked under the last foregoing subsection any provision thereof as to payment of costs shall not cease to have effect by reason only of the revocation; but the court may, if it thinks fit, revoke or vary any such provision or, where no costs have been awarded in the proceedings for the revoked order, award such costs.

(4) A lease executed or agreement made under this section, in a case where the interest of the lessor is subject to a mortgage, shall be deemed to be one authorised by section 99 of the Law of Property Act 1925 (which confers certain powers of leasing on mortgagors in possession), and subsection (13) of that section (which allows those powers to be restricted or excluded by agreement) shall not have effect in relation to such a lease or agreement.

Compensation where order for new tenancy precluded on certain grounds

C–22   **37.**—(1) Subject to the provisions of this Act, in a case specified in subsection (1A), (1B) or (1C) below (a 'compensation case') the tenant shall be entitled on quitting the holding to recover from the landlord by way of compensation an amount determined in accordance with this section.

(1A) The first compensation case is where on the making of an application by the tenant under section 24(1) of this Act the court is precluded (whether by subsection (1) or subsection (2) of section 31 of this Act) from making an order for the grant of a new tenancy by reason of any of the grounds specified in paragraphs (e), (f) and (g) of section 30(1) of this Act (the 'compensation grounds') and not of any grounds specified in any other paragraph of section 30(1).

(1B) The second compensation case is where on the making of an application under section 29(2) of this Act the court is precluded (whether by section 29(4)(a) or section 31(2) of this Act) from making an order for the grant of a new tenancy by reason of any of the compensation grounds and not of any other grounds specified in section 30(1) of this Act.

(1C) The third compensation case is where—

(a)   the landlord's notice under section 25 of this Act or, as the case may be, under section 26(6) of this Act, states his opposition to the grant of a new tenancy on any of the compensation grounds and not on any other grounds specified in section 30(1) of this Act; and

(b)   either—

(i)   no application is made by the tenant under section 24(1) of this Act or by the landlord under section 29(2) of this Act; or

(ii)   such an application is made but is subsequently withdrawn.

(2) Subject to the following provisions of this section compensation under this section shall be as follows, that is to say,—

(a)   where the conditions specified in the next following subsection are satisfied in relation to the whole of the holding it shall be the product of the appropriate multiplier and twice the rateable value of the holding,

(b)   in any other case it shall be the product of the appropriate multiplier and the rateable value of the holding.

(3) The said conditions are—

(a)   that, during the whole of the fourteen years immediately preceding the termination of the current tenancy, premises being or comprised in the holding have been occupied for the purposes of a business carried on by the occupier or for those and other purposes;

(b)   that, if during those fourteen years there was a change in the occupier of the premises, the person who was the occupier immediately after the change was the successor to the business carried on by the person who was the occupier immediately before the change.

(3A) If the conditions specified in subsection (3) above are satisfied in relation to part of the holding but not in relation to the other part, the amount of compensation shall be the aggregate of sums calculated separately as compensation in respect of each part, and accordingly, for the purpose of calculating compensation in respect of a part any reference in this section to the holding shall be construed as a reference to that part.

(3B) Where section 44(1A) of this Act applies, the compensation shall be determined separately for each part and compensation determined for any part shall be recoverable only from the person who is the owner of an interest in that part which fulfils the conditions specified in section 44(1) of this Act.

(4) Where the court is precluded from making an order for the grant of a new tenancy under this Part of this Act in a compensation case, the court shall on the application of the tenant certify that fact.

(5) For the purposes of subsection (2) of this section the rateable value of the holding shall be determined as follows:—

(a) where in the valuation list in force at the date on which the landlord's notice under section 25 or, as the case may be, subsection (6) of section 26 of this Act is given a value is then shown as the annual value (as hereinafter defined) of the holding, the rateable value of the holding shall be taken to be that value;

(b) where no such value is so shown with respect to the holding but such a value or such values is or are so shown with respect to premises comprised in or comprising the holding or part of it, the rateable value of the holding shall be taken to be such value as is found by a proper apportionment or aggregation of the value or values so shown;

(c) where the rateable value of the holding cannot be ascertained in accord-ance with the foregoing paragraphs of this subsection, it shall be taken to be the value which, apart from any exemption from assessment to rates, would on a proper assessment be the value to be entered in the said valuation list as the annual value of the holding;

and any dispute arising, whether in proceedings before the court or otherwise, as to the determination for those purposes of the rateable value of the holding shall be referred to the Commissioners of Inland Revenue for decision by a valuation officer.

An appeal shall lie to the Lands Tribunal from any decision of a valuation officer under this subsection, but subject thereto any such decision shall be final.

(5A) If any part of the holding is domestic property as defined in section 66 of the Local Government Finance Act 1988,—

(a) The domestic property shall be disregarded in determining the rateable value of the holding under subsection (5) of this section; and

(b) if, on the date specified in subsection 5(a) of this section, the tenant occupied the whole or any part of the domestic property, the amount of compensation to which he is entitled under subsection (1) of this section shall be increased by the addition of a sum equal to his reasonable expenses in removing from the domestic property.

(5B) Any question as to the amount of the sum referred to in paragraph (b) of subsection (5A) of this section shall be determined by agreement between the landlord and the tenant or, in default of agreement, by the court.

(5C) If the whole of the holding is domestic property, as defined in section 66 of the Local Government Finance Act 1988, for the purpose of subsection (2) of this section the rateable value of the holding shall be taken to be an amount equal to the rent at which it is estimated the holding might reasonably be expected to let from year to year if the tenant undertook to pay all usual tenant's rates and taxes and to bear the cost of the repairs and insurance and the other expenses (if any) necessary to maintain the holding in a state to command that rent.

(5D) The following provisions shall have effect as regards a determination of an amount mentioned in subsection (5C) of this section—

(a) the date by reference to which such a determination is to be made is the date on which the landlord's notice under section 25 or, as the case may be, subsection (6) of section 26 of this Act is given;

(b) any dispute arising, whether in proceedings before the court or otherwise, as to such a determination shall be referred to the Commissioners of Inland Revenue for decision by a valuation officer;

(c) an appeal shall lie to the Lands Tribunal from such a decision but, subject to that, such a decision shall be final.

(5E) Any deduction made under paragraph 2A of Schedule 6 to the Local Government Finance Act 1988 (deduction from valuation of hereditaments used for breeding horses etc) shall be disregarded, to the extent that it relates to the holding, in determining the rateable value of the holding under subsection (5) of this section.

(6) The Commissioners of Inland Revenue may by statutory instrument make rules prescribing the procedure in connection with references under this section.

(7) In this section—

the reference to the termination of the current tenancy is a reference to the date of termination specified in the landlord's notice under section 25 of this Act or, as the case may be, the date specified in the tenant's request for a new tenancy as the date from which the new tenancy is to begin;

the expression 'annual value' means rateable value except that where the rateable value differs from the net annual value the said expression means net annual value;

the expression 'valuation officer' means any officer of the Commissioners of Inland Revenue for the time being authorised by a certificate of the Commissioners to act in relation to a valuation list.

(8) In subsection (2) of this section 'the appropriate multiplier' means such multiplier as the Secretary of State may by order made by statutory instrument prescribe and different multipliers may be so prescribed in relation to different cases.

(9) A statutory instrument containing an order under subsection (8) of this section shall be subject to annulment in pursuance of a resolution of either House or Parliament.

Compensation for possession obtained by misrepresentation

C–23   **37A.**—(1) Where the court—

(a)   makes an order for the termination of the current tenancy but does not make an order for the grant of a new tenancy, or

(b)   refuses an order for the grant of a new tenancy,

and it subsequently made to appear to the court that the order was obtained, or the court was induced to refuse the grant, by misrepresentation or the concealment of material facts, the court may order the landlord to pay to the tenant such sum as appears sufficient as compensation for damage or loss sustained by the tenant as the result of the order or refusal.

(2) Where—

(a)   the tenant has quit the holding—

(i)   after making but withdrawing an application under section 24(1) of this Act; or

(ii)   without making such an application; and

(b)   it is made to appear to the court that he did so by reason of misrepresentation or the concealment of material facts,

the court may order the landlord to pay to the tenant such sum as appears sufficient as compensation for damage or loss sustained by the tenant as the result of quitting the holding.

Restriction on agreements excluding provisions of Part II

C–24   **38.**—(1) Any agreement relating to a tenancy to which this Part of this Act applies (whether contained in the instrument creating the tenancy or not) shall be void (except as provided by section 38A of this Act) in so far as it purports to preclude the tenant from making an application or request under this Part of this Act or provides for the termination or the surrender of the tenancy in the event of his making such an application or request or for the imposition of any penalty or disability on the tenant in that event.

(2) Where—

(a)   during the whole of the five years immediately preceding the date on which the tenant under a tenancy to which this Part of this Act applies is to quit the holding, premises being or comprised in the holding have been occupied for the purposes of a business carried on by the occupier or for those and other purposes, and

(b)   if during those five years there was a change in the occupier of the premises, the person who was the occupier immediately after the change was the successor to the business carried on by the person who was the occupier immediately before the change,

any agreement (whether contained in the instrument creating the tenancy or not and whether made before or after the termination of that tenancy) which purports to exclude or reduce compensation under section 37 of this Act shall to that extent be void, so however that this subsection shall not affect any agreement as to the amount of any such compensation which is made after the right to compensation has accrued.

(3) In a case not falling within the last foregoing subsection the right to compensation conferred by section 37 of this Act may be excluded or modi-fied by agreement.

Agreements to exclude provisions of Part 2

38A.—(1) The persons who will be the landlord and the tenant in rela-   C–25
tion to a tenancy to be granted for a term of years certain which will be a tenancy to which this Part of this Act applies may agree that the provisions of sections 24 to 28 of this Act shall be excluded in relation to that tenancy.

(2) The persons who are the landlord and the tenant in relation to a tenancy to which this Part of this Act applies may agree that the tenancy shall be surrendered on such date or in such circumstances as may be specified in the agreement and on such terms (if any) as may be so specified.

(3) An agreement under subsection (1) above shall be void unless—

(a)   the landlord has served on the tenant a notice in the form, or substantially in the form, set out in Schedule 1 to the Regulatory Reform (Business Tenancies) (England and Wales) Order 2003 ('the 2003 Order'); and

(b)   the requirements specified in Schedule 2 to that Order are met.

(4) An agreement under subsection (2) above shall be void unless—

(a)   the landlord has served on the tenant a notice in the form, or substantially in the form, set out in Schedule 3 to the 2003 Order; and

(b)   the requirements specified in Schedule 4 to that Order are met.

General and supplementary provisions

Saving for compulsory acquisitions

C–26   **39.**—(1) [. . .]¹

(2) If the amount of the compensation which would have been payable under section 37 of this Act if the tenancy had come to an end in circumstances giving rise to compensation under that section and the date at which the acquiring authority obtained possession had been the termination of the current tenancy exceeds the amount of the compensation payable under section 121 of the Lands Clauses Consolidation Act 1845, or section 20 of the Compulsory Purchase Act 1965, in the case of a tenancy to which this Part of this Act applies, that compensation shall be increased by the amount of the excess.

(3) Nothing in section 24 of this Act shall affect the operation of the said section 121.

Duties of tenants and landlords of business premises to give information to each other

C–27   **40.**—(1) Where a person who is an owner of an interest in reversion expectant (whether immediately or not) on a tenancy of any business premises has served on the tenant a notice in the prescribed form requiring him to do so, it shall be the duty of the tenant to give the appropriate person in writing the information specified in subsection (2) below.

(2) That information is—

(a)   whether the tenant occupies the premises or any part of them wholly or partly for the purposes of a business carried on by him;

(b)   whether his tenancy has effect subject to any sub-tenancy on which his tenancy is immediately expectant and, if so—

(i)   what premises are comprised in the sub-tenancy;

(ii)   for what term it has effect (or, if it is terminable by notice, by what notice it can be terminated);

¹Repealed by Land Compensation Act 1973 (c. 26) Sch. 3.

    (iii)   what is the rent payable under it;

    (iv)   who is the sub-tenant;

    (v)   (to the best of his knowledge and belief) whether the sub-tenant is in occupation of the premises or of part of the premises comprised in the sub-tenancy and, if not, what is the sub-tenant's address;

    (vi)   whether an agreement is in force excluding in relation to the sub-tenancy the provisions of sections 24 to 28 of this Act; and

    (vii)   whether a notice has been given under section 25 or 26(6) of this Act, or a request has been made under section 26 of this Act, in relation to the sub-tenancy and, if so, details of the notice or request; and

(c)   (to the best of his knowledge and belief) the name and address of any other person who owns an interest in reversion in any part of the premises.

(3) Where the tenant of any business premises who is a tenant under such a tenancy as is mentioned in section 26(1) of this Act has served on a reversioner or a reversioner's mortgagee in possession a notice in the prescribed form requiring him to do so, it shall be the duty of the person on whom the notice is served to give the appropriate person in writing the information specified in subsection (4) below.

(4) That information is—

(a)   whether he is the owner of the fee simple in respect of the premises or any part of them or the mortgagee in possession of such an owner,

(b)   if he is not, then (to the best of his knowledge and belief)—

    (i)   the name and address of the person who is his or, as the case may be, his mortgagor's immediate landlord in respect of those premises or of the part in respect of which he or his mortgagor is not the owner in fee simple;

    (ii)   for what term his or his mortgagor's tenancy has effect and what is the earliest date (if any) at which that tenancy is terminable by notice to quit given by the landlord; and

    (iii)   whether a notice has been given under section 25 or 26(6) of this Act, or a request has been made under section 26 of this Act, in relation to the tenancy and, if so, details of the notice or request;

(c)   (to the best of his knowledge and belief) the name and address of any other person who owns an interest in reversion in any part of the premises; and

(d)   if he is a reversioner, whether there is a mortgagee in possession of his interest in the premises and, if so, (to the best of his knowledge and belief) what is the name and address of the mortgagee.

(5) A duty imposed on a person by this section is a duty—

(a) to give the information concerned within the period of one month beginning with the date of service of the notice; and

(b) if within the period of six months beginning with the date of service of the notice that person becomes aware that any information which has been given in pursuance of the notice is not, or is no longer, correct, to give the appropriate person correct information within the period of one month beginning with the date on which he becomes aware.

(6) This section shall not apply to a notice served by or on the tenant more than two years before the date on which apart from this Act his tenancy would come to an end by effluxion of time or could be brought to an end by notice to quit given by the landlord.

(7) Except as provided by section 40A of this Act, the appropriate person for the purposes of this section and section 40A(1) of this Act is the person who served the notice under subsection (1) or (3) above.

(8) In this section—

'business premises' means premises used wholly or partly for the purposes of a business;

'mortgagee in possession' includes a receiver appointed by the mortgagee or by the court who is in receipt of the rents and profits, and 'his mortgagor' shall be construed accordingly;

'reversioner' means any person having an interest in the premises, being an interest in reversion expectant (whether immediately or not) on the tenancy;

'reversioner's mortgagee in possession' means any person being a mortgagee in possession in respect of such an interest; and

'sub-tenant' includes a person retaining possession of any premises by virtue of the Rent (Agriculture) Act 1976 or the Rent Act 1977 after the coming to an end of a sub-tenancy, and 'sub-tenancy' includes a right so to retain possession.

Duties in transfer cases

C–28 **40A.**—(1) If a person on whom a notice under section 40(1) or (3) of this Act has been served has transferred his interest in the premises or any part of them to some other person and gives the appropriate person notice in writing—

(a) of the transfer of his interest; and

(b) of the name and address of the person to whom he transferred it,

on giving the notice he ceases in relation to the premises or (as the case may be) to that part to be under any duty imposed by section 40 of this Act.

(2) If—

(a)   the person who served the notice under section 40(1) or (3) of this Act ('the transferor') has transferred his interest in the premises to some other person ('the transferee'); and

(b)   the transferor or the transferee has given the person required to give the information notice in writing—

(i)   of the transfer; and
(ii)   of the transferee's name and address,

the appropriate person for the purposes of section 40 of this Act and subsection (1) above is the transferee.

(3) If—

(a)   a transfer such as is mentioned in paragraph (a) of subsection (2) above has taken place; but

(b)   neither the transferor nor the transferee has given a notice such as is mentioned in paragraph (b) of that subsection,

any duty imposed by section 40 of this Act may be performed by giving the information either to the transferor or to the transferee.

Proceedings for breach of duties to give information

40B. A claim that a person has broken any duty imposed by section 40 of this Act may be made the subject of civil proceedings for breach of statutory duty; and in any such proceedings a court may order that person to comply with that duty and may make an award of damages.   C–29

Trusts

41.—(1) Where a tenancy is held on trust, occupation by all or any of the beneficiaries under the trust, and the carrying on of a business by all or any of the beneficiaries, shall be treated for the purposes of section 23 of this Act as equivalent to occupation or the carrying on of a business by the tenant; and in relation to a tenancy to which this Part of this Act applies by virtue of the foregoing provisions of this subsection—   C–30

(a)   references (however expressed) in this Part of this Act and in the Ninth Schedule to this Act to the business of, or to carrying on of business, use, occupation or enjoyment by, the tenant shall be construed as including references to the business of, or to carrying on of business, use, occupation or enjoyment by, the beneficiaries or beneficiary;

(b)   the reference in paragraph (d) of subsection (1) of section 34 of this Act to the tenant shall be construed as including the beneficiaries or beneficiary; and

(c)   a change in the persons of the trustees shall not be treated as a change in the person of the tenant.

(2) Where the landlord's interest is held on trust the references in paragraph (g) of subsection (1) of section 30 of this Act to the landlord shall be construed as including references to the beneficiaries under the trust or any of them; but, except in the case of a trust arising under a will or on the intestacy of any person, the reference in subsection (2) of that section to the creation of the interest therein mentioned shall be construed as including the creation of the trust.

Partnerships

C–31   **41A.**—(1) The following provisions of this section shall apply where—

(a)   a tenancy is held jointly by two or more persons (in this section referred to as the joint tenants); and

(b)   the property comprised in the tenancy is or includes premises occupied for the purposes of a business; and

(c)   the business (or some other business) was at some time during the existence of the tenancy carried on in partnership by all the persons who were then the joint tenants or by those and other persons and the joint tenants' interest in the premises was then partnership property; and

(d)   the business is carried on (whether alone or in partnership with other persons) by one or some only of the joint tenants and no part of the property comprised in the tenancy is occupied, in right of the tenancy, for the purposes of a business carried on (whether alone or in partnership with other persons) by the other or others.

(2) In the following provisions of this section those of the joint tenants who for the time being carry on the business are referred to as the business tenants and the others as the other joint tenants.

(3) Any notice given by the business tenants which, had it been given by all the joint tenants, would have been—

(a)   a tenant's request for a new tenancy made in accordance with section 26 of this Act; or

(b)   a notice under subsection (1) or subsection (2) of section 27 of this Act;

shall be treated as such if it states that it is given by virtue of this section and sets out the facts by virtue of which the persons giving it are the business tenants; and references in those sections and in section 24A of this Act to the tenant shall be construed accordingly.

(4) A notice given by the landlord to the business tenants which, had it been given to all the joint tenants, would have been a notice under section 25 of this Act shall be treated as such a notice, and references in that section to the tenant shall be construed accordingly.

(5) An application under section 24(1) of this Act for a new tenancy may, instead of being made by all the joint tenants, be made by the business tenants alone; and where it is so made—

(a)   this Part of this Act shall have effect, in relation to it, as if the references therein to the tenant included references to the business tenants alone; and

(b)   the business tenants shall be liable, to the exclusion of the other joint tenants, for the payment of rent and the discharge of any other obligation under the current tenancy for any rental period beginning after the date specified in the landlord's notice under section 25 of this Act, or as the case may be, beginning on or after the date specified in their request for a new tenancy.

(6) Where the court makes an order under section 29 of this Act for the grant of a new tenancy it may order the grant to be made to the business tenants or to them jointly with the persons carrying on the business in partnership with them, and may order the grant to be made subject to the satisfaction, within a time specified by the order, of such conditions as to guarantors, sureties or otherwise as appear to the court equitable, having regard to the omission of the other joint tenants from the persons who will be the tenants under the new tenancy.

(7) The business tenants shall be entitled to recover any amount payable by way of compensation under section 37 or section 59 of this Act.

Groups of companies

42.—(1) For the purposes of this section two bodies corporate shall be   **C–32** taken to be members of a group if and only if one is a subsidiary of the other or both are subsidiaries of a third body corporate or the same person has a controlling interest in both.

(2) Where a tenancy is held by a member of a group, occupation by another member of the group, and the carrying on of a business by another member of the group, shall be treated for the purposes of section 23 of this Act as equivalent to occupation or the carrying on of a business by the member of the group holding the tenancy; and in relation to a tenancy to which this Part of this Act applies by virtue of the foregoing provisions of this subsection—

(a)   references (however expressed) in this Part of this Act and in the Ninth Schedule to this Act to the business of or to use occupation or enjoyment by the tenant shall be construed as including references to the business of or to use occupation or enjoyment by the said other member;

(b)   the reference in paragraph (d) of subsection (1) of section 34 of this Act to the tenant shall be construed as including the said other member; and

(c)   an assignment of the tenancy from one member of the group to another shall not be treated as a change in the person of the tenant.

(3) Where the landlord's interest is held by a member of a group—

(a)   the reference in paragraph (g) of subsection (1) of section 30 of this Act to intended occupation by the landlord for the purposes of a business to be carried on by him shall be construed as including intended occupation by any member of the group for the purposes of a business to be carried on by that member; and

(b)   the reference in subsection (2) of that section to the purchase or creation of any interest shall be construed as a reference to a purchase from or creation by a person other than a member of the group.

Tenancies excluded from Part II

C–33   **43.**—(1) This part of this Act does not apply—

(a)   to a tenancy of an agricultural holding which is a tenancy in relation to which the Agricultural Holdings Act 1986 applies or a tenancy which would be a tenancy of an agricultural holding in relation to which that Act applied if subsection (3) of section 2 of that Act did not have effect or, in a case where approval was given under subsection (1) of that section if that approval had not been given;

(aa)   to a farm business tenancy;

(b)   to a tenancy created by a mining lease;

(2) This Part of this Act does not apply to a tenancy granted by reason that the tenant was the holder of an office, appointment or employment from the grantor thereof and continuing only so long as the tenant holds the office, appointment or employment, or terminable by the grantor on the tenant's ceasing to hold it, or coming to an end at a time fixed by reference to the time at which the tenant ceases to hold it:

Provided that this subsection shall not have effect in relation to a tenancy granted after the commencement of this Act unless the tenancy was granted by an instrument in writing which expressed the purpose for which the tenancy was granted.

(3) This Part of this Act does not apply to a tenancy granted for a term certain not exceeding six months unless—

(a)   the tenancy contains provision for renewing the term or for extending it beyond six months from its beginning; or

(b)   the tenant has been in occupation for a period which, together with any period during which any predecessor in the carrying on of the business carried on by the tenant was in occupation, exceeds twelve months.

Jurisdiction of county court to make declaration

43A. Where the rateable value of the holding is such that the jurisdiction conferred on the court by any other provision of this Part of this Act is, by virtue of section 63 of this Act, exercisable by the county court, the county court shall have jurisdiction (but without prejudice to the jurisdiction of the High Court) to make any declaration as to any matter arising under this Part of this Act, whether or not any other relief is sought in the proceedings.   **C–34**

Meaning of 'the landlord' in Part II, and provisions as to mesne landlords, etc

44.—(1) Subject to subsections (1A) and (2) below, in this Part of this Act the expression 'the landlord', in relation to a tenancy (in this section referred to as 'the relevant tenancy'), means the person (whether or not he is the immediate landlord) who is the owner of that interest in the property comprised in the relevant tenancy which for the time being fulfils the following conditions, that is to say—   **C–35**

(a)   that it is an interest in reversion expectant (whether immediately or not) on the termination of the relevant tenancy, and

(b)   that it is either the fee simple or a tenancy which will not come to an end within fourteen months by effluxion of time and, if it is such a tenancy, that no notice has been given by virtue of which it will come to an end within fourteen months or any further time by which it may be continued under section 36(2) or section 64 of this Act,

and is not itself in reversion expectant (whether immediately or not) on an interest which fulfils those conditions.

(1A) The reference in subsection (1) above to a person who is the owner of an interest such as is mentioned in that subsection is to be construed, where different persons own such interests in different parts of the property, as a reference to all those persons collectively.

(2) References in this Part of this Act to a notice to quit given by the landlord are references to a notice to quit given by the immediate landlord.

(3) The provisions of the Sixth Schedule to this Act shall have effect

for the application of this Part of this Act to cases where the immediate landlord of the tenant is not the owner of the fee simple in respect of the holding.

*   *   *   *   *

Interpretation of Part II

C–36   **46.**—(1) In this Part of this Act:—

'business' has the meaning assigned to it by subsection (2) of section 23 of this Act;

'current tenancy' means the tenancy under which the tenant holds for the time being;

'date of termination' has the meaning assigned to it by subsection (1) of section 25 of this Act;

subject to the provisions of section 32 of this Act, 'the holding' has the meaning assigned to it by subsection (3) of section 23 of this Act;

'interim rent' has the meaning given by section 24A(1) of this Act;

'mining lease' has the same meaning as the Landlord and Tenant Act 1927.

(2) For the purposes of this Part of this Act, a person has a controlling interest in a company, if, had he been a company, the other company would have been its subsidiary; and in this Part—

'company' has the meaning given by section 735 of the Companies Act 1985; and

'subsidiary' has the meaning given by section 736 of that Act.

Part III

Compensation For Improvements

Time for making claims for compensation for improvements

C–37   **47.**—(1) Where a tenancy is terminated by notice to quit, whether given by the landlord or by the tenant, or by a notice given by any person under Part I or Part II of this Act, the time for making a claim for compensation at the termination of the tenancy shall be a time falling within the period of three months beginning on the date on which the notice is given:

Provided that where the tenancy is terminated by a tenant's request for a new tenancy under section 26 of this Act, the said time shall be a time falling within the period of three months beginning on the date on which the landlord gives notice, or (if he has not given such a notice) the latest date on which he could have given notice, under subsection (6) of the said section 26 or, as the case may be, paragraph (a) of subsection (4) of section 57 or paragraph (b) of subsection (1) of section 58 of this Act.

(2) Where a tenancy comes to an end by effluxion of time, the time for making such a claim shall be a time not earlier than six nor later than three months before the coming to an end of the tenancy.

(3) Where a tenancy is terminated by forfeiture or re-entry, the time for making such a claim shall be a time falling within the period of three months beginning with the effective date of the order of the court for the recovery of possession of the land comprised in the tenancy or, if the tenancy is terminated by re-entry without such an order, the period of three months beginning with the date of the re-entry.

(4) In the last foregoing subsection the reference to the effective date of an order is a reference to the date on which the order is to take effect according to the terms thereof or the date on which it ceases to be subject to appeal, whichever is the later.

* * * * *

Amendments as to limitations on tenant's right to compensation

48.—(1) So much of paragraph (b) of subsection (1) of section 2 of   C–38
the Act of 1927 as provides that a tenant shall not be entitled to compensation in respect of any improvement made in pursuance of a statutory obligation shall not apply to any improvement begun after the commencement of this Act, but section 3 of the Act of 1927 (which enables a landlord to object to a proposed improvement) shall not have effect in relation to an improvement made in pursuance of a statutory obligation except so much thereof as—

(a)   requires the tenant to serve on the landlord notice of his intention to make the improvement together with such a plan and specification as are mentioned in that section and to supply copies of the plan and specification at the request of any superior landlord; and

(b)   enables the tenant to obtain at his expense a certificate from the landlord or the tribunal that the improvement has been duly executed.

(2) Paragraph (c) of the said subsection (1) (which provides that a tenant shall not be entitled to compensation in respect of any improvement made less than three years before the termination of the tenancy) shall not apply to any improvement begun after the commencement of this Act.

(3) No notice shall be served after the commencement of this Act under paragraph (d) of the said subsection (1) (which excludes rights to compensation where the landlord serves on the tenant notice offering a renewal of the tenancy on reasonable terms).

Restrictions on contracting out

C–39   **49.** In section 9 of the Act of 1927 (which provides that Part I of that Act shall apply notwithstanding any contract to the contrary made after the date specified in that section) the proviso (which requires effect to be given to such a contract where it appears to the tribunal that the contract was made for adequate consideration) shall cease to have effect except as respects a contract made before the tenth day of December nineteen hundred and fifty-three.

Interpretation of Part III

C–40   **50.** In this Part of this Act the expression 'Act of 1927' means the Landlord and Tenant Act 1927, the expression 'compensation' means compensation under Part I of that Act in respect of an improvement, and other expressions used in this Part of this Act and in the Act of 1927 have the same meanings in this Part of this Act as in that Act.

PART IV

MISCELLANEOUS AND SUPPLEMENTARY

*   *   *   *   *

Compensations for possession obtained by misrepresentation

C–41   **55.**[. . .]

Application to Crown

C–42   **56.**—(1) Subject to the provisions of this and the four next following sections, Part II of this Act shall apply where there is an interest belonging to Her Majesty in right of the Crown or the Duchy of Lancaster or belonging to the Duchy of Cornwall, or belonging to a Government department or held on behalf of Her Majesty for the purposes of a Government department, in like manner as if that interest were an interest not so belonging or held.

(2) The provisions of the Eighth Schedule to this Act shall have effect as respects the application of Part II of this Act to cases where the interest of the landlord belongs to Her Majesty in right of the Crown or the Duchy of Lancaster or to the Duchy of Cornwall.

(3) Where a tenancy is held by or on behalf of a Government depart-

ment and the property comprised therein is or includes premises occupied for any purposes of a Government department, the tenancy shall be one to which Part II of this Act applies; and for the purposes of any provision of the said Part II or the Ninth Schedule to this Act which is applicable only if either or both of the following conditions are satisfied, that is to say—

(a)   that any premises have during any period been occupied for the purposes of the tenant's business;

(b)   that on any change of occupier of any premises the new occupier succeeded to the business of the former occupier,

the said conditions shall be deemed to be satisfied respectively, in relation to such a tenancy, if during that period or, as the case may be, immediately before and immediately after the change, the premises were occupied for the purposes of a Government department.

(4) The last foregoing subsection shall apply in relation to any premises provided by a Government department without any rent being payable to the department therefore as if the premises were occupied for the purposes of a Government department.

(5) The provisions of Parts III and IV of this Act, amending any other enactment which binds the Crown or applies to land belonging to Her Majesty in right of the Crown or the Duchy of Lancaster, or land belonging to the Duchy of Cornwall, or to land belonging to any Government department, shall bind the Crown or apply to such land.

(6) Sections 53 and 54 of this Act shall apply where the interest of the landlord, or any other interest in the land in question, belongs to Her Majesty in right of the Crown or the Duchy of Lancaster or to the Duchy of Cornwall, or belongs to a Government department or is held on behalf of Her Majesty for the purposes of a Government department, in like manner as if that interest were an interest not so belonging or held.

(7) Part I of this Act shall apply where—

(a)   there is an interest belonging to Her Majesty in right of the Crown and that interest is under the management of the Crown Estate Commissioners; or

(b)   there is an interest belonging to Her Majesty in right of the Duchy of Lancaster or belonging to the Duchy of Cornwall;

as if it were an interest not so belonging.

*   *   *   *   *

Modification on grounds of public interest of rights under Part II

57.—(1) Where the interest of the landlord or any superior landlord in the property comprised in any tenancy belongs to or is held for the purposes of a Government department or is held by a local authority, statutory

C–43

undertakers or a development corporation, the Minister or Board in charge of any Government department may certify that it is requisite for the purposes of the first-mentioned department, or, as the case may be, of the authority, undertakers or corporation, that the use or occupation of the property or a part thereof shall be changed by a specified date.

(2) A certificate under the last foregoing subsection shall not be given unless the owner of the interest belonging or held as mentioned in the last foregoing subsection has given to the tenant a notice stating—

(a)   that the question of the giving of such a certificate is under consideration by the Minister or Board specified in the notice, and

(b)   that if within twenty-one days of the giving of the notice the tenant makes to that Minister or Board representations in writing with respect to that question, they will be considered before the question is determined.

and if the tenant makes any such representations within the said twenty-one days the Minister or Board shall consider them before determining whether to give the certificate.

(3) Where a certificate has been given under subsection (1) of this section in relation to any tenancy, then—

(a)   if a notice given under subsection (1) of section 25 of this Act specifies as the date of termination a date not earlier than the date specified in the certificate and contains a copy of the certificate subsection (6) of that section shall not apply to the notice and no application for a new tenancy shall be made by the tenant under subsection (1) of section 24 of this Act;

(b)   if such a notice specifies an earlier date as the date of termination and contains a copy of the certificate, then if the court makes an order under Part II of this Act for the grant of a new tenancy the new tenancy shall be for a term expiring not later than the date specified in the certificate and shall not be a tenancy to which Part II of this Act applies.

(4) Where a tenant makes a request for a new tenancy under section 26 of this Act, and the interest of the landlord or any superior landlord in the property comprised in the current tenancy belongs or is held as mentioned in subsection (1) of this section, the following provisions shall have effect—

(a)   if a certificate has been given under the said subsection (1) in relation to the current tenancy, and within two months after the making of the request the landlord gives notice to the tenant that the certificate has been given and the notice contains a copy of the certificate, then,—

(i)   if the date specified in the certificate is not later than that specified in the tenant's request for a new tenancy, the tenant shall not make an application under section 24 of this Act for the grant of a new tenancy;

(ii)   if, in any other case, the court makes an order under Part II of this Act for the grant of a new tenancy the new tenancy shall be for a term expiring not later than the date specified in the certificate and shall not be a tenancy to which Part II of this Act applies;

(b)   if no such certificate has been given but notice under subsection (2) of this section has been given before the making of the request or within two months thereafter, the request shall not have effect, without prejudice however, to the making of a new request when the Minister or Board has determined whether to give a certificate.

(5) Where application is made to the court under Part II of this Act for the grant of a new tenancy and the landlord's interest in the property comprised in the tenancy belongs or is held as mentioned in subsection (1) of this section, the Minister or Board in charge of any Government department may certify that it is necessary in the public interest that if the landlord makes an application in that behalf the court shall determine as a term of the new tenancy that it shall be terminable by six months' notice to quit given by the landlord.

Subsection (2) of this section shall apply in relation to a certificate under this subsection, and if notice under the said subsection (2) has been given to the tenant—

(a)   the court shall not determine the application for the grant of a new tenancy until the Minister or Board has determined whether to give a certificate.

(b)   if a certificate is given, the court shall on the application of the landlord determine as a term of the new tenancy that it shall be terminable as afore said, and section 25 of this Act shall apply accordingly.

(6) The foregoing provisions of this section shall apply to an interest held by a Health Authority or Special Health Authority as they apply to an interest held by a local authority but with the substitution, for the reference to the purposes of the authority, of a reference to the purposes of the National Health Service Act 1977.

(7) Where the interest of the landlord or any superior landlord in the property comprised in any tenancy belongs to the National Trust the Minister of Works[1] may certify that it is requisite, for the purpose of securing that the property will as from a specified date be used or occupied in a manner better suited to the nature thereof, that the use or occupation of the property should be changed: and subsections (2) to (4) of this section shall apply in relation to certificates under this subsection, and to cases where the interest of the landlord or any superior landlord belongs to the National Trust, as those subsections apply in relation to certificates under subsection (1) of this section and to cases where the interest of the landlord or any superior landlord belongs or is held as mentioned in that subsection.

[1]Now the Secretary of State for the Environment.

(8) In this and the next following section the expression 'Government department' does not include the Commissioners of Crown Lands[1] and the expression 'landlord' has the same meaning as in Part II of this Act; and in the last foregoing subsection the expression 'National Trust' means the National Trust for Places of Historic Interest or Natural Beauty.

Termination on special grounds of tenancies to which Part II applies

C–44   58.—(1) Where the landlord's interest in the property comprised in any tenancy belongs to or is held for the purposes of a Government department, and the Minister or Board in charge of any Government department certifies that for reasons of national security it is necessary that the use or occupation of the property should be discontinued or changed, then—

    (a)   if the landlord gives a notice under subsection (1) of section 25 of this Act containing a copy of the certificate, subsection (6) of that section shall not apply to the notice and no application for a new tenancy shall be made by the tenant under subsection (1) of section 24 of this Act;

    (b)   if (whether before or after the giving of the certificate) the tenant makes a request for a new tenancy under section 26 of this Act, and within two months after the making of the request the landlord gives notice to the tenant that the certificate has been given and the notice contains a copy of the certificate—

        (i)   the tenant shall not make an application under section 24 of this Act for the grant of a new tenancy, and

        (ii)   if the notice specifies as the date on which the tenancy is to terminate a date earlier than that specified in the tenant's request as the date on which the new tenancy is to begin but neither earlier than six months from the giving of the notice nor earlier than the earliest date at which apart from this Act the tenancy would come to an end or could be brought to an end, the tenancy shall terminate on the date specified in the notice instead of that specified in the request.

(2) Where the landlord's interest in the property comprised in any tenancy belongs to or is held for the purposes of a Government department, nothing in this Act shall invalidate an agreement to the effect—

    (a)   that on the giving of such a certificate as is mentioned in the last foregoing subsection the tenancy may be terminated by notice to quit given by the landlord of such length as may be specified in the agreement, if the notice contains a copy of the certificate; and

    (b)   that after the giving of such a notice containing such a copy the tenancy shall not be one to which Part II of this Act applies.

[1]Now the Crown Estate Commissioners.

(3) Where the landlord's interest in the property comprised in any tenancy is held by statutory undertakers, nothing in this Act shall invalidate an agreement to the effect—

(a)   that where the Minister or Board in charge of a Government department certifies that possession of the property comprised in the tenancy or a part thereof is urgently required for carrying out repairs (whether on that property or elsewhere) which are needed for the proper operation of the landlord's undertaking, the tenancy may be terminated by notice to quit given by the landlord of such length as may be specified in the agreement, if the notice contains a copy of the certificate; and

(b)   that after the giving of such a notice containing such a copy, the tenancy shall not be one to which Part II of this Act applies.

(4) Where the court makes an order under Part II of this Act for the grant of a new tenancy and the Minister or Board in charge of any Government department certifies that the public interest requires the tenancy to be subject to such a term as is mentioned in paragraph (a) or (b) of this subsection, as the case may be, then—

(a)   if the landlord's interest in the property comprised in the tenancy belongs to or is held for the purposes of a Government department, the court shall on the application of the landlord determine as a term of the new tenancy that such an agreement as is mentioned in subsection (2) of this section and specifying such length of notice as is mentioned in the certificate shall be embodied in the new tenancy;

(b)   if the landlord's interest in that property is held by statutory undertakers, the court shall on the application of the landlord determine as a term of the new tenancy that such an agreement as is mentioned in subsection (3) of this section and specifying such length of notice as is mentioned in the certificate shall be embodied in the new tenancy.

Compensation for exercise of powers under ss.57 and 58

59.—(1) Where by virtue of any certificate given for the purposes of   C–45
either of the two last foregoing sections or, subject to subsection (1A)
below, section 60A below[1] the tenant is precluded from obtaining an order
for the grant of a new tenancy, or of a new tenancy for a term expiring
later than a specified date, the tenant shall be entitled on quitting the
premises to recover from the owner of the interest by virtue of which the
certificate was given an amount by way of compensation, and subsections
(2), (3) to (3B) and (5) to (7) of section 37 of this Act shall with the necessary modifications apply for the purposes of ascertaining the amount.

[1]Substituted by Government of Wales Act 1998, Sch.15, para.1.

(1A) No compensation shall be recoverable under subsection (1) above where the certificate was given under section 60A below and either—

    (a)   the premises vested in the Welsh Development Agency under section 7 (property of Welsh Industrial Estates Corporation) or 8 (land held under Local Employment Act 1972) of the Welsh Development Agency Act 1975, or

    (b)   the tenant was not tenant of the premises when the said Agency acquired the interest by virtue of which the certificate was given.[2]

(1B) No compensation shall be recoverable under subsection (1) above while the certificate was given under section 60B below and either—

    (a)   the premises are premises which—

        (i)   were vested in the Welsh Development Agency by section 8 of the Welsh Development Agency Act 1975 or were acquired by the Agency when no tenancy subsisted in the premises; and

        (ii)   vested in the Development Board for Rural Wales under section 24 of the Development of Rural Wales Act 1976; or

    (b)   the tenant was not the tenant of the premises when the Board acquired the interest by virtue of which the certificate was given.

(2) Subsections (2) and (3) of section 38 of this Act shall apply to compensation under this section as they apply to compensation under section 37 of this Act.

Special provisions as to premises Provided under Distribution of Industry Acts 1945 and 1950, etc

C–46   **60.**—(1) Where the property comprised in a tenancy consists of premises of which the Secretary of State or the English Industrial Estates Corporation is the landlord, being premises situated in a locality which is either—

    (a)   a development area; or
    (b)   an intermediate area;

and the Secretary of State certifies that it is necessary or expedient for achieving the purpose mentioned in section 2(1) of the Local Employment Act 1972 that the use or occupation of the property should be changed, paragraphs (a) and (b) of subsection (1) of section 58 of this

---

[1]Repealed by Government of Wales Act 1998, Sch.18, Part IV.

Act shall apply as they apply where such a certificate is given as is mentioned in that subsection.

(2) Where the court makes an order under Part II of this Act for the grant of a new tenancy of any such premises as aforesaid, and the Secretary of State certifies that it is necessary or expedient as aforesaid that the tenancy should be subject to a term, specified in the certificate, prohibiting or restricting the tenant from assigning the tenancy or subletting, charging or parting with possession of the premises or any part thereof or changing the use of the premises or any part thereof, the court shall determine that the terms of the tenancy shall include the terms specified in the certificate.

(3) In this section 'development area' and 'intermediate area' mean an area for the time being specified as a development area or, as the case may be, as an intermediate area by an order made, or having effect as if made, under section 1 of the Industrial Development Act 1982.

Welsh Development Agency premises

60A.—(1) Where the property comprised in a tenancy consists of   **C–47** premises of which the Welsh Development Agency is the landlord, and the Secretary of State certifies that it is necessary or expedient, for the purpose of providing employment appropriate to the needs of the area in which the premises are situated, that the use or occupation of the property should be changed, paragraphs (a) and (b) of section 58(1) above shall apply as they apply where such a certificate is given as is mentioned in that subsection.

(2) Where the court makes an order under Part II of this Act for the grant of a new tenancy of any such premises as aforesaid, and the Secretary of State certifies that it is necessary or expedient as aforesaid that the tenancy should be subject to a term, specified in the certificate, prohibiting or restricting the tenant from assigning the tenancy or subletting, charging or parting with possession of the premises or any part of the premises or changing the use of the premises or any part of the premises, the court shall determine that the terms of the tenancy shall include the terms specified in the certificate.

Development Board for Rural Wales premises

60B.(1) Where the property comprised in a tenancy consists of   **C–48** premises of which the Welsh Development Agency is the landlord, and the Secretary of State certifies that it is necessary or expedient, for the purpose of providing employment appropriate to the needs of the area in which the premises are situated, that the use or occupation of the property should be changed, paragraphs (a) and (b) of section 58(1) above shall apply as they apply where such a certificate is given as is mentioned in that subsection.

(2) Where the court makes an order under Part II of this Act for the grant of a new tenancy of any such premises as aforesaid, and the Secretary of State certifies that is is necessary or expedient as aforesaid that the tenancy should be subject to a term, specified in the certificate, prohibiting or restricting the tenant from assigning the tenancy or subletting, charging or parting with possession of the premises or any part of the premises or changing the use of the premises or any part of the premises, the court shall determine that the terms of the tenancy shall include the terms specified in the certificate.

*   *   *   *   *

Jurisdiction of court for purposes of Parts I and II and of Part I of Landlord and Tenant Act 1927

C–49   **63.**—(1) Any jurisdiction conferred on the court by any provision of Part I of this Act shall be exercised by the county court.

(2) Any jurisdiction conferred on the court by any provision of Part II of this Act or conferred on the tribunal by Part I of the Landlord and Tenant Act 1927, shall, subject to the provisions of this section, be exercised by the High Court or a county court.

*   *   *   *   *

(4) The following provisions shall have effect as respects transfer of proceedings from or to the High Court or the county court, that is to say—

(a)   where an application is made to the one but by virtue of an order under section 1 of the Courts and Legal Services Act 1990 cannot be entertained except by the other, the application shall not be treated as improperly made but any proceedings thereon shall be transferred to the other court;

(b)   any proceedings under the provisions of Part II of this Act or of Part I of the Landlord and Tenant Act 1927, which are pending before one of those courts may by order of that court made on the application of any person interested be transferred to the other court, if it appears to the court making the order that it is desirable that the proceedings and any proceedings before the other court should both be entertained by the other court.

(5) In any proceedings where in accordance with the foregoing provisions of this section the county court exercises jurisdiction the powers of the judge of summoning one or more assessors under subsection (1) of section 63 of the County Courts Act 1984, may be exercised notwith-

¹Repealed by Government of Wales Act 1998, Sch.18, Part IV.

standing that no application is made in that behalf by any party to the proceedings.

(6) Where in any such proceedings an assessor is summoned by a judge under the said subsection (1),—

(a) he may, if so directed by the judge, inspect the land to which the proceedings relate without the judge and report to the judge in writing thereon;

(b) the judge may on consideration of the report and any observations of the parties thereon give such judgment or make such order in the proceedings as may be just;

(c) the remuneration of the assessor shall be at such rate as may be determined by the Lord Chancellor with the approval of the Treasury and shall be defrayed out of moneys provided by Parliament.

(7) In this section the expression 'the holding'—

(a) in relation to proceedings under Part II of this Act, has the meaning assigned to it by subsection (3) of section 23 of this Act.

(b) in relation to proceedings under Part I of the Landlord and Tenant Act 1927, has the same meaning as in the said Part I.

*   *   *   *   *

(9) Nothing in this section shall prejudice the operation of section 41 of the County Courts Act 1984 (which relates to the removal into the High Court of proceedings commenced in a county court).

*   *   *   *   *

Interim continuation of tenancies pending determination by court

64.—(1) In any case where—   **C–50**

(a) a notice to terminate a tenancy has been given under Part I or Part II of this Act or a request for a new tenancy has been made under Part II thereof, and

(b) an application to the court has been made under the said Part I or under section 24(1) or 29(2) of this Act, as the case may be, and

(c) apart from this section the effect of the notice or request would be to terminate the tenancy before the expiration of the period of three months beginning with the date on which the application is finally disposed of,

the effect of the notice or request shall be to terminate the tenancy at the expiration of the said period of three months and not at any other time.

(2) The reference in paragraph (c) of subsection (1) of this section to the

date on which an application is finally disposed of shall be construed as a reference to the earliest date by which the proceedings on the application (including any proceedings on or in consequence of an appeal) have been determined and any time for appealing or further appealing has expired, except that if the application is withdrawn or any appeal is abandoned the reference shall be construed as a reference to the date of the withdrawal or abandonment.

Provisions as to reversions

C–51   **65.**—(1) Where by virtue of any provision of this Act a tenancy (in this subsection referred to as 'the inferior tenancy') is continued for a period such as to extend to or beyond the end of the term of a superior tenancy, the superior tenancy shall, for the purposes of this Act and of any any other enactment and of any rule of law, be deemed so long as it subsists to be an interest in reversion expectant upon the termination of the inferior tenancy and, if there is no intermediate tenancy, to be the interest in reversion immediately expectant upon the termination thereof.

(2) In the case of a tenancy continuing by virtue of any provision of this Act after the coming to an end of the interest in reversion immediately expectant upon the termination thereof, subsection (1) of section 139 of the Law of Property Act 1925 (which relates to the effect of the extinguishment of a reversion) shall apply as if references in the said subsection (1) to the surrender or merger of the reversion included references to the coming to an end of the reversion for any reason other than surrender or merger.

(3) Where by virtue of any provision of this Act a tenancy (in this subsection referred to as 'the continuing tenancy') is continued beyond the beginning of a reversionary tenancy which was granted (whether before or after the commencement of this Act) so as to begin on or after the date on which apart from this Act the continuing tenancy would have come to an end, the reversionary tenancy shall have effect as if it had been granted subject to the continuing tenancy.

(4) Where by virtue of any provision of this Act a tenancy (in this subsection referred to as 'the new tenancy') is granted for a period beginning on the same date as a reversionary tenancy or for a period such as to extend beyond the beginning of the term of a reversionary tenancy, whether the reversionary tenancy in question was granted before or after the commencement of this Act, the reversionary tenancy shall have effect as if it had been granted subject to the new tenancy.

Provisions as to notices

C–52   **66.**—(1) Any form of notice required by this Act to be prescribed shall be prescribed by regulations made by the Secretary of State by statutory instrument.

(2) Where the form of a notice to be served on persons of any description is to be prescribed for any of the purposes of this Act, the form to be prescribed shall include such an explanation of the reluctant provisions of this Act as appears to the Secretary of State requisite for informing persons of that description of their rights and obligations under those provisions.

(3) Different forms of notice may be prescribed for the purposes of the operation of any provision of this Act in relation to different cases.

(4) Section 23 of the Landlord and Tenant Act 1927 (which relates to the service of notices) shall apply for the purposes of this Act.

(5) Any statutory instrument under this section shall be subject to annulment in pursuance of a resolution of either House of Parliment.

Provisions as to mortgagees in possession

67. Anything authorised or required by the provisions of this Act,   **C–53** other than subsection (3) of section 40, to be done at any time by, to or with the landlord, or a landlord of a specified description, shall, if at that time the interest of the landlord in question is subject to a mortgage and the mortgagee is in possession or a receiver appointed by the mortgagee or by the court is in receipt of the rents and profits, be deemed to be authorised or required to be done by, to or with the mortgagee instead of that landlord.

*   *   *   *   *

Interpretation

69.—(1) In this Act the following expressions have the meanings   **C–54** hereby assigned to them respectively, that is to say—

'agricultural holding' has the same meaning as in the Agricultural Holdings Act 1986;

'development corporation' has the same meaning as in the New Towns Act 1946;

'farm business tenancy' has the same meaning as in the Agricultural Tenancies Act 1995;

'local authority' means any local authority within the meaning of the Town and Country Planning Act 1990, any National Park Authority, the Broads Authority, the London Fire and Emergency Planning Authority[1] or a joint authority established by Part IV of the Local Government Act 1985;

'mortgage' includes a charge or lien and 'mortgagor' and 'mortgagee' shall be construed accordingly;

'notice to quit' means a notice to terminate a tenancy (whether a period-

---

[1] Inserted by Greater London Authority Act 1999, Sch.29, para.1.

ical tenancy or a tenancy for a term of years certain) given in accordance with the provisions (whether express or implied) of that tenancy;

'repairs' includes any work of maintenance, decoration or restoration, and references to repairing, to keeping up in repair and to state of repair shall be construed accordingly;

'statutory undertakers' has the same meaning or yielding as in the Town and Country Planning Act 1947;

'tenancy' means a tenancy created either immediately or derivatively out of the freehold, whether by a lease or underlease, by an agreement for a lease or underlease or by a tenancy agreement or in pursuance of any enactment (including this Act), but does not include a mortgage term or any interest arising in favour of a mortgagor by his attorning tenant to his mortgagee, and references to the granting of a tenancy and to demised property shall be construed accordingly;

'terms', in relation to a tenancy, includes conditions.

(2) References in this Act to an agreement between the landlord and the tenant (except in section 17) and subsections (1) and (2) of section 38 thereof) shall be construed as references to an agreement in writing between them.

(3) References in this Act to an action for any relief shall be construed as including references to a claim for that relief by way of counter-claim in any proceedings.

Short title and citation, commencement and extent

C–55   **70.**—(1) This Act may be cited as the Landlord and Tenant Act, 1954, and the Landlord and Tenant Act, 1927, and this Act may be cited together as the Landlord and Tenant Acts, 1927 and 1954.

(2) This Act shall come into operation on the first day of October, nineteen hundred and fifty-four.

(3) This Act shall not extend to Scotland or to Northern Ireland.

*   *   *   *   *

SIXTH SCHEDULE   Section 44

PROVISIONS FOR PURPOSES OF PART II WHERE IMMEDIATE LANDLORD IS NOT THE FREEHOLDER

Definitions

C–56   **1.** In this Schedule the following expressions have the meanings hereby assigned to them in relation to a tenancy (in this Schedule referred to as 'the relevant tenancy'), that is to say—

'the competent landlord' means the person who in relation to the tenancy is for the time being the landlord (as defined by section 44 of this Act) for the purposes of Part II of this Act;

'mesne landlord' means a tenant whose interest is intermediate between the relevant tenancy and the interest of the competent landlord; and

'superior landlord' means a person (whether the owner of the fee simple or a tenant) whose interest is superior to the interest of the competent landlord.

Power of court to order reversionary tenancies

2. Where the period for which in accordance with the provisions of Part II of this Act it is agreed or determined by the court that a new tenancy should be granted thereunder will extend beyond the date on which the interest of the immediate landlord will come to an end, the power of the court under Part II of this Act to order such a grant shall include power to order the grant of a new tenancy until the expiration of that interest and also to order the grant of such a reversionary tenancy or reversionary tenancies as may be required to secure that the combined effects of those grants will be equivalent to the grant of a tenancy for that period; and the provisions of Part II of this Act shall, subject to the necessary modifications, apply in relation to the grant of a tenancy together with one or more reversionary tenancies as they apply in relation to the grant of one new tenancy.

C–57

Acts of competent landlord binding on other landlords

3.—(1) Any notice given by the competent landlord, under Part II of this Act to terminate the relevant tenancy, and any agreement made between that landlord and the tenant as to the granting, duration, or terms of a future tenancy, being an agreement made for the purposes of the said Part II, shall bind the interest of any mesne landlord notwithstanding that he has not consented to the giving of the notice or was not a party to the agreement.

C–58

(2) The competent landlord shall have power for the purposes of Part II of this Act to give effect to any agreement with the tenant for the grant of a new tenancy beginning with the coming to an end of the relevant tenancy, notwithstanding that the competent landlord will not be the immediate landlord at the commencement of the new tenancy, and any instrument made in the exercise of the power conferred by this subparagraph shall have effect as if the mesne landlord had been a party thereto.

(3) Nothing in the foregoing provisions of this paragraph shall prejudice the provisions of the next following paragraph.

Provisions as to consent of mesne landlord to acts of competent landlord

C–59   **4.**—(1) If the competent landlord, not being the immediate landlord, gives any such notice or makes any such agreement as is mentioned in sub-paragraph (1) of the last foregoing paragraph without the consent of every mesne landlord, any mesne landlord whose consent has not been given thereto shall be entitled to compensation from the competent landlord for any loss arising in consequence of the giving of the notice or the making of the agreement;

(2) If the competent landlord applies to any mesne landlord for his consent to such a notice or agreement, that consent shall not be unreasonably withheld, but may be given subject to any conditions which may be reasonable (including conditions as to the modification of the proposed notice or agreement or as to the payment of compensation by the competent landlord).

(3) Any question arising under this paragraph whether consent has been unreasonably withheld or whether any conditions imposed on the giving of consent are unreasonable shall be determined by the court.

Consent of superior landlord required for agreements affecting his interest

C–60   **5.** An agreement between the competent landlord and the tenant made for the purposes of Part II of this Act in a case where—

(a)   the competent landlord is himself a tenant, and
(b)   the agreement would apart from this paragraph operate as respects any period after the coming to an end of the interest of the competent landlord,

shall not have effect unless every superior landlord who will be the immediate landlord of the tenant during any part of that period is a party to the agreement.

Withdrawal by competent landlord of notice given by mesne landlord

C–61   **6.** Where the competent landlord has given a notice under section 25 of this Act to terminate the relevant tenancy and, within two months after the giving of the notice, a superior landlord—

(a)   becomes the competent landlord; and
(b)   gives to the tenant notice in the prescribed form that he withdraws the notice previously given,

the notice under section 25 of this Act shall cease to have effect, but without prejudice to the giving of a further notice under that section by the competent landlord.

Duty to inform superior landlords

7. If the competent landlord's interest in the property comprised in the   **C–62**
relevant tenancy is a tenancy which will come or can be brought to an end within sixteen months (or any further time by which it may be continued under section 36(2) or section 64 of this Act) and he gives to the tenant under the relevant tenancy a notice under section 25 of this Act to terminate the tenancy or is given by him a notice under section 26(3) of this Act:—

(a)   the competent landlord shall forthwith send a copy of the notice to his immediate landlord; and

(b)   any superior landlord whose interest in the property is a tenancy shall forthwith send to his immediate landlord any copy which has been sent to him in pursuance of the preceding sub-paragraph or this sub-paragraph.

*   *   *   *   *

EIGHTH SCHEDULE   **Section 56**

APPLICATION OF PART II TO THE LAND BELONGING TO CROWN AND DUCHIES OF LANCASTER AND CORNWALL

1. Where an interest in any property comprised in a tenancy belongs   **C–63**
to Her Majesty in right of the Duchy of Lancaster, then for the purposes of Part II of this Act the Chancellor of the Duchy shall represent Her Majesty and shall be deemed to be the owner of the interest.

2. Where an interest in any property comprised in a tenancy belongs to the Duchy of Cornwall, then for the purposes of Part II of this Act such person as the Duke of Cornwall, or other the possessor for the time being of the Duchy of Cornwall, appoints shall represent the Duke of Cornwall or other the possessor aforesaid, and shall be deemed to be the owner of the interest and may do any act or thing under the said Part II which the owner of that interest is authorised or required to do thereunder.

*   *   *   *   *

4. The amount of any compensation payable under section 37 of this Act by the Chancellor of the Duchy of Lancaster shall be raised and paid as an expense incurred in improvement of land belonging to Her Majesty in right of the Duchy within section 25 of the Act of the fifty-seventh year of King George the Third, Chapter ninety-seven.

5. Any compensation payable under section 37 of this Act by the person representing the Duke of Cornwall or other the possessor for the time being of the Duchy of Cornwall shall be paid, and advances therefor made, in the manner and subject to the provisions of section 8 of the Duchy of Cornwall Management Act 1863 with respect to improvements of land mentioned in that section.

Appendix D

The Agricultural Tenancies Act 1995

Part I

General Provisions

Farm business tenancies

Meaning of 'farm business tenancy'

1.—(1) A tenancy is a 'farm business tenancy' for the purposes of this **D–01**
Act if—

(a)   it meets the business conditions together with either the agriculture condition or the notice conditions, and
(b)   it is not a tenancy which, by virtue of section 2 of this Act,
cannot be a farm business tenancy.

(2) The business conditions are—

(a)   that all or part of the land comprised in the tenancy is farmed
for the purposes of a trade or business, and
(b)   that, since the beginning of the tenancy, all or part of the land
so comprised has been so farmed.

(3) The agriculture condition is that, having regard to—

(a)   the terms of the tenancy,
(b)   the use of the land comprised in the tenancy,
(c)   the nature of any commercial activities carried on on that land,
and
(d)   any other relevant circumstances,

the character of the tenancy is primarily or wholly agricultural.

(4) The notice conditions are—

(a) that, on or before the relevant day, the landlord and the tenant each gave the other a written notice—

  (i) identifying (by name or otherwise) the land to be comprised in the tenancy or proposed tenancy, and

  (ii) containing a statement to the effect that the person giving the notice intends that the tenancy or proposed tenancy is to be, and remain, a farm business tenancy, and

(b) that, at the beginning of the tenancy, having regard to the terms of the tenancy and any other relevant circumstances, the character of the tenancy was primarily or wholly agricultural.

(5) In subsection (4) above 'the relevant day' means whichever is the earlier of the following—

(a) the day on which the parties enter into any instrument creating the tenancy, other than an agreement to enter into a tenancy on a future date, or

(b) the beginning of the tenancy.

(6) The written notice referred to in subsection (4) above must not be included in any instrument creating the tenancy.

(7) If in any proceedings—

(a) any question arises as to whether a tenancy was a farm business tenancy at any time, and

(b) it is proved that all or part of the land comprised in the tenancy was farmed for the purposes of a trade or business at that time,

it shall be presumed, unless the contrary is proved, that all or part of the land so comprised has been so farmed since the beginning of the tenancy.

(8) Any use of land in breach of the terms of the tenancy, any commercial activities carried on in breach of those terms, and any cessation of such activities in breach of those terms, shall be disregarded in determining whether at any time the tenancy meets the business conditions or the agriculture condition, unless the landlord or his predecessor in title has consented to the breach or the landlord has acquiesced in the breach.

Tenancies which cannot be farm business tenancies

D–02 **2.**—(1) A tenancy cannot be a farm business tenancy for the purposes of this Act if—

(a) the tenancy begins before 1st September 1995, or

(b) it is a tenancy of an agricultural holding beginning on or after that date with respect to which, by virtue of section 4 of this Act, the Agricultural Holdings Act 1986 applies.

(2) In this section 'agricultural holding' has the same meaning as in the Agricultural Holdings Act 1986.

Compliance with notice conditions in cases of surrender and regrant

3.—(1) This section applies where—   D–03

(a) a tenancy ('the new tenancy') is granted to a person who, immediately before the grant, was the tenant under a farm business tenancy ('the old tenancy') which met the notice conditions specified in section 1(4) of this Act,

(b) the condition in subsection (2) below or the condition in subsection (3) below is met, and

(c) except as respects the matters mentioned in subsections (2) and (3) below and matters consequential on them, the terms of the new tenancy are substantially the same as the terms of the old tenancy.

(2) The first condition referred to in subsection (1)(b) above is that the land comprised in the new tenancy is the same as the land comprised in the old tenancy, apart from any changes in area which are small in relation to the size of the holding and do not affect the character of the holding.

(3) The second condition referred to in subsection (1)(b) above is that the old tenancy and the new tenancy are both fixed term tenancies, but the term date under the new tenancy is earlier than the term date under the old tenancy.

(4) Where this section applies, the new tenancy shall be taken for the purposes of this Act to meet the notice conditions specified in section 1(4) of this Act.

(5) In subsection (3) above, 'the term date', in relation to a fixed term tenancy, means the date fixed for the expiry of the term.

Exclusion of Agricultural Holdings Act 1986

Agricultural Holdings Act 1986 not to aply in relation to new tenancies except in special cases

4.—(1) The Agricultural Holdings Act 1986 (in this section referred to   D–04
as 'the 1986 Act') shall not apply in relation to any tenancy beginning on or after 1st September 1995 (including any agreement to which section 2 of that Act would otherwise apply beginning on or after that date), except any tenancy of an agricultural holding which—

(a) is granted by a written contract of tenancy entered into before 1st September 1995 and indicating (in whatever terms) that the 1986 Act is to apply in relation to the tenancy,

(b)   is obtained by virtue of a direction of an Agricultural Land Tribunal under section 39 or 53 of the 1986 Act,

(c)   is granted (following a direction under section 39 of that Act) in circumstances falling within section 45(6) of that Act,

(d)   is granted on an agreed succession by a written contract of tenancy indicating (in whatever terms) that Part IV of the 1986 Act is to apply in relation to the tenancy,

(e)   is created by the acceptance of a tenant, in accordance with the provisions as to compensation known as the 'Evesham custom' and set out in subsections (3) to (5) of section 80 of the 1986 Act, on the terms and conditions of the previous tenancy, or

(f)   is granted to a person who, immediately before the grant of the tenancy, was the tenant of the holding, or of any agricultural holding which comprised the whole or a substantial part of the land comprised in the holding, under a tenancy in relation to which the 1986 Act applied ('the previous tenancy') and is so granted merely because a purported variation of the previous tenancy (not being an agreement expressed to take effect as a new tenancy between the parties) has effect as an implied surrender followed by the grant of the tenancy.

D–05   (2) For the purposes of subsection (1)(d) above, a tenancy ('the current tenancy') is granted on an agreed succession if, and only if—

(a)   the previous tenancy of the holding or a related holding was a tenancy in relation to which Part IV of the 1986 Act applied, and

(b)   the current tenancy is granted otherwise than as mentioned in paragraph (b) or (c) of subsection (1) above but in such circumstances that if—

(i)   Part IV of the 1986 Act applied in relation to the current tenancy, and

(ii)   a sole (or sole surviving) tenant under the current tenancy were to die and be survived by a close relative of his,

the occasion on which the current tenancy is granted would for the purposes of subsection (1) of section 37 of the 1986 Act be taken to be an occasion falling within paragraph (a) or (b) of that subsection.

(3) In this section—

(a)   'agricultural holding' and 'contract of tenancy' have the same meaning as in the 1986 Act, and

(b)   'close relative' and 'related holding' have the meaning given by section 35(2) of that Act.

Termination of the tenancy

Tenancies for more than two years to continue from year to year unless terminated by notice

5.—(1) A farm business tenancy for a term of more than two years **D–06** shall, instead of terminating on the term date, continue (as from that date) as a tenancy from year to year, but otherwise on the terms of the original tenancy so far as applicable, unless at least twelve months but less than twenty-four months before the term date a written notice has been given by either party to the other of his intention to terminate the tenancy.

(2) In subsection (1) above 'the term date', in relation to a fixed term tenancy, means the date fixed for the expiry of the term.

(3) For the purposes of section 140 of the Law of Property Act 1925 (apportionment of conditions on severance of reversion), a notice under subsection (1) above shall be taken to be a notice to quit.

(4) This section has effect notwithstanding any agreement to the contrary.

Length of notice to quit

6.—(1) Where a farm business tenancy is a tenancy from year to year, **D–07** a notice to quit the holding or part of the holding shall (notwithstanding any provision to the contrary in the tenancy) be invalid unless—

(a) it is in writing,

(b) it is to take effect at the end of a year of the tenancy, and

(c) it is given at least twelve months but less than twenty-four months before the date on which it is to take effect.

(2) Where, by virtue of section 5(1) of this Act, a farm business tenancy for a term of more than two years is to continue (as from the term date) as a tenancy from year to year, a notice to quit which complies with subsection (1) above and which is to take effect on the first anniversary of the term date shall not be invalid merely because it is given before the term date; and in this subsection 'the term date' has the meaning given by section 5(2) of this Act.

(3) Subsection (1) above does not apply in relation to a counter-notice given by the tenant by virtue of subsection (2) of section 140 of the Law of Property Act 1925 (apportionment of conditions on severance of reversion).

Notice required for exercise of option to terminate tenancy or resume
possession of part

D–08   **7.**—(1) Where a farm business tenancy is a tenancy for a term of more than two years, any notice to quit the holding or part of the holding given in pursuance of any provision of the tenancy shall (notwithstanding any provision to the contrary in the tenancy) be invalid unless it is in writing and is given at least twelve months but less than twenty-four months before the date on which it is to take effect.

(2) Subsection (1) above does not apply in relation to a counter-notice given by the tenant by virtue of subsection (2) of section 140 of the Law of Property Act 1925 (apportionment of conditions on severance of reversion).

(3) Subsection (1) above does not apply to a tenancy which, by virtue of subsection (6) of section 149 of the Law of Property Act 1925 (lease for life or lives or for a term determinable with life or lives or on the marriage of the lessee), takes effect as such a term of years as is mentioned in that subsection.

Tenant's right to remove fixtures and buildings

Tenant's right to remove fixtures and buildings

D–09   **8.**—(1) Subject to the provisions of this section—

(a)   any fixture (of whatever description) affixed, whether for the purposes of agriculture or not, to the holding by the tenant under a farm business tenancy, and

(b)   any building erected by him on the holding,

may be removed by the tenant at any time during the continuance of the tenancy or at any time after the termination of the tenancy when he remains in possession as tenant (whether or not under a new tenancy), and shall remain his property so long as he may remove it by virtue of this subsection.

(2) Subsection (1) above shall not apply—

(a)   to a fixture affixed or a building erected in pursuance of some obligation,

(b)   to a fixture affixed or a building erected instead of some fixture or building belonging to the landlord,

(c)   to a fixture or building in respect of which the tenant has obtained compensation under section 16 of this Act or otherwise, or

(d)   to a fixture or building in respect of which the landlord has given his consent under section 17 of this Act on condition that the tenant agrees not to remove it and which the tenant has agreed not to remove.

(3) In the removal of a fixture or building by virtue of subsection (1) above, the tenant shall not do any avoidable damage to the holding.

(4) Immediately after removing a fixture or building by virtue of subsection (1) above, the tenant shall make good all damage to the holding that is occasioned by the removal.

(5) This section applies to a fixture or building acquired by a tenant as it applies to a fixture or building affixed or erected by him.

(6) Except as provided by subsection (2)(d) above, this section has effect notwithstanding any agreement or custom to the contrary.

(7) No right to remove fixtures that subsists otherwise than by virtue of this section shall be exercisable by the tenant under a farm business tenancy.

PART II

RENT REVIEW UNDER FARM BUSINESS TENANCY

Application of Part II

9. This Part of this Act applies in relation to a farm business tenancy (notwithstanding any agreement to the contrary) unless the tenancy is created by an instrument which—   **D–10**

(a)   expressly states that the rent is not to be reviewed during the tenancy, or

(b)   provides that the rent is to be varied, at a specified time or times during the tenancy—

    (i)   by or to a specified amount, or

    (ii)   in accordance with a specified formula which does not preclude a reduction and which does not require or permit the exercise by any person of any judgment or discretion in relation to the determination of the rent of the holding,

but otherwise is to remain fixed.

Notice requiring statutory rent review

10.—(1) The landlord or tenant under a farm business tenancy in relation to which this Part of this Act applies may by notice in writing given to the other (in this Part of this Act referred to as a 'statutory review notice') require that the rent to be payable in respect of the holding as   **D–11**

from the review date shall be referred to arbitration in accordance with this Act.

(2) In this Part of this Act 'the review date', in relation to a statutory review notice, means a date which—

(a)   is specified in the notice, and
(b)   complies with subsections (3) to (6) below.

(3) The review date must be at least twelve months but less than twenty-four months after the day on which the statutory review notice is given.

(4) If the parties have agreed in writing that the rent is to be, or may be, varied as from a specified date or dates, or at specified intervals, the review date must be a date as from which the rent could be varied under the agreement.

(5) If the parties have agreed in writing that the review date for the purposes of this Part of this Act is to be a specified date or dates, the review date must be that date or one of those dates.

(6) If the parties have not agreed as mentioned in subsection (4) or (5) above, the review date—

(a)   must be an anniversary of the beginning of the tenancy or, where the landlord and the tenant have agreed in writing that the review date for the purposes of this Act is to be some other day of the year, that day of the year, and
(b)   must not fall before the end of the period of three years beginning with the latest of any of the following dates—

(i)   the beginning of the tenancy,
(ii)   any date as from which there took effect a previous direction of an arbitrator as to the amount of the rent,
(iii) any date as from which there took effect a previous determination as to the amount of the rent made, otherwise than as arbitrator, by a person appointed under an agreement between the landlord and the tenant, and
(iv)   any date as from which there took effect a previous agreement in writing between the landlord and the tenant, entered into since the grant of the tenancy, as to the amount of the rent.

Review date where new tenancy of severed part of reversion

D–12   **11.**—(1) This section applies in any case where a farm business tenancy ('the new tenancy') arises between—

(a)   a person who immediately before the date of the beginning of the tenancy was entitled to a severed part of the reversionary estate in the land comprised in a farm business tenancy ('the original tenancy') in which the land to which the new tenancy relates was then comprised, and

(b)   the person who immediately before that date was the tenant under the original tenancy,

and the rent payable under the new tenancy at its beginning represents merely the appropriate portion of the rent payable under the original tenancy immediately before the beginning of the new tenancy.

(2) In any case where this section applies—

(a)   references to the beginning of the tenancy in subsection (6) of section 10 of this Act shall be taken to be references to the beginning of the original tenancy, and

(b)   references to rent in that subsection shall be taken to be references to the rent payable under the original tenancy,

until the first occasion following the beginning of the new tenancy on which any such direction, determination or agreement with respect to the rent of the new holding as is mentioned in that subsection takes effect.

Appointment of arbitrator

12. Where a statutory review notice has been given in relation to a   **D–13**
farm business tenancy, but—

(a)   no arbitrator has been appointed under an agreement made since the notice was given, and

(b)   no person has been appointed under such an agreement to determine the question of the rent (otherwise than as arbitrator) on a basis agreed by the parties,

either party may, at any time during the period of six months ending with the review date, apply to the President of the Royal Institution of Chartered Surveyors (in this Act referred to as 'the RICS') for the appointment of an arbitrator by him.

Amount of rent

13.—(1) On any reference made in pursuance of a statutory review   **D–14**
notice, the arbitrator shall determine the rent properly payable in respect of the holding at the review date and accordingly shall, with effect from that date, increase or reduce the rent previously payable or direct that it shall continue unchanged.

(2) For the purposes of subsection (1) above, the rent properly payable in respect of a holding is the rent at which the holding might reasonably

be expected to be let on the open market by a willing landlord to a willing tenant, taking into account (subject to subsections (3) and (4) below) all relevant factors, including (in every case) the terms of the tenancy (including those which are relevant for the purposes of section 10(4) to (6) of this Act, but not those relating to the criteria by reference to which any new rent is to be determined).

(3) The arbitrator shall disregard any increase in the rental value of the holding which is due to tenant's improvement other than—

(a)   any tenant's improvement provided under an obligation which was imposed on the tenant by the terms of his tenancy or any previous tenancy and which arose on or before the beginning of the tenancy in question,

(b)   any tenant's improvement to the extent that any allowance or benefit has been made or given by the landlord in consideration of its provision, and

(c)   any tenant's improvement to the extent that the tenant has received any compensation from the landlord in respect of it.

(4) The arbitrator—

(a)   shall disregard any effect on the rent of the fact that the tenant who is a party to the arbitration is in occupation of the holding, and

(b)   shall not fix the rent at a lower amount by reason of any dilapidation or deterioration of, or damage to, buildings or land caused or permitted by the tenant.

(5) In this section 'tenant's improvement', and references to the provision of such an improvement, have the meaning given by section 15 of this Act.

Interpretation of Part II

D–15   **14.** In this Part of this Act, unless the context otherwise requires—
'the review date', in relation to a statutory review notice, has the meaning given by section 10(2) of this Act;
'statutory review notice' has the meaning given by section 10(1) of this Act.

PART III

COMPENSATION ON TERMINATION OF FARM BUSINESS TENANCY

Tenant's entitlement to compensation

Meaning of 'tenant's improvement'

15. For the purposes of this Part of this Act a 'tenant's improvement', **D–16**
in relation to any farm business tenancy, means—

    (a)   any physical improvement which is made on the holding by the
tenant by his own effort or wholly or partly at his own expense,
or

    (b)   any intangible advantage which—

        (i)   is obtained for the holding by the tenant by his own effort
or wholly or partly at his own expense, and

        (ii)   becomes attached to the holding,

and references to the provision of a tenant's improvement are references
to the making by the tenant of any physical improvement falling within
paragraph (*a*) above or the obtaining by the tenant of any intangible
advantage falling within paragraph (*b*) above.

Tenant's right to compensation for tenant's improvement

16.—(1) The tenant under a farm business tenancy shall, subject to the **D–17**
provisions of this Part of this Act, be entitled on the termination of the
tenancy, on quitting the holding, to obtain from his landlord compensation in respect of any tenant's improvement.

(2) A tenant shall not be entitled to compensation under this section
in respect of—

    (a)   any physical improvement which is removed from the holding,
or

    (b)   any intangible advantage which does not remain attached to the
holding.

(3) Section 13 of, and Schedule 1 to, the Agriculture Act 1986 (compensation to outgoing tenants for milk quota) shall not apply in relation
to a farm business tenancy.

Conditions of eligibility

Consent of landlord as condition of compensation for tenant's improvement

D–18   **17.**—(1) A tenant shall not be entitled to compensation under section 16 of this Act in respect of any tenant's improvement unless the landlord has given his consent in writing to the provision of the tenant's improvement.

(2) Any such consent may be given in the instrument creating the tenancy or elsewhere.

(3) Any such consent may be given either unconditionally or on condition that the tenant agrees to a specified variation in the terms of the tenancy.

(4) The variation referred to in subsection (3) above must be related to the tenant's improvement in question.

(5) This section does not apply in any case where the tenant's improvement consists of planning permission.

Conditions in relation to compensation for planning permission

D–19   **18.**—(1) A tenant shall not be entitled to compensation under section 16 of this Act in respect of a tenant's improvement which consists of planning permission unless—

(a)   the landlord has given his consent in writing to the making of the application for planning permission,

(b)   that consent is expressed to be given for the purpose—

(i)   of enabling a specified physical improvement falling within paragraph (a) of section 15 of this Act lawfully to be provided by the tenant, or

(ii)   of enabling the tenant lawfully to effect a specified change of use, and

(c)   on the termination of the tenancy, the specified physical improvement has not been completed or the specified change of use has not been effected.

(2) Any such consent may be given either unconditionally or on condition that the tenant agrees to a specified variation in the terms of the tenancy.

(3) The variation referred to in subsection (2) above must be related to the physical improvement or change of use in question.

*Reference to arbitration of refusal or failure to give consent or of
condition attached to consent*

19.—(1) Where, in relation to any tenant's improvement, the tenant   **D–20**
under a farm business tenancy is aggrieved by—

(a)   the refusal of his landlord to give his consent under section 17(1)
       of this Act,
(b)   the failure of his landlord to give such consent within two
       months of a written request by the tenant for such consent, or
(c)   any variation in the terms of the tenancy required by the land-
       lord as a condition of giving such consent,

the tenant may by notice in writing given to the landlord demand that the
question shall be referred to arbitration under this section; but this subsection has effect subject to subsections (2)and (3) below.

(2) No notice under subsection (1) above may be given in relation to
any tenant's improvement which the tenant has already provided or begun
to provide, unless that improvement is a routine improvement.

(3) No notice under subsection (1) above may be given—

(a)   in a case falling within paragraph (a) or (c) of that subsection,
       after the end of the period of two months beginning with the day
       on which notice of the refusal or variation referred to in that
       paragraph was given to the tenant, or
(b)   in a case falling within paragraph (b) of that subsection, after
       the end of the period of four months beginning with the day on
       which the written request referred to in that paragraph was given
       to the landlord.

(4) Where the tenant has given notice under subsection (1) above but   **D–21**
no arbitrator has been appointed under an agreement made since the
notice was given, the tenant or the landlord may apply to the President of
the RICS, subject to subsection (9) below, for the appointment of an arbitrator by him.

(5) The arbitrator shall consider whether, having regard to the terms
of the tenancy and any other relevant circumstances (including the
circumstances of the tenant and the landlord), it is reasonable for the
tenant to provide the tenant's improvement.

(6) Subject to subsection (9) below, the arbitrator may unconditionally approve the provision of the tenant's improvement or may withhold
his approval, but may not give his approval subject to any condition or
vary any condition required by the landlord under section 17(3) of this
Act.

(7) If the arbitrator gives his approval, that approval shall have effect
for the purposes of this Part of this Act and for the purposes of the
terms of the farm business tenancy as if it were the consent of the landlord.

(8) In a case falling within subsection (1)(*c*) above, the withholding by the arbitrator of his approval shall not affect the validity of the landlord's consent or of the condition subject to which it was given.

(9) Where, at any time after giving a notice under subsection (1) above in relation to any tenant's improvement which is not a routine improvement, the tenant begins to provide the improvement—

    (a)   no application may be made under subsection (4) above after that time,

    (b)   where such an application has been made but no arbitrator has been appointed before that time, the application shall be ineffective, and

    (c)   no award may be made by virtue of subsection (6) above after that time except as to the costs of the reference and award in a case where the arbitrator was appointed before that time.

(10) For the purposes of this section—

'fixed equipment' includes any building or structure affixed to land and any works constructed on, in, over or under land, and also includes anything grown on land for a purpose other than use after severance from the land, consumption of the thing grown or its produce, or amenity;

'routine improvement', in relation to a farm business tenancy, means any tenant's improvement which—

    (a)   is a physical improvement made in the normal course of farming the holding or any part of the holding, and

    (b)   does not consist of fixed equipment or an improvement to fixed equipment,

but does not include any improvement whose provision is prohibited by the terms of the tenancy.

Amount of compensation

Amount of compensation for tenant's improvement not consisting of planning permission

D–22   **20.**—(1) The amount of compensation payable to the tenant under section 16 of this Act in respect of any tenant's improvement shall be an amount equal to the increase attributable to the improvement in the value of the holding at the termination of the tenancy as land comprised in a tenancy.

(2) Where the landlord and the tenant have entered into an agreement in writing whereby any benefit is given or allowed to the tenant in consideration of the provision of a tenant's improvement, the amount of compensation otherwise payable in respect of that improvement shall be

reduced by the proportion which the value of the benefit bears to the amount of the total cost of providing the improvement.

(3) Where a grant has been or will be made to the tenant out of public money in respect of a tenant's improvement, the amount of compensation otherwise payable in respect of that improvement shall be reduced by the proportion which the amount of the grant bears to the amount of the total cost of providing the improvement.

(4) Where a physical improvement which has been completed or a change of use which has been effected is authorised by any planning permission granted on an application made by the tenant, section 18 of this Act does not prevent any value attributable to the fact that the physical improvement or change of use is so authorised from being taken into account under this section in determining the amount of compensation payable in respect of the physical improvement or in respect of any intangible advantage obtained as a result of the change of use.

(5) This section does not apply where the tenant's improvement consists of planning permission.

Amount of compensation for planning permission

21.—(1) The amount of compensation payable to the tenant under section 16 of this Act in respect of a tenant's improvement which consists of planning permission shall be an amount equal to the increase attributable to the fact that the relevant development is authorised by the planning permission in the value of the holding at the termination of the tenancy as land comprised in a tenancy.   **D–23**

(2) In subsection (1) above, 'the relevant develoment' means the physical improvement or change of use specified in the landlord's consent under section 18 of this Act in accordance with subsection (1)(*b*) of that section.

(3) Where the landlord and the tenant have entered into an agreement in writing wherby any benefit is given or allowed to the tenant in consideration of the obtaining of planning permission by the tenant, the amount of compensation otherwise payable in respect of that permission shall be reduced by the proportion which the value of the benefit bears to the amount of the total cost of obtaining the permission.

Settlement of claims for compensation

22.—(1) Any claim by the tenant under a farm business tenancy for compensation under section 16 of this Act shall, subject to the provisions of this section, be determined by arbitration under this section.   **D–24**

(2) No such claim for compensation shall be enforceable unless before the end of the period of two months beginning with the date of the termination of the tenancy the tenant has given notice in writing to

his landlord of his intention to make the claim and of the nature of the claim.

(3) Where—

(a) the landlord and the tenant have not settled the claim by agreement in writing, and

(b) no arbitrator has been appointed under an agreement made since the notice under subsection (2) above was given,

either party may, after the end of the period of four months beginning with the date of the termination of the tenancy, apply to the President of the RICS for the appointment of an arbitrator by him.

(4) Where—

(a) an application under subsection (3) above relates wholly or partly to compensation in respect of a routine improvement (within the meaning of section 19 of this Act) which the tenant has provided or has begun to provide, and

(b) that application is made at the same time as an application under section 19(4) of this Act relating to the provision of that improvement,

the President of the RICS shall appoint the same arbitrator on both applications and, if both applications are made by the same person, only one fee shall be payable by virtue of section 30(2) of this Act in respect of them.

(5) Where a tenant lawfully remains in occupation of part of the holding after the termination of a farm business tenancy, references in subsections (2) and (3) above to the termination of the tenancy shall, in the case of a claim relating to that part of the holding, be construed as references to the termination of the occupation.

Supplementary provisions with respect to compensation

Successive tenancies

D–25   **23.**—(1) Where the tenant under a farm business tenancy has remained in the holding during two or more such tenancies, he shall not be deprived of his right to compensation under section 16 of this Act by reason only that any tenant's improvement was provided during a tenancy other than the one at the termination of which he quits the holding.

(2) The landlord and tenant under a farm business tenancy may agree that the tenant is to be entitled to compensation under section 16 of this Act on the termination of the tenancy even though at that termination the tenant remains in the holding under a new tenancy.

(3) Where the landlord and the tenant have agreed as mentioned in subsection (2) above in relation to any tenancy ('the earlier tenancy'), the tenant shall not be entitled to compensation at the end of any subse-

quent tenancy in respect of any tenant's improvement provided during the earlier tenancy in relation to the land comprised in the earlier tenancy.

Resumption of possession of part of holding

24.—(1) Where—   **D–26**

(a)   the landlord under a farm business tenancy resumes possession of part of the holding in pursuance of any provision of the tenancy, or

(b)   a person entitled to a severed part of the reversionary estate in a holding held under a farm business tenancy resumes possession of part of the holding by virtue of a notice to quit that part given to the tenant by virtue of section 140 of the Law of Property Act 1925,

the provisions of this Part of this Act shall, subject to subsections (2) and (3) below, apply to that part of the holding (in this section referred to as 'the relevant part') as if it were a separate holding which the tenant had quitted in consequence of a notice to quit and, in a case falling within paragraph (b) above, as if the person resuming possession were the landlord of that separate holding.

(2) The amount of compensation payable to the tenant under section 16 of this Act in respect of any tenant's improvement provided for the relevant part by the tenant and not consisting of planning permission shall, subject to section 20(2) to (4) of this Act, be an amount equal to the increase attributable to the tenant's improvement in the value of the original holding on the termination date as land comprised in a tenancy.

(3) The amount of compensation payable to the tenant under section 16 of this Act in respect of any tenant's improvement which consists of planning permission relating to the relevant part shall, subject to section 21(3) of this Act, be an amount equal to the increase attributable to the fact that the relevant development is authorised by the planning permission in the value of the original holding on the termination date as land comprised in a tenancy.

(4) In a case falling within paragraph (a) or (b) of subsection (1) above, sections 20 and 21 of this Act shall apply on the termination of the tenancy, in relation to the land then comprised in the tenancy, as if the reference in subsection (1) of each of those sections to the holding were a reference to the original holding.

(5) In subsections (2) to (4) above—
'the original holding' means the land comprised in the farm business tenancy—

(a)   on the date when the landlord gave his consent under section 17 or 18 of this Act in relation to the tenant's improvement, or

(b)   where approval in relation to the tenant's improvement was given by an arbitrator, on the date on which that approval was given,

'the relevant development', in relation to any tenant's improvement which consists of planning permission, has the meaning given by section 21(2) of this Act, and

'the termination date' means the date on which possession of the relevant part was resumed.

Compensation where reversionary estate in holding is severed

D–27 **25.**—(1) Where the reversionary estate in the holding comprised in a farm business tenancy is for the time being vested in more than one person in several parts, the tenant shall be entitled, on quitting the entire holding, to require that any compensation payable to him under section 16 of this Act shall be determined as if the reversionary estate were not so severed.

(2) Where subsection (1) applies, the arbitrator shall, where necessary, apportion the amount awarded between the persons who for the purposes of this Part of this Act together constitute the landlord of the holding, and any additional costs of the award caused by the apportionment shall be directed by the arbitrator to be paid by those persons in such proportions as he shall determine.

Extent to which compensation recoverable under agreements

D–28 **26.**—(1) In any case for which apart from this section the provisions of this Part of this Act provide for compensation, a tenant shall be entitled to compensation in accordance with those provisions and not otherwise, and shall be so entitled notwithstanding any agreement to the contrary.

(2) Nothing in the provisions of this Part of this Act, apart from this section, shall be construed as disentitling a tenant to compensation in any case for which those provisions do not provide for compensation.

Interpretation of Part III

27. In this Part of this Act, unless the context otherwise requires—
'planning permission' has the meaning given by section 336(1) of the Town and Country Planning Act 1990;
'tenant's improvement', and references to the provision of such an improvement, have the meaning given by section 15 of this Act.

PART IV

MISCELLANEOUS AND SUPPLEMENTAL

Resolution of disputes

Resolution of disputes

28.—(1) Subject to subsections (4) and (5) below and to section 29 of **D–29** this Act, any dispute between the landlord and the tenant under a farm business tenancy, being a dispute concerning their rights and obligations under this Act, under the terms of the tenancy or under any custom, shall be determined by arbitration.

(2) Where such a dispute has arisen, the landlord or the tenant may give notice in writing to the other specifying the dispute and stating that, unless before the end of the period of two months beginning with the day on which the notice is given the parties have appointed an arbitrator by agreement, he proposes to apply to the President of the RICS for the appointment of an arbitrator by him.

(3) Where a notice has been given under subsection (2) above, but no arbitrator has been appointed by agreement, either party may, after the end of the period of two months referred to in that subsection, apply to the President of the RICS for the appointment of an arbitrator by him.

(4) [. . .]¹

(5) Subsections (1) to (3) above do not apply in relation to—

(a) the determination of rent in pursuance of a statutory review notice (as defined in section 10(1) of this Act),

(b) any case falling within section 19(1) of this Act, or

(c) any claim for compensation under Part III of this Act.

Cases where right to refer claim to arbitration under section 28 does not apply

29.—(1) Section 28 of this Act does not apply in relation to any **D–30** dispute if—

(a) the tenancy is created by an instrument which includes provision for disputes to be resolved by any person other than—

(i) the landlord or the tenant, or

(ii) a third party appointed by either of them without the consent or concurrence of the other, and

¹Repealed by Arbitration Act 1996, Sch.4.

(b) either of the following has occurred—

    (i) the landlord and the tenant have jointly referred the dispute to the third party under the provision, or

    (ii) the landlord or the tenant has referred the dispute to the third party under the provision and notified the other in writing of the making of the reference, the period of four weeks beginning with the date on which the other was so notified has expired and the other has not given a notice under section 28(2) of this Act in relation to the dispute before the end of that period.

(2) For the purposes of subsection (1) above, a term of the tenancy does not provide for disputes to be 'resolved' by any person unless that person (whether or not acting as arbitrator) is enabled under the terms of the tenancy to give a decision which is binding in law on both parties.

General provisions applying to arbitrations under Act

D–31   **30.**—(1) Any matter which is required to be determined by arbitration under this Act shall be determined by the arbitration of a sole arbitrator.

(2) Any application under this Act to the President of the RICS for the appointment of an arbitrator by him must be made in writing and must be accompanied by such reasonable fee as the President may determine in respect of the costs of making the appointment.

(3) Where an arbitrator appointed for the purposes of this Act dies or is incapable of acting and no new arbitrator has been appointed by agreement, either party may apply to the President of the RICS for the appointment of a new arbitrator by him.

Miscellaneous

Mortgages of agricultural land

D–32   **31.**—(1) Section 99 of the Law of Property Act 1925 (leasing powers of mortgagor and mortgagee in possession) shall be amended in accordance with subsections (2) and (3) below.

(2) At the beginning of subsection (13), there shall be inserted 'Subject to subsection (13A) below,'.

(3) After that subsection, there shall be inserted—

'(13A) Subsection (13) of this section—

(a) shall not enable the application of any provision of this section to be excluded or restricted in relation to any mortgage of agricultural land made after 1st March 1948 but before 1st September 1995, and

(b)   shall not enable the power to grant a lease of an agricultural holding to which, by virtue of section 4 of the Agricultural Tenancies Act 1995, the Agricultural Holdings Act 1986 will apply, to be excluded or restricted in relation to any mortgage of agricultural land made on or after 1st September 1995.

(13B) In subsection (13A) of this section—
'agricultural holding' has the same meaning as in the Agricultural Holdings Act 1986; and
'agricultural land' has the same meaning as in the Agriculture Act 1947.'

(4) Paragraph 12 of Schedule 14 to the Agricultural Holdings Act 1986 (which excludes the application of subsection (13) of section 99 of the Law of Property Act 1925 in relation to a mortgage of agricultural land and is superseded by the amendments made by subsections (1) to (3) above) shall cease to have effect.

Power of limited owners to give consents etc

32. The landlord under a farm business tenancy, whatever his estate or interest in the holding, may, for the purposes of this Act, give any consent, make any agreement or do or have done to him any other act which he might give, make, do or have done to him if he were owner in fee simple or, if his interest is an interest in a leasehold, were absolutely entitled to that leasehold.   **D–33**

Power to apply and raise capital money

33.—(1) The purposes authorised by section 73 of the Settled Land Act 1925 or section 26 of the Universities and College Estates Act 1925 for the application of capital money shall include—

(a)   the payment of expenses incurred by a landlord under a farm business tenancy in, or in connection with, the making of any physical improvement on the holding,

(b)   the payment of compensation under section 16 of this Act, and

(c)   the payment of the costs, charges and expenses incurred by him on a reference to arbitration under section 19 or 22 of this Act.

(2) The purposes authorised by section 71 of the Settled Land Act 1925 as purposes for which money may be raised by mortgage shall include the payment of compensation under section 16 of this Act.

(3) Where the landlord under a farm business tenancy—

(a)　is a tenant for life or in a fiduciary position, and
(b)　is liable to pay compensation under section 16 of this Act,

he may require the sum payable as compensation and any costs, charges and expenses incurred by him in connection with the tenant's claim under that section to be paid out of any capital money held on the same trusts as the settled land.

(4) In subsection (3) above—
'capital money' includes any personal estate held on the same trusts as the land.

Estimation of best rent for purposes of Acts and other instruments

D–34　　34.—(1) In estimating the best rent or reservation in the nature of rent of land comprised in a farm business tenancy for the purposes of a relevant instrument, it shall not be necessary to take into account against the tenant any increase in the value of that land arising from any tenant's improvements.

(2) In subsection (1) above—
'a relevant instrument' means any Act of Parliament, deed or other instrument which authorises a lease to be made on the condition that the best rent or reservation in the nature of rent is reserved;
'tenant's improvement' has the meaning given by section 15 of this Act.

Preparation of documents etc by valuers and surveyors

D–35　　35.—(1) Section 22 of the Solicitors Act 1974 (unqualified person not to prepare certain instruments) shall be amended as follow.

(2) In subsection (2), after paragraph (ab) there shall be inserted—
'(ac) any accredited person drawing or preparing any instrument—

(i)　which creates, or which he believes on reasonable grounds will create, a farm business tenancy (within the meaning of the Agricultural Tenancies Act 1995), or
(ii)　which relates to an existing tenancy which is, or which he believes on reasonable grounds to be, such a tenancy;'.

(3) In subsection (3A), immediately before the definition of 'registered trade mark agent' there shall be inserted—
''accredited person' means any person who is—

(a) a Full Member of the Central Association of Agricultural Valuers.

(b) an Associate or Fellow of the Incorporated Society of Valuers and Auctioneers, or

(c) an Associate or Fellow of the Royal Institution of Chartered Surveyors;'.

Supplemental

Service of notices

36.—(1) This section applies to any notice or other document required or authorised to be given under this Act.   **D–36**

(2) A notice or other document to which this section applies is duly given to a person if—

(a) it is delivered to him,

(b) it is left at his proper address, or

(c) it is given to him in a manner authorised by a written agreement made, at any time before the giving of the notice, between him and the person giving the notice.

(3) A notice or other document to which this section applies is not duly given to a person if its text is transmitted to him by facsimile or other electronic means otherwise than by virtue of subsection (2)(c) above.

(4) Where a notice or other document to which this section applies is to be given to a body corporate, the notice or document is duly given if it is given to the secretary or clerk of that body.

(5) Where—

(a) a notice or other document to which this section applies is to be given to a landlord under a farm business tenancy and an agent or servant of his is responsible for the control of the management of the holding, or

(b) such a document is to be given to a tenant under a farm business tenancy and an agent or servant of his is responsible for the carrying on of a business on the holding,

the notice or document is duly given if it is given to that agent or servant.

(6) For the purposes of this section, the proper address of any person to whom a notice or other document to which this section applies is to be given is—

(a) in the case of the secretary or clerk of a body corporate, the registered or principal office of that body, and

(b) in any other case, the last known address of the person in question.

(7) Unless or until the tenant under a farm business tenancy has received—

(a) notice that the person who before that time was entitled to receive the rents and profits of the holding ('the original landlord') has ceased to be so entitled, and

(b) notice of the name and address of the person who has become entitled to receive the rents and profits,

any notice or other document given to the original landlord by the tenant shall be deemed for the purposes of this Act to have been given to the landlord under the tenancy.

Crown land

D–37 37.—(1) This Act shall apply in relation to land in which there subsists, or has at any material time subsisted, a Crown interest as it applies in relation to land in which no such interest subsists or has ever subsisted.

(2) For the purposes of this Act—

(a) where an interest belongs to Her Majesty in right of the Crown and forms part of the Crown Estate, the Crown Estate Commissioners shall be treated as the owner of the interest,

(b) where an interest belongs to Her Majesty in right of the Crown and does not form part of the Crown Estate, the government department having the management of the land or, if there is no such department, such person as Her Majesty may appoint in writing under the Royal Sign Manual shall be treated as the owner of the interest,

(c) where an interest belongs to Her Majesty in right of the Duchy of Lancaster, the Chancellor of the Duchy shall be treated as the owner of the interest,

(d) where an interest belongs to a government department or is held in trust for Her Majesty for the purposes of a government department, that department shall be treated as the owner of the interest, and

(e) where an interest belongs to the Duchy of Cornwall, such person as the Duke of Cornwall or the possessor for the time being of the Duchy of Cornwall appoints shall be treated as the owner of the interest and, in the case where the interest is that of landlord, may do any act or thing which a landlord is authorised or required to do under this Act.

D–38 (3) If any question arises as to who is to be treated as the owner of a Crown interest, that question shall be referred to the Treasury, whose decision shall be final.

(4) In subsections (1) and (3) above 'Crown interest' means an interest which belongs to Her Majesty in right of the Crown or of the Duchy of

2346593031714923215588148681

THE AGRICULTURAL TENANCIES ACT 1995   253

Lancaster or to the Duchy of Cornwall, or to a government department, or which is held in trust for Her Majesty for the purposes of a government department.

(5) Any compensation payable under section 16 of this Act by the Chancellor of the Duchy of Lancaster may be raised and paid under section 25 of the Duchy of Lancaster Act 1817 (application of monies) as an expense incurred in improvement of land belonging to Her Majesty in right of the Duchy.

(6) In the case of land belonging to the Duchy of Cornwall, the purposes authorised by section 8 of the Duchy of Cornwall Management Act 1863 (application of monies) for the advancement of parts of such gross sums as are there mentioned shall include the payment of compensation under section 16 of this Act.

(7) Nothing in subsection (6) above shall be taken as prejudicing the operation of the Duchy of Cornwall Management Act 1982.

Interpretation

38.—(1) In this Act, unless the context otherwise requires—   **D–39**

'agriculture' includes horticulture, fruit growing, seed growing, dairy farming and livestock breeding and keeping, the use of land as grazing land, meadow land, osier land, market gardens and nursery grounds, and the use of land for woodlands where that use is ancillary to the farming of land for other agricultural purposes, and 'agricultural' shall be construed accordingly;

'building' includes any part of a building;

'fixed term tenancy' means any tenancy other than a periodic tenancy;

'holding', in relation to a farm business tenancy, means the aggregate of the land comprised in the tenancy;

'landlord' includes any person from time to time deriving title from the original landlord;

'livestock' includes any creature kept for the production of food, wool, skins or fur or for the purpose of its use in the farming of land;

'the RICS' means the Royal Institution of Chartered Surveyors;

'tenancy' means any tenancy other than a tenancy at will, and includes a sub-tenancy and an agreement for a tenancy or subtenancy;

'tenant' includes a sub-tenant and any person deriving title from the original tenant or sub-tenant;

'termination', in relation to a tenancy, means the cesser of the tenancy by reason of effluxion of time or from any other cause.

(2) References in this Act to the farming of land include references to the carrying on in relation to land of any agricultural activity.

(3) A tenancy granted pursuant to a contract shall be taken for the purposes of this Act to have been granted when the contract was entered into.

(4) For the purposes of this Act a tenancy begins on the day on which, under the terms of the tenancy, the tenant is entitled to possession under that tenancy; and references in this Act to the beginning of the tenancy are references to that day.

(5) The designations of landlord and tenant shall continue to apply until the conclusion of any proceedings taken under this Act in respect of compensation.

Index of defined expressions

D–40   **39.** In this Act the expressions listed below are defined by or otherwise fall to be construed in accordance with the provisions indicated—

agriculture, agricultural	section 38(1)
begins, beginning (in relation to a tenancy)	section 38(4)
building	section 38(1)
farm business tenancy	section 1
farming (or land)	section 38(2)
fixed term tenancy	section 38(1)
grant (of a tenancy)	section 38(3)
holding (in relation to a farm business tenancy)	section 38(1)
landlord	section 38(1) and (5)
livestock	section 38(1)
planning permission (in Part III)	section 27
provision (of a tenant's improvement) (in Part III)	section 15
the review date (in Part II)	section 10(2)
the RICS	section 38(1)
statutory review notice (in Part II)	section 10(1)
tenancy	section 38(1)
tenant	section 38(1) and (5)
tenant's improvement (in Part III)	section 15
termination (of a tenancy)	section 38(1).

*   *   *   *   *

Short title, commencement and extent

D–41   **41.**—(1) This Act may be cited as the Agricultural Tenancies Act 1995.

(2) This Act shall come into force on 1st September 1995.

(3) Subject to subsection (4) below, this Act extends to England and Wales only.

(4) The amendment by a provision of the Schedule to this Act of an enactment which extends to Scotland or Northern Ireland also extends there, except that paragraph 9 of the Schedule does not extend to Northern Ireland.

*   *   *   *   *

Appendix E

The Landlord and Tenant (Covenants) Act 1995

Preliminary

Tenancies to which the Act applies

1.—(1) Sections 3 to 16 and 21 apply only to new tenancies. **E–01**

(2) Sections 17 to 20 apply to both new and other tenancies.

(3) For the purposes of this section a tenancy is a new tenancy if it is granted on or after the date on which this Act comes into force otherwise than in pursuance of—

(a)   an agreement entered into before that date, or

(b)   an order of a court made before that date.

(4) Subsection (3) has effect subject to section 20(1) in the case of overriding leases granted under section 19.

(5) Without prejudice to the generality of subsection (3), that subsection applies to the grant of a tenancy where by virtue of any variation of a tenancy there is a deemed surrender and regrant as it applies to any other grant of a tenancy.

(6) Where a tenancy granted on or after the date on which this Act comes into force is so granted in pursuance of an option granted before that date, the tenancy shall be regarded for the purposes of subsection (3) as granted in pursuance of an agreement entered into before that date (and accordingly is not a new tenancy), whether or not the option was exercised before that date.

(7) In subsection (6) 'option' includes right of first refusal.

Covenants to which the Act applies

2.—(1) This Act applies to a landlord covenant or a tenant covenant **E–02** of a tenancy—

(a) whether or not the covenant has reference to the subject matter of the tenancy, and

(b) whether the covenant is express, implied or imposed by law, but does not apply to a covenant falling within subsection (2).

(2) Nothing in this Act affects any covenant imposed in pursuance of—

(a) section 35 or 155 of the Housing Act 1985 (covenants for repayment of discount on early disposals);

(b) paragraph 1 of Schedule 6A to that Act (covenants requiring redemption of landlord's share); or

(c) section 11 or 13 of the Housing Act 1996 or paragraph 1 or 3 of Schedule 2 to the Housing Associations Act 1985 (covenants for repayment of discount on early disposals or for restricting disposals).

Transmission of covenants

Transmission of benefit and burden of covenants

E–03   **3.**—(1) The benefit and burden of all landlord and tenant covenants of a tenancy—

(a) shall be annexed and incident to the whole, and to each and every part, of the premises demised by the tenancy and of the reversion in them, and

(b) shall in accordance with this section pass on an assignment of the whole or any part of those premises or of the reversion in them.

(2) Where the assignment is by the tenant under the tenancy, then as from the assignment the assignee—

(a) becomes bound by the tenant covenants of the tenancy except to the extent that—

(i) immediately before the assignment they did not bind the assignor, or

(ii) they fall to be complied with in relation to any demised premises not comprised in the assignment; and

(b) becomes entitled to the benefit of the landlord covenants of the tenancy except to the extent that they fall to be complied with in relation to any such premises.

(3) Where the assignment is by the landlord under the tenancy, then as from the assignment the assignee—

(a) becomes bound by the landlord covenants of the tenancy except to the extent that—

    (i) immediately before the assignment they did not bind the assignor, or

    (ii) they fall to be complied with in relation to any demised premises not comprised in the assignment; and

(b) becomes entitled to the benefit of the tenant covenants of the tenancy except to the extent that they fall to be complied with in relation to any such premises.

(4) In determining for the purposes of subsection (2) or (3) whether any covenant bound the assignor immediately before the assignment, any waiver or release of the covenant which (in whatever terms) is expressed to be personal to the assignor shall be disregarded.

(5) Any landlord or tenant covenant of a tenancy which is restrictive of the user of land shall, as well as being capable of enforcement against an assignee, be capable of being enforced against any other person who is the owner or occupier of any demised premises to which the covenant relates, even though there is no express provision in the tenancy to that effect.

(6) Nothing in this section shall operate—

(a) in the case of a covenant which (in whatever terms) is expressed to be personal to any person, to make the covenant enforceable by or (as the case may be) against any other person; or

(b) to make a covenant enforceable against any person if, apart from this section, it would not be enforceable against him by reason of its not having been registered under the Land Registration Act 2002 or the Land Charges Act 1972.

(7) To the extent that there remains in force any rule of law by virtue of which the burden of a covenant whose subject matter is not in existence at the time when it is made does not run with the land affected unless the covenantor covenants on behalf of himself and his assigns, that rule of law is hereby abolished in relation to tenancies.

Transmission of rights of re-entry

4. The benefit of a landlord's right of re-entry under a tenancy—   **E–04**

(a) shall be annexed and incident to the whole, and to each and every part, of the reversion in the premises demised by the tenancy, and

(b) shall pass on an assignment of the whole or any part of the reversion in those premises.

Release of covenants on assignment

Tenant released from covenants on assignment of tenancy

E–05 **5.**—(1) This section applies where a tenant assigns premises demised to him under a tenancy.

(2) If the tenant assigns the whole of the premises demised to him, he—

(a) is released from the tenant covenants of the tenancy, and
(b) ceases to be entitled to the benefit of the landlord covenants of the tenancy,

as from the assignment.

(3) If the tenant assigns part only of the premises demised to him, then as from the assignment he—

(a) is released from the tenant covenants of the tenancy, and
(b) ceases to be entitled to the benefit of the landlord covenants of the tenancy,

only to the extent that those covenants fall to be complied with in relation to that part of the demised premises.

(4) This section applies as mentioned in subsection (1) whether or not the tenant is tenant of the whole of the premises comprised in the tenancy.

Landlord may be released from covenants on assignment of reversion

E–06 **6.**—(1) This section applies where a landlord assigns the reversion in premises of which he is the landlord under a tenancy.

(2) If the landlord assigns the reversion in the whole of the premises of which he is the landlord—

(a) he may apply to be released from the landlord covenants of the tenancy in accordance with section 8; and
(b) if he is so released from all of those covenants, he ceases to be entitled to the benefit of the tenant covenants of the tenancy as from the assignment.

(3) If the landlord assigns the reversion in part only of the premises of which he is the landlord—

(a)   he may apply to be so released from the landlord covenants of the tenancy to the extent that they fall to be complied with in relation to that part of those premises; and

(b)   if he is, to that extent, so released from all of those covenants, then as from the assignment he ceases to be entitled to the benefit of the tenant covenants only to the extent that they fall to be complied with in relation to that part of those premises.

(4) This section applies as mentioned in subsection (1) whether or not the landlord is landlord of the whole of the premises comprised in the tenancy.

Former landlord may be released from covenants on assignment of reversion

7.—(1) This section applies where—   E–07

(a)   a landlord assigns the reversion in premises of which he is the landlord under a tenancy, and

(b)   immediately before the assignment a former landlord of the premises remains bound by a landlord covenant of the tenancy ('the relevant covenant').

(2) If immediately before the assignment the former landlord does not remain the landlord of any other premises demised by the tenancy, he may apply to be released from the relevant covenant in accordance with section 8.

(3) In any other case the former landlord may apply to be so released from the relevant covenant to the extent that it falls to be complied with in relation to any premises comprised in the assignment.

(4) If the former landlord is so released from every landlord covenant by which he remained bound immediately before the assignment, he ceases to be entitled to the benefit of the tenant covenants of the tenancy.

(5) If the former landlord is so released from every such landlord covenant to the extent that it falls to be complied with in relation to any premises comprised in the assignment, he ceases to be entitled to the benefit of the tenant covenants of the tenancy to the extent that they fall to be so complied with.

(6) This section applies as mentioned in subsection (1)—

(a)   whether or not the landlord making the assignment is landlord of the whole of the premises comprised in the tenancy; and

(b)   whether or not the former landlord has previously applied (whether under section 6 or this section) to be released from the relevant covenant.

Procedure for seeking release from a covenant under section 6 or 7

E–08   **8.**—(1) For the purposes of section 6 or 7 an application for the release of a covenant to any extent is made by serving on the tenant, either before or within the period of four weeks beginning with the date of the assignment in question, a notice informing him of—

(a)   the proposed assignment or (as the case may be) the fact that the assignment has taken place, and

(b)   the request for the covenant to be released to that extent.

(2) Where an application for the release of a covenant is made in accordance with subsection (1), the covenant is released to the extent mentioned in the notice if—

(a)   the tenant does not, within the period of four weeks beginning with the day on which the notice is served, serve on the landlord or former landlord a notice in writing objecting to the release, or

(b)   the tenant does so serve such a notice but the court, on the application of the landlord or former landlord, makes a declaration that it is reasonable for the covenant to be so released, or

(c)   the tenant serves on the landlord or former landlord a notice in writing consenting to the release and, if he has previously served a notice objecting to it, stating that that notice is withdrawn.

(3) Any release from a covenant in accordance with this section shall be regarded as occurring at the time when the assignment in question takes place.

(4) In this section—

(a)   'the tenant' means the tenant of the premises comprised in the assignment in question (or, if different parts of those premises are held under the tenancy by different tenants, each of those tenants);

(b)   any reference to the landlord or the former landlord is a reference to the landlord referred to in section 6 or the former landlord referred to in section 7, as the case may be; and

(c)   'the court' means a county court.

Apportionment of liability between assignor and assignee

Apportionment of liability under covenants binding both assignor and assignee of tenancy or reversion

E–09   **9.**—(1) This section applies where—

(a)   a tenant assigns part only of the premises demised to him by a tenancy;

(b)   after the assignment both the tenant and his assignee are to be bound by a non-attributable tenant covenant of the tenancy; and

(c)   the tenant and his assignee agree that as from the assignment liability under the covenant is to be apportioned between them in such manner as is specified in the agreement.

(2) This section also applies where—

(a)   a landlord assigns the reversion in part only of the premises of which he is the landlord under a tenancy;

(b)   after the assignment both the landlord and his assignee are to be bound by a non-attributable landlord covenant of the tenancy; and

(c)   the landlord and his assignee agree that as from the assignment liability under the covenant is to be apportioned between them in such manner as is specified in the agreement.

(3) Any such agreement as is mentioned in subsection (1) or (2) may apportion liability in such a way that a party to the agreement is exonerated from all liability under a covenant.

(4) In any case falling within subsection (1) or (2) the parties to the agreement may apply for the apportionment to become binding on the appropriate person in accordance with section 10.

(5) In any such case the parties to the agreement may also apply for the apportionment to become binding on any person (other than the appropriate person) who is for the time being entitled to enforce the covenant in question; and section 10 shall apply in relation to such an application as it applies in relation to an application made with respect to the appropriate person.

(6) For the purposes of this section a covenant is, in relation to an assignment, a 'non-attributable' covenant if it does not fall to be complied with in relation to any premises comprised in the assignment.

(7) In this section 'the appropriate person' means either—

(a)   the landlord of the entire premises referred to in subsection (1)(a) (or, if different parts of those premises are held under the tenancy by different landlords, each of those landlords), or

(b)   the tenant of the entire premises referred to in subsection (2)(a) (or, if different parts of those premises are held under the tenancy by different tenants, each of those tenants),

depending on whether the agreement in question falls within subsection (1) or subsection (2).

Procedure for making apportionment bind other party to lease

10.—(1) For the purposes of section 9 the parties to an agreement falling within subsection (1) or (2) of that section apply for an apportionment to   **E–10**

become binding on the appropriate person if, either before or within the period of four weeks beginning with the date of the assignment in question, they serve on that person a notice informing him of—

(a)   the proposed assignment or (as the case may be) the fact that the assignment has taken place;

(b)   the prescribed particulars of the agreement; and

(c)   their request that the apportionment should become binding on him.

(2) Where an application for an apportionment to become binding has been made in accordance with subsection (1), the apportionment becomes binding on the appropriate person if—

(a)   he does not, within the period of four weeks beginning with the day on which the notice is served under subsection (1), serve on the parties to the agreement a notice in writing objecting to the apportionment becoming binding on him, or

(b)   he does so serve such a notice but the court, on the application of the parties to the agreement, makes a declaration that it is reasonable for the apportionment to become binding on him, or

(c)   he serves on the parties to the agreement a notice in writing consenting to the apportionment becoming binding on him and, if he has previously served a notice objecting thereto, stating that that notice is withdrawn.

(3) Where any apportionment becomes binding in accordance with this section, this shall be regarded as occurring at the time when the assignment in question takes place.

(4) In this section—

'the appropriate person' has the same meaning as in section 9;

'the court' means a county court;

'prescribed' means prescribed by virtue of section 27.

Excluded assignments

Assignments in breach of covenant or by operation of law

E–11   **11.**—(1) This section provides for the operation of sections 5 to 10 in relation to assignments in breach of a covenant of a tenancy or assignments by operation of law ('excluded assignments').

(2) In the case of an excluded assignment subsection (2) or (3) of section 5—

(a)   shall not have the effect mentioned in that subsection in relation to the tenant as from that assignment, but

(b)   shall have that effect as from the next assignment (if any) of the premises assigned by him which is not an excluded assignment.

(3) In the case of an excluded assignment subsection (2) or (3) of section 6 or 7—

(a)   shall not enable the landlord or former landlord to apply for such a release as is mentioned in that subsection as from that assignment, but

(b)   shall apply on the next assignment (if any) of the reversion assigned by the landlord which is not an excluded assignment so as to enable the landlord or former landlord to apply for any such release as from that subsequent assignment.

(4) Where subsection (2) or (3) of section 6 or 7 does so apply—

(a)   any reference in that section to the assignment (except where it relates to the time as from which the release takes effect) is a reference to the excluded assignment; but

(b)   in that excepted case and in section 8 as it applies in relation to any application under that section made by virtue of subsection (3) above, any reference to the assignment or proposed assignment is a reference to any such subsequent assignment as is mentioned in that subsection.

(5) In the case of an excluded assignment section 9—

(a)   shall not enable the tenant or landlord and his assignee to apply for an agreed apportionment to become binding in accordance with section 10 as from that assignment, but

(b)   shall apply on the next assignment (if any) of the premises or reversion assigned by the tenant or landlord which is not an excluded assignment so as to enable him and his assignee to apply for such an apportionment to become binding in accordance with section 10 as from that subsequent assignment.

(6) Where section 9 does so apply—

(a)   any reference in that section to the assignment or the assignee under it is a reference to the excluded assignment and the assignee under that assignment; but

(b)   in section 10 as it applies in relation to any application under section 9 made by virtue of subsection (5) above, any reference to the assignment or proposed assignment is a reference to any such subsequent assignment as is mentioned in that subsection.

(7) If any such subsequent assignment as is mentioned in subsection (2), (3) or (5) above comprises only part of the premises assigned by the tenant or (as the case may be) only part of the premises the reversion in which was assigned by the landlord on the excluded assignment—

(a) the relevant provision or provisions of section 5, 6, 7 or 9 shall only have the effect mentioned in that subsection to the extent that the covenants or covenant in question fall or falls to be complied with in relation to that part of those premises; and

(b) that subsection may accordingly apply on different occasions in relation to different parts of those premises.

Third party covenants

Covenants with management companies etc

E–12 **12.**—(1) This section applies where—

(a) a person other than the landlord or tenant ('the third party') is under a covenant of a tenancy liable (as principal) to discharge any function with respect to all or any of the demised premises ('the relevant function'); and

(b) that liability is not the liability of a guarantor or any other financial liability referable to the performance or otherwise of a covenant of the tenancy by another party to it.

(2) To the extent that any covenant of the tenancy confers any rights against the third party with respect to the relevant function, then for the purposes of the transmission of the benefit of the covenant in accordance with this Act it shall be treated as if it were—

(a) a tenant covenant of the tenancy to the extent that those rights are exercisable by the landlord; and

(b) a landlord covenant of the tenancy to the extent that those rights are exercisable by the tenant.

(3) To the extent that any covenant of the tenancy confers any rights exercisable by the third party with respect to the relevant function, then for the purposes mentioned in subsection (4), it shall be treated as if it were—

(a) a tenant covenant of the tenancy to the extent that those rights are exercisable against the tenant; and

(b) a landlord covenant of the tenancy to the extent that those rights are exercisable against the landlord.

(4) The purposes mentioned in subsection (3) are—

(a) the transmission of the burden of the covenant in accordance with this Act; and

(b) any release from, or apportionment of liability in respect of, the covenant in accordance with this Act.

(5) In relation to the release of the landlord from any covenant which is to be treated as a landlord covenant by virtue of subsection (3), section 8 shall apply as if any reference to the tenant were a reference to the third party.

Joint liability under covenants

Covenants binding two or more persons

13.—(1) Where in consequence of this Act two or more persons are bound by the same covenant, they are so bound both jointly and severally.   **E–13**

(2) Subject to section 24(2), where by virtue of this Act—

(a) two or more persons are bound jointly and severally by the same covenant, and

(b) any of the persons so bound is released from the covenant,

the release does not extend to any other of those persons.

(3) For the purpose of providing for contribution between persons who, by virtue of this Act, are bound jointly and severally by a covenant, the Civil Liability (Contribution) Act 1978 shall have effect as if—

(a) liability to a person under a covenant were liability in respect of damage suffered by that person;

(b) references to damage accordingly included a breach of a covenant of a tenancy; and

(c) section 7(2) of that Act were omitted.

Abolition of indemnity covenants implied by statute

14. The following provisions (by virtue of which indemnity covenants are implied on the assignment of a tenancy) shall cease to have effect—   **E–14**

(a) subsections (1)(C) and (D) of section 77 of the Law of Property Act 1925; and

(b) subsections (1)(b) and (2) of section 24 of the Land Registration Act 1925.

Enforcement of covenants

Enforcement of covenants

E–15   **15.**—(1) Where any tenant covenant of a tenancy, or any right of re-
entry contained in a tenancy, is enforceable by the reversioner in respect
of any premises demised by the tenancy, it shall also be so enforceable
by—

> (a)   any person (other than the reversioner) who, as the holder of the
>   immediate reversion in those premises, is for the time being enti-
>   tled to the rents and profits under the tenancy in respect of those
>   premises, or
> (b)   any mortgagee in possession of the reversion in those premises
>   who is so entitled.

(2) Where any landlord covenant of a tenancy is enforceable against
the reversioner in respect of any premises demised by the tenancy, it shall
also be so enforceable against any person falling within subsection (1)(a)
or (b).

(3) Where any landlord covenant of a tenancy is enforceable by the
tenant in respect of any premises demised by the tenancy, it shall also be
so enforceable by any mortgagee in possession of those premises under a
mortgage granted by the tenant.

(4) Where any tenant covenant of a tenancy, or any right of re-entry
contained in a tenancy, is enforceable against the tenant in respect of any
premises demised by the tenancy, it shall also be so enforceable against any
such mortgagee.

(5) Nothing in this section shall operate—

> (a)   in the case of a covenant which (in whatever terms) is expressed
>   to be personal to any person, to make the covenant enforceable
>   by or (as the case may be) against any other person; or
> (b)   to make a covenant enforceable against any person if, apart from
>   this section, it would not be enforceable against him by reason
>   of its not having been registered under the Land Registration
>   Act 2002 or the Land Charges Act 1972.

(6) In this section—
'mortgagee' and 'mortgage' include 'chargee' and 'charge' respectively;
'the reversioner', in relation to a tenancy, means the holder for the time
being of the interest of the landlord under the tenancy.

Liability of former tenant etc in respect of covenants

Tenant guaranteeing performance of covenant by assignee

16.—(1) Where on an assignment a tenant is to any extent released   **E–16**
from a tenant covenant of a tenancy by virtue of this Act ('the relevant
covenant'), nothing in this Act (and in particular section 25) shall preclude him from entering into an authorised guarantee agreement with
respect to the performance of that covenant by the assignee.

(2) For the purposes of this section an agreement is an authorised
guarantee agreement if—

(a)   under it the tenant guarantees the performance of the relevant
      covenant to any extent by the assignee; and
(b)   it is entered into in the circumstances set out in subsection (3); and
(c)   its provisions conform with subsections (4) and (5).

(3) Those circumstances are as follows—

(a)   by virtue of a covenant against assignment (whether absolute or
      qualified) the assignment cannot be effected without the consent
      of the landlord under the tenancy or some other person;
(b)   any such consent is given subject to a condition (lawfully
      imposed) that the tenant is to enter into an agreement guaran-
      teeing the performance of the covenant by the assignee; and
(c)   the agreement is entered into by the tenant in pursuance of that
      condition.

(4) An agreement is not an authorised guarantee agreement to the   **E–17**
extent that it purports—

(a)   to impose on the tenant any requirement to guarantee in any
      way the performance of the relevant covenant by any person
      other than the assignee; or
(b)   to impose on the tenant any liability, restriction or other require-
      ment (of whatever nature) in relation to any time after the
      assignee is released from that covenant by virtue of this Act.

(5) Subject to subsection (4), an authorised guarantee agreement may—

(a)   impose on the tenant any liability as sole or principal debtor in
      respect of any obligation owed by the assignee under the rele-
      vant covenant;
(b)   impose on the tenant liabilities as guarantor in respect of the
      assignee's performance of that covenant which are no more
      onerous than those to which he would be subject in the event of
      his being liable as sole or principal debtor in respect of any obli-
      gation owed by the assignee under that covenant;

(c) require the tenant, in the event of the tenancy assigned by him being disclaimed, to enter into a new tenancy of the premises comprised in the assignment—

    (i) whose term expires not later than the term of the tenancy assigned by the tenant, and

    (ii) whose tenant covenants are no more onerous than those of that tenancy;

(d) make provision incidental or supplementary to any provision made by virtue of any of paragraphs (a) to (c).

E–18   (6) Where a person ('the former tenant') is to any extent released from a covenant of a tenancy by virtue of section 11(2) as from an assignment and the assignor under the assignment enters into an authorised guarantee agreement with the landlord with respect to the performance of that covenant by the assignee under the assignment—

(a) the landlord may require the former tenant to enter into an agreement under which he guarantees, on terms corresponding to those of that authorised guarantee agreement, the performance of that covenant by the assignee under the assignment; and

(b) if its provisions conform with subsections (4) and (5), any such agreement shall be an authorised guarantee agreement for the purposes of this section; and

(c) in the application of this section in relation to any such agreement—

    (i) subsections (2)(b) and (c) and (3) shall be omitted, and

    (ii) any reference to the tenant or to the assignee shall be read as a reference to the former tenant or to the assignee under the assignment.

(7) For the purposes of subsection (1) it is immaterial that—

(a) the tenant has already made an authorised guarantee agreement in respect of a previous assignment by him of the tenancy referred to in that subsection, it having been subsequently revested in him following a disclaimer on behalf of the previous assignee, or

(b) the tenancy referred to in that subsection is a new tenancy entered into by the tenant in pursuance of an authorised guarantee agreement;

and in any such case subsections (2) to (5) shall apply accordingly.

(8) It is hereby declared that the rules of law relating to guarantees (and in particular those relating to the release of sureties) are, subject to its terms, applicable in relation to any authorised guarantee agreement as in relation to any other guarantee agreement.

                *   *   *   *   *

Supplemental

Effects of becoming subject to liability under, or entitled to benefit of, covenant etc

23.—(1) Where as a result of an assignment a person becomes, by virtue of this Act, bound by or entitled to the benefit of a covenant, he shall not by virtue of this Act have any liability or rights under the covenant in relation to any time falling before the assignment.   **E–19**

(2) Subsection (1) does not preclude any such rights being expressly assigned to the person in question.

(3) Where as a result of an assignment a person becomes, by virtue of this Act, entitled to a right of re-entry contained in a tenancy, that right shall be exercisable in relation to any breach of a covenant of the tenancy occurring before the assignment as in relation to one occurring thereafter, unless by reason of any waiver or release it was not so exercisable immediately before the assignment.

Effects of release from liability under, or loss of benefit of, covenant

24.—(1) Any release of a person from a covenant by virtue of this Act does not affect any liability of his arising from a breach of the covenant occurring before the release.   **E–20**

(2) Where—

(a)   by virtue of this Act a tenant is released from a tenant covenant of a tenancy, and

(b)   immediately before the release another person is bound by a covenant of the tenancy imposing any liability or penalty in the event of a failure to comply with that tenant covenant,

then, as from the release of the tenant, that other person is released from the covenant mentioned in paragraph (b) to the same extent as the tenant is released from that tenant covenant.

(3) Where a person bound by a landlord or tenant covenant of a tenancy—

(a)   assigns the whole or part of his interest in the premises demised by the tenancy, but

(b)   is not released by virtue of this Act from the covenant (with the result that subsection (1) does not apply),

the assignment does not affect any liability of his arising from a breach of the covenant occurring before the assignment.

(4) Where by virtue of this Act a person ceases to be entitled to the benefit of a covenant, this does not affect any rights of his arising from a breach of the covenant occurring before he ceases to be so entitled.

Agreement void if it restricts operation of the Act

E–21   **25.**—(1) Any agreement relating to a tenancy is void to the extent that—

(a)   it would apart from this section have effect to exclude, modify or otherwise frustrate the operation of any provision of this Act, or

(b)   it provides for—

(i)   the termination or surrender of the tenancy, or

(ii)   the imposition on the tenant of any penalty, disability or liability, in the event of the operation of any provision of this Act, or

(c)   it provides for any of the matters referred to in paragraph (b)(i) or (ii) and does so (whether expressly or otherwise) in connection with, or in consequence of, the operation of any provision of this Act.

(2) To the extent that an agreement relating to a tenancy constitutes a covenant (whether absolute or qualified) against the assignment, or parting with the possession, of the premises demised by the tenancy or any part of them—

(a)   the agreement is not void by virtue of subsection (1) by reason only of the fact that as such the covenant prohibits or restricts any such assignment or parting with possession; but

(b)   paragraph (a) above does not otherwise affect the operation of that subsection in relation to the agreement (and in particular does not preclude its application to the agreement to the extent that it purports to regulate the giving of, or the making of any application for, consent to any such assignment or parting with possession).

(3) In accordance with section 16(1) nothing in this section applies to any agreement to the extent that it is an authorised guarantee agreement; but (without prejudice to the generality of subsection (1) above) an agreement is void to the extent that it is one falling within section 16(4)(a) or (b).

(4) This section applies to an agreement relating to a tenancy whether or not the agreement is—

(a)   contained in the instrument creating the tenancy; or

(b)   made before the creation of the tenancy.

Miscellaneous savings etc

E–22   **26.**—(1) Nothing in this Act is to be read as preventing—

(a)   a party to a tenancy from releasing a person from a landlord covenant or a tenant covenant of the tenancy; or

(b)   the parties to a tenancy from agreeing to an apportionment of liability under such a covenant.

(2) Nothing in this Act affects the operation of section 3(3A) of the Landlord and Tenant Act 1985 (preservation of former landlord's liability until tenant notified of new landlord).

(3) No apportionment which has become binding in accordance with section 10 shall be affected by any order or decision made under or by virtue of any enactment not contained in this Act which relates to apportionment.

Notices for the purposes of the Act

27.—(1) The form of any notice to be served for the purposes of   **E–23** section 8, 10 or 17 shall be prescribed by regulations made by the Lord Chancellor by statutory instrument.

(2) The regulations shall require any notice served for the purposes of section 8(1) or 10(1) ('the initial notice') to include—

(a)   an explanation of the significance of the notice and the options available to the person on whom it is served;

(b)   a statement that any objections to the proposed release, or (as the case may be) to the proposed binding effect of the apportionment, must be made by notice in writing served on the person or persons by whom the initial notice is served within the period of four weeks beginning with the day on which the initial notice is served; and

(c)   an address in England and Wales to which any such objections may be sent.

(3) The regulations shall require any notice served for the purposes of section 17 to include an explanation of the significance of the notice.

(4) If any notice purporting to be served for the purposes of section 8(1), 10(1) or 17 is not in the prescribed form, or in a form substantially to the same effect, the notice shall not be effective for the purposes of section 8, section 10 or section 17 (as the case may be).

(5) Section 23 of the Landlord and Tenant Act 1927 shall apply in relation to the service of notices for the purposes of section 8, 10 or 17.

(6) Any statutory instrument made under this section shall be subject to annulment in pursuance of a resolution of either House of Parliament.

Interpretation

28.—(1) In this Act (unless the context otherwise requires)—   **E–24** 'assignment' includes equitable assignment and in addition (subject to section 11) assignment in breach of a covenant of a tenancy or by operation of law;

'authorised guarantee agreement' means an agreement which is an authorised guarantee agreement for the purposes of section 16;

'collateral agreement', in relation to a tenancy, means any agreement collateral to the tenancy, whether made before or after its creation;

'consent' includes licence;

'covenant' includes term, condition and obligation, and references to a covenant (or any description of covenant) of a tenancy include a covenant (or a covenant of that description) contained in a collateral agreement;

'landlord' and 'tenant', in relation to a tenancy, mean the person for the time being entitled to the reversion expectant on the term of the tenancy and the person so entitled to that term respectively;

'landlord covenant', in relation to a tenancy, means a covenant falling to be complied with by the landlord of premises demised by the tenancy;

'new tenancy' means a tenancy which is a new tenancy for the purposes of section 1;

'reversion' means the interest expectant on the termination of a tenancy;

'tenancy' means any lease or other tenancy and includes—

(a)   a sub-tenancy, and
(b)   an agreement for a tenancy,

but does not include a mortgage term;

'tenant covenant', in relation to a tenancy, means a covenant falling to be complied with by the tenant of premises demised by the tenancy.

E–25   (2) For the purposes of any reference in this Act to a covenant falling to be complied with in relation to a particular part of the premises demised by a tenancy, a covenant falls to be so complied with if—

(a)   it in terms applies to that part of the premises, or
(b)   in its practical application it can be attributed to that part of the premises (whether or not it can also be so attributed to other individual parts of those premises).

(3) Subsection (2) does not apply in relation to covenants to pay money; and, for the purposes of any reference in this Act to a covenant falling to be complied with in relation to a particular part of the premises demised by a tenancy, a covenant of a tenancy which is a covenant to pay money falls to be so complied with if—

(a)   the covenant in terms applies to that part; or
(b)   the amount of the payment is determinable specifically by reference—

   (i)   to that part, or
   (ii)   to anything falling to be done by or for a person as tenant or occupier of that part (if it is a tenant covenant), or
   (iii) to anything falling to be done by or for a person as landlord of that part (if it is a landlord covenant).

(4) Where two or more persons jointly constitute either the landlord or the tenant in relation to a tenancy, any reference in this Act to the landlord or the tenant is a reference to both or all of the persons who jointly constitute the landlord or the tenant, as the case may be (and accordingly nothing in section 13 applies in relation to the rights and liabilities of such persons between themselves).

(5) References in this Act to the assignment by a landlord of the reversion in the whole or part of the premises demised by a tenancy are to the assignment by him of the whole of his interest (as owner of the reversion) in the whole or part of those premises. **E–26**

(6) For the purposes of this Act—

(a) any assignment (however effected) consisting in the transfer of the whole of the landlord's interest (as owner of the reversion) in any premises demised by a tenancy shall be treated as an assignment by the landlord of the reversion in those premises even if it is not effected by him; and

(b) any assignment (however effected) consisting in the transfer of the whole of the tenant's interest in any premises demised by a tenancy shall be treated as an assignment by the tenant of those premises even if it is not effected by him.

Crown application

29.—(1) This Act binds the Crown. **E–27**

Consequential amendments and repeals

*   *   *   *   *

(4) In consequence of this Act nothing in the following provisions, namely—

(a) sections 78 and 79 of the Law of Property Act 1925 (benefit and burden of covenants relating to land), and

(b) sections 141 and 142 of that Act (running of benefit and burden of covenants with reversion),

shall apply in relation to new tenancies.

(5) The Lord Chancellor may by order made by statutory instrument make, in the case of such enactments as may be specified in the order, such amendments or repeals in, or such modifications of, those enactments as appear to him to be necessary or expedient in consequence of any provision of this Act.

(6) Any statutory instrument made under subsection (5) shall be subject to annulment in pursuance of a resolution of either House of Parliament.

Commencement

E–28   **31.**—(1) The provisions of this Act come into force on such day as the
Lord Chancellor may appoint by order made by statutory instrument.
     (2) An order under this section may contain such transitional provi-
sions and savings (whether or not involving the modification of any enactment) as appear to the Lord Chancellor necessary or expedient in
connection with the provisions brought into force by the order.

Short title and extent

E–29   **32.**—(1) This Act may be cited as the Landlord and Tenant (Covenants)
Act 1995.
     (2) This Act extends to England and Wales only.

                    *   *   *   *   *

Appendix F

SI 2003/3096
Landlord and Tenant, England and Wales Regulatory Reform
The Regulatory Reform (Business Tenancies) (England and Wales) Order 2003

Approved by both Houses of Parliament

Made . . . . *1st December 2003*
Coming into force . . . . *1st June 2004*

Whereas
    (a) the First Secretary of State has consulted—

    (i)   such organisations as appear to him to be representative of interests substantially affected by his proposals for this Order,
    (ii)   the National Assembly for Wales,
    (iii) the Law Commission, and
    (iv) such other persons as he considered appropriate;

    (b) as a result of that consultation it appeared to the First Secretary of State that it was appropriate to vary part of his proposals, and he undertook such further consultation with respect to the variations as appeared to him appropriate;

    (c) following the consultation mentioned in recitals (a) and (b) the First Secretary of State considered it appropriate to proceed with the making of this Order;

    (d) a document containing the First Secretary of State's proposals was laid before Parliament as required by section 6 of the Regulatory Reform Act 2001 and the period for Parliamentary consideration under section 8 of that Act expired;

    (e) the First Secretary of State had regard to the representations made during that period and, in particular, to the reports of the House of

Commons Regulatory Reform Committee (Second Report, Session 2002–03, HC182) and the House of Lords Select Committee on Delegated Powers and Regulatory Reform (Fourth Report, Session 2002–03), HL Paper 22);

(f) a draft of this Order was laid before Parliament with a statement giving details of those representations and the changes to the First Secretary of State's proposals in the light of them;

(g) the draft was approved by a resolution of each of House of Parliament;

(h) this Order modifies a function of the National Assembly for Wales and the Assembly has agreed that it be made;

(i) the First Secretary of State is of the opinion that this Order does not remove any necessary protection or prevent any person from continuing to exercise any right or freedom which he might reasonably expect to continue to exercise; and

(j) this Order creates burdens affecting persons in the carrying on of certain activities, and the First Secretary of State is of the opinion that—

(i)   the provisions of this Order, taken as a whole, strike a fair balance between the public interest and the interests of the persons affected by the burdens being created, and

(ii)   the extent to which this Order removes or reduces one or more burdens, or has other beneficial effects for persons affected by the burdens imposed by the existing law, makes it desirable for this Order to be made;

Now therefore the First Secretary of State, in exercise of the powers conferred by sections 1 and 4 of the Regulatory Reform Act 2001, hereby makes the following Order:—

Introduction

Citation, commencement and interpretation

1.—(1) This Order may be cited as the Regulatory Reform (Business Tenancies) (England and Wales) Order 2003.

(2) This Order extends to England and Wales only.

(3) This Order shall come into force at the end of the period of 6 months beginning with the day on which it is made.

(4) In this Order, 'the Act' means the Landlord and Tenant Act 1954

Amendment of the Landlord and Tenant Act 1954

2. The Act shall be amended as follows.

Applications to court by landlord or tenant

Amendments to section 24

3.—(1) In section 24(1) (continuation of business tenancies), for the words 'provisions of section twenty-nine of this Act, the tenant under such a tenancy may apply to the court for' substitute the words 'following provisions of this Act either the tenant or the landlord under such a tenancy may apply to the court for an order for the grant of'.

(2) Insert the following subsections after section 24(2)—

'(2A) Neither the tenant nor the landlord may make an application under subsection (1) above if the other has made such an application and the application has been served.

(2B) Neither the tenant nor the landlord may make such an application if the landlord has made an application under section 29(2) of this Act and the application has been served.

(2C) The landlord may not withdraw an application under subsection (1) above unless the tenant consents to its withdrawal.'

Amendments to section 25

4.—(1) Omit section 25(5) (requirement for tenant to notify landlord whether he is willing to give up possession).

(2) For section 25(6) substitute—

'(6) A notice under this section shall not have effect unless it states whether the landlord is opposed to the grant of a new tenancy to the tenant.

(7) A notice under this section which states that the landlord is opposed to the grant of a new tenancy to the tenant shall not have effect unless it also specifies one or more of the grounds specified in section 30(1) of this Act as the ground or grounds for his opposition.

(8) A notice under this section which states that the landlord is not opposed to the grant of a new tenancy to the tenant shall not have effect unless it sets out the landlord's proposals as to—

(a)   the property to be comprised in the new tenancy (being either the whole or part of the property comprised in the current tenancy);

(b)   the rent to be payable under the new tenancy; and

(c)   the other terms of the new tenancy.'

Landlord's application to terminate tenancy

5. For section 29 (order by court for grant of a new tenancy) and the cross-heading immediately preceding it substitute—

'Applications to court

Order by court for grant of new tenancy or termination of current tenancy

29.—(1) Subject to the provisions of this Act, on an application under section 24(1) of this Act, the court shall make an order for the grant of a new tenancy and accordingly for the termination of the current tenancy immediately before the commencement of the new tenancy.

(2) Subject to the following provisions of this Act, a landlord may apply to the court for an order for the termination of a tenancy to which this Part of this Act applies without the grant of a new tenancy—

    (a)   if he has given notice under section 25 of this Act that he is opposed to the grant of a new tenancy to the tenant; or

    (b)   if the tenant has made a request for a new tenancy in accordance with section 26 of this Act and the landlord has given notice under subsection (6) of that section.

(3) The landlord may not make an application under subsection (2) above if either the tenant or the landlord has made an application under section 24(1) of this Act.

(4) Subject to the provisions of this Act, where the landlord makes an application under subsection (2) above—

    (a)   if he establishes, to the satisfaction of the court, any of the grounds on which he is entitled to make the application in accordance with section 30 of this Act, the court shall make an order for the termination of the current tenancy in accordance with section 64 of this Act without the grant of a new tenancy; and

    (b)   if not, it shall make an order for the grant of a new tenancy and accordingly for the termination of the current tenancy immediately before the commencement of the new tenancy.

(5) The court shall dismiss an application by the landlord under section 24(1) of this Act if the tenant informs the court that he does not want a new tenancy.

(6) The landlord may not withdraw an application under subsection (2) above unless the tenant consents to its withdrawal.'.

Amendments to section 30

6.—(1) In section 30(1) (grounds of opposition by landlord to renewal of tenancy), for the words 'subsection (1) of section twenty-four of this Act' substitute 'section 24(1) of this Act, or make an application under section 29(2) of this Act,'.

(2) In section 30(2), after the words 'oppose an application' insert 'under section 24(1) of this Act, or make an application under section 29(2) of this Act,'.

Amendment to section 31

7. In section 31(2) (declaration and order of the court in certain cases where landlord opposes renewal) for the words from the beginning to 'any of those grounds' substitute 'Where the landlord opposes an application under section 24(1) of this Act, or makes an application under section 29(2) of this Act, on one or more of the grounds specified in section 30(1)(d) to (f) of this Act but establishes none of those grounds, and none of the other grounds specified in section 30(1) of this Act, to the satisfaction of the court, then if the court would have been satisfied on any of the grounds specified in section 30(1)(d) to (f) of this Act'.

Amendment to section 31A

8. In section 31A(1) (grant of new tenancy in some cases where section 30(1)(f) applies), after the words '30(1) of this Act' insert ', or makes an application under section 29(2) of this Act on that ground,'.

Amendment to section 34

9. In section 34(2)(a) (rent under new tenancy), for the words 'for the new tenancy' substitute the words 'to the court'.

Time limits for applications to court

10. After section 29 insert the following sections—

'Time limits for applications to court
29A.—(1) Subject to section 29B of this Act, the court shall not entertain an application—

(a)   by the tenant or the landlord under section 24(1) of this Act; or

(b)   by the landlord under section 29(2) of this Act,

if it is made after the end of the statutory period.

(2) In this section and section 29B of this Act 'the statutory period' means a period ending—

(a)   where the landlord gave a notice under section 25 of this Act, on the date specified in his notice; and

(b)   where the tenant made a request for a new tenancy under section 26 of this Act, immediately before the date specified in his request.

(3) Where the tenant has made a request for a new tenancy under section 26 of this Act, the court shall not entertain an application under section 24(1) of this Act which is made before the end of the period of two months beginning with the date of the making of the request, unless the application is made after the landlord has given a notice under section 26(6) of this Act.

Agreements extending time limits

29B.—(1) After the landlord has given a notice under section 25 of this Act, or the tenant has made a request under section 26 of this Act, but before the end of the statutory period, the landlord and tenant may agree that an application such as is mentioned in section 29A(1) of this Act, may be made before the end of a period specified in the agreement which will expire after the end of the statutory period.

(2) The landlord and tenant may from time to time by agreement further extend the period for making such an application, but any such agreement must be made before the end of the period specified in the current agreement.

(3) Where an agreement is made under this section, the court may entertain an application such as is mentioned in section 29A(1) of this Act if it is made before the end of the period specified in the agreement.

(4) Where an agreement is made under this section, or two or more agreements are made under this section, the landlord's notice under section 25 of this Act or tenant's request under section 26 of this Act shall be treated as terminating the tenancy at the end of the period specified in the agreement or, as the case may be, at the end of the period specified in the last of those agreements.'.

Amendment to section 25

11. In section 25(1) (termination of tenancy subject to provisions of Part 4) after 'subject to' insert 'the provisions of section 29B(4) of this Act and'.

Amendment to section 26

12. In section 26(5) (termination of tenancy subject to section 36(2) and Part 4) for 'subsection (2) of section thirty-six' substitute 'sections 29B(4) and 36(2)'.

Companies and their controlling shareholders

Amendment to section 23

13. After section 23(1) (tenancies to which Part 2 applies) insert—

'(1A) Occupation or the carrying on of a business—

(a)   by a company in which the tenant has a controlling interest; or

(b)   where the tenant is a company, by a person with a controlling interest in the company,

shall be treated for the purposes of this section as equivalent to occupation or, as the case may be, the carrying on of a business by the tenant. (1B) Accordingly references (however expressed) in this Part of this Act to the business of, or to use, occupation or enjoyment by, the tenant shall be construed as including references to the business of, or to use, occupation or enjoyment by, a company falling within subsection (1A)(a) above or a person falling within subsection (1A)(b) above.'.

Amendments to section 30

14.—(1) After section 30(1) (opposition by landlord to renewal of tenancy) insert—

'(1A) Where the landlord has a controlling interest in a company, the reference in subsection (1)(g) above to the landlord shall be construed as a reference to the landlord or that company. (1B) Subject to subsection (2A) below, where the landlord is a company and a person has a controlling interest in the company, the reference in subsection (1)(g) above to the landlord shall be construed as a reference to the landlord or that person.'

(2) After section 30(2) insert—

'(2A) Subsection (1B) above shall not apply if the controlling interest was acquired after the beginning of the period of five years which ends with the termination of the current tenancy, and at all times since the acquisition of the controlling interest the holding has been comprised in a tenancy or successive tenancies of the description specified in section 23(1) of this Act.'.

Amendment to section 34

15. After section 34(2) (improvements to which subsection (1)(c) applies) insert—

'(2A) If this Part of this Act applies by virtue of section 23(1A) of this Act, the reference in subsection (1)(d) above to the tenant shall be construed as including—

(a) a company in which the tenant has a controlling interest, or
(b) where the tenant is a company, a person with a controlling interest in the company.'.

Amendment to section 42

16. At the end of the first paragraph of section 42(1) (groups of companies) add 'or the same person has a controlling interest in both'.

Amendments to section 46

17.—(1) Section 46 (interpretation of Part 2) shall become section 46(1). (2) After that subsection add—

'(2) For the purposes of this Part of this Act, a person has a controlling interest in a company, if, had he been a company, the other company would have been its subsidiary; and in this Part—

"company" has the meaning given by section 735 of the Companies Act 1985; and
"subsidiary" has the meaning given by section 736 of that Act.'.

Interim rent

Rent while tenancy continues by virtue of section 24

18. For section 24A (interim rent) substitute—

'*Applications for determination of interim rent while tenancy continues*
24A.—(1) Subject to subsection (2) below, if—

(a)   the landlord of a tenancy to which this Part of this Act applies has given notice under section 25 of this Act to terminate the tenancy; or

(b)   the tenant of such a tenancy has made a request for a new tenancy in accordance with section 26 of this Act,

either of them may make an application to the court to determine a rent (an 'interim rent') which the tenant is to pay while the tenancy ('the relevant tenancy') continues by virtue of section 24 of this Act and the court may order payment of an interim rent in accordance with section 24C or 24D of this Act.

(2) Neither the tenant nor the landlord may make an application under subsection (1) above if the other has made such an application and has not withdrawn it.

(3) No application shall be entertained under subsection (1) above if it is made more than six months after the termination of the relevant tenancy.

Date from which interim rent is payable

24B.—(1) The interim rent determined on an application under section 24A(1) of this Act shall be payable from the appropriate date.

(2) If an application under section 24A(1) of this Act is made in a case where the landlord has given a notice under section 25 of this Act, the appropriate date is the earliest date of termination that could have been specified in the landlord's notice.

(3) If an application under section 24A(1) of this Act is made in a case where the tenant has made a request for a new tenancy under section 26 of this Act, the appropriate date is the earliest date that could have been specified in the tenant's request as the date from which the new tenancy is to begin.

Amount of interim rent where new tenancy of whole premises granted and landlord not opposed

24C.—(1) This section applies where—

(a)   the landlord gave a notice under section 25 of this Act at a time when the tenant was in occupation of the whole of the property comprised in the relevant tenancy for purposes such as are mentioned in section 23(1) of this Act and stated in the notice that he was not opposed to the grant of a new tenancy; or

(b)   the tenant made a request for a new tenancy under section 26 of this Act at a time when he was in occupation of the whole of that property for such purposes and the landlord did not give notice under subsection (6) of that section,

and the landlord grants a new tenancy of the whole of the property comprised in the relevant tenancy to the tenant (whether as a result of an order for the grant of a new tenancy or otherwise).

(2) Subject to the following provisions of this section, the rent payable

under and at the commencement of the new tenancy shall also be the interim rent.

(3) Subsection (2) above does not apply where—

(a)   the landlord or the tenant shows to the satisfaction of the court that the interim rent under that subsection differs substantially from the relevant rent; or

(b)   the landlord or the tenant shows to the satisfaction of the court that the terms of the new tenancy differ from the terms of the relevant tenancy to such an extent that the interim rent under that subsection is substantially different from the rent which (in default of such agreement) the court would have determined under section 34 of this Act to be payable under a tenancy which commenced on the same day as the new tenancy and whose other terms were the same as the relevant tenancy.

(4) In this section 'the relevant rent' means the rent which (in default of agreement between the landlord and the tenant) the court would have determined under section 34 of this Act to be payable under the new tenancy if the new tenancy had commenced on the appropriate date (within the meaning of section 24B of this Act).

(5) The interim rent in a case where subsection (2) above does not apply by virtue only of subsection (3)(a) above is the relevant rent.

(6) The interim rent in a case where subsection (2) above does not apply by virtue only of subsection (3)(b) above, or by virtue of subsection (3)(a) and (b) above, is the rent which it is reasonable for the tenant to pay while the relevant tenancy continues by virtue of section 24 of this Act.

(7) In determining the interim rent under subsection (6) above the court shall have regard—

(a)   to the rent payable under the terms of the relevant tenancy; and

(b)   to the rent payable under any sub-tenancy of part of the property comprised in the relevant tenancy,

but otherwise subsections (1) and (2) of section 34 of this Act shall apply to the determination as they would apply to the determination of a rent under that section if a new tenancy of the whole of the property comprised in the relevant tenancy were granted to the tenant by order of the court and the duration of that new tenancy were the same as the duration of the new tenancy which is actually granted to the tenant.

(8) In this section and section 24D of this Act 'the relevant tenancy' has the same meaning as in section 24A of this Act.

Amount of interim rent in any other case
    24D.— (1) The interim rent in a case where section 24C of this Act does not apply is the rent which it is reasonable for the tenant to pay while the relevant tenancy continues by virtue of section 24 of this Act.

(2) In determining the interim rent under subsection (1) above the court shall have regard—

(a)   to the rent payable under the terms of the relevant tenancy; and
(b)   to the rent payable under any sub-tenancy of part of the property comprised in the relevant tenancy,

but otherwise subsections (1) and (2) of section 34 of this Act shall apply to the determination as they would apply to the determination of a rent under that section if a new tenancy from year to year of the whole of the property comprised in the relevant tenancy were granted to the tenant by order of the court.

(3) If the court—

(a)   has made an order for the grant of a new tenancy and has ordered payment of interim rent in accordance with section 24C of this Act, but
(b)   either—

(i)   it subsequently revokes under section 36(2) of this Act the order for the grant of a new tenancy; or
(ii) the landlord and tenant agree not to act on the order,

the court on the application of the landlord or the tenant shall determine a new interim rent in accordance with subsections (1) and (2) above without a further application under section 24A(1) of this Act.'.

Compensation

Compensation for refusal of new tenancy

19.— (1) For section 37(1) (compensation where new tenancy precluded on certain grounds) substitute—

'(1) Subject to the provisions of this Act, in a case specified in subsection (1A), (1B) or (1C) below (a "compensation case") the tenant shall be entitled on quitting the holding to recover from the landlord by way of compensation an amount determined in accordance with this section.

(1A) The first compensation case is where on the making of an application by the tenant under section 24(1) of this Act the court is precluded (whether by subsection (1) or subsection (2) of section 31 of this Act) from making an order for the grant of a new tenancy by reason of any of the grounds specified in paragraphs (e), (f) and (g) of section 30(1) of this Act (the "compensation grounds") and not of any grounds specified in any other paragraph of section 30(1).

(1B) The second compensation case is where on the making of an application under section 29(2) of this Act the court is precluded (whether by section 29(4)(a) or section 31(2) of this Act) from making an order for the grant of a new tenancy by reason of any of the compensation grounds and not of any other grounds specified in section 30(1) of this Act.

(1C) The third compensation case is where—

(a) the landlord's notice under section 25 of this Act or, as the case may be, under section 26(6) of this Act, states his opposition to the grant of a new tenancy on any of the compensation grounds and not on any other grounds specified in section 30(1) of this Act; and

(b) either—

(i) no application is made by the tenant under section 24(1) of this Act or by the landlord under section 29(2) of this Act; or

(ii) such an application is made but is subsequently withdrawn.'.

(2) In section 37(2)—

(a) for the words 'subsections (5A) to (5E) of this section the said amount' substitute 'the following provisions of this section, compensation under this section'; and

(b) in paragraph (a), after the word 'satisfied' insert 'in relation to the whole of the holding'.

(3) After section 37(3) insert—

'(3A) If the conditions specified in subsection (3) above are satisfied in relation to part of the holding but not in relation to the other part, the amount of compensation shall be the aggregate of sums calculated separately as compensation in respect of each part, and accordingly, for the purpose of calculating compensation in respect of a part any reference in this section to the holding shall be construed as a reference to that part.

(3B) Where section 44(1A) of this Act applies, the compensation shall be determined separately for each part and compensation determined for any part shall be recoverable only from the person who is the owner of an interest in that part which fulfils the conditions specified in section 44(1) of this Act.'.

(4) In section 37(4), for the words 'the circumstances mentioned in subsection (1) of this section' substitute 'a compensation case'.

Compensation for misrepresentation

20. After section 37 insert—

'*Compensation for possession obtained by misrepresentation*
37A.—(1) Where the court—

(a) makes an order for the termination of the current tenancy but does not make an order for the grant of a new tenancy, or

(b) refuses an order for the grant of a new tenancy,

and it subsequently made to appear to the court that the order was obtained, or the court was induced to refuse the grant, by misrepresentation or the concealment of material facts, the court may order the landlord to pay to the tenant such sum as appears sufficient as compensation for damage or loss sustained by the tenant as the result of the order or refusal.

(2) Where—

(a) the tenant has quit the holding—

(i) after making but withdrawing an application under section 24(1) of this Act; or

(ii) without making such an application; and

(b) it is made to appear to the court that he did so by reason of misrepresentation or the concealment of material facts,

the court may order the landlord to pay to the tenant such sum as appears sufficient as compensation for damage or loss sustained by the tenant as the result of quitting the holding.'.

Agreements to exclude security of tenure

Amendments to section 38

21.— In section 38(1) (restrictions on agreements excluding provisions of Part 2)or 'subsection (4) of this section' substitute 'section 38A of this Act'.

(2) Omit section 38(4).

Agreements to exclude sections 24 to 28

22.—1) After section 38 insert—

'*Agreements to exclude provisions of Part 2*
38A.—(1) The persons who will be the landlord and the tenant in relation to a tenancy to be granted for a term of years certain which will be a tenancy to which this Part of this Act applies may agree that the provisions of sections 24 to 28 of this Act shall be excluded in relation to that tenancy.

(2) The persons who are the landlord and the tenant in relation to a tenancy to which this Part of this Act applies may agree that the tenancy shall be surrendered on such date or in such circumstances as may be specified in the agreement and on such terms (if any) as may be so specified.

(3) An agreement under subsection (1) above shall be void unless—

(a)   the landlord has served on the tenant a notice in the form, or substantially in the form, set out in Schedule 1 to the Regulatory Reform (Business Tenancies) (England and Wales) Order 2003 ('the 2003 Order'); and

(b)   the requirements specified in Schedule 2 to that Order are met.

(4) An agreement under subsection (2) above shall be void unless—

(a)   the landlord has served on the tenant a notice in the form, or substantially in the form, set out in Schedule 3 to the 2003 Order; and

(b)   the requirements specified in Schedule 4 to that Order are met.'

(2) Schedules 1 to 4 to this Order shall have effect.

Duties to give information

Provision of information

23. For section 40 substitute—

'*Duties of tenants and landlords of business premises to give information to each other*
40.—(1) Where a person who is an owner of an interest in reversion expectant (whether immediately or not) on a tenancy of any business premises has served on the tenant a notice in the prescribed form requiring him to do so, it shall be the duty of the tenant to give the appropriate person in writing the information specified in subsection (2) below.
(2) That information is—

(a)   whether the tenant occupies the premises or any part of them wholly or partly for the purposes of a business carried on by him;

(b)   whether his tenancy has effect subject to any sub-tenancy on which his tenancy is immediately expectant and, if so—

(i)   what premises are comprised in the sub-tenancy;
(ii)   for what term it has effect (or, if it is terminable by notice, by what notice it can be terminated);
(iii) what is the rent payable under it;
(iv)   who is the sub-tenant;
(v)   (to the best of his knowledge and belief) whether the sub-tenant is in occupation of the premises or of part of the premises comprised in the sub-tenancy and, if not, what is the sub-tenant's address;
(vi)   whether an agreement is in force excluding in relation to the sub-tenancy the provisions of sections 24 to 28 of this Act; and

(vii) whether a notice has been given under section 25 or 26(6) of this Act, or a request has been made under section 26 of this Act, in relation to the sub-tenancy and, if so, details of the notice or request; and

(c) (to the best of his knowledge and belief) the name and address of any other person who owns an interest in reversion in any part of the premises.

(3) Where the tenant of any business premises who is a tenant under such a tenancy as is mentioned in section 26(1) of this Act has served on a reversioner or a reversioner's mortgagee in possession a notice in the prescribed form requiring him to do so, it shall be the duty of the person on whom the notice is served to give the appropriate person in writing the information specified in subsection (4) below.

(4) That information is—

(a) whether he is the owner of the fee simple in respect of the premises or any part of them or the mortgagee in possession of such an owner,

(b) if he is not, then (to the best of his knowledge and belief)—

    (i) the name and address of the person who is his or, as the case may be, his mortgagor's immediate landlord in respect of those premises or of the part in respect of which he or his mortgagor is not the owner in fee simple;

    (ii) for what term his or his mortgagor's tenancy has effect and what is the earliest date (if any) at which that tenancy is terminable by notice to quit given by the landlord; and

    (iii) whether a notice has been given under section 25 or 26(6) of this Act, or a request has been made under section 26 of this Act, in relation to the tenancy and, if so, details of the notice or request;

(c) (to the best of his knowledge and belief) the name and address of any other person who owns an interest in reversion in any part of the premises; and

(d) if he is a reversioner, whether there is a mortgagee in possession of his interest in the premises and, if so, (to the best of his knowledge and belief) what is the name and address of the mortgagee.

(5) A duty imposed on a person by this section is a duty—

(a) to give the information concerned within the period of one month beginning with the date of service of the notice; and

(b) if within the period of six months beginning with the date of service of the notice that person becomes aware that any information which has been given in pursuance of the notice is not, or is no longer, correct, to give the appropriate person correct information within the period of one month beginning with the date on which he becomes aware.

(6) This section shall not apply to a notice served by or on the tenant more than two years before the date on which apart from this Act his tenancy would come to an end by effluxion of time or could be brought to an end by notice to quit given by the landlord.

(7) Except as provided by section 40A of this Act, the appropriate person for the purposes of this section and section 40A(1) of this Act is the person who served the notice under subsection (1) or (3) above.

(8) In this section—

'business premises' means premises used wholly or partly for the purposes of a business;

'mortgagee in possession' includes a receiver appointed by the mortgagee or by the court who is in receipt of the rents and profits, and 'his mortgagor' shall be construed accordingly;

'reversioner' means any person having an interest in the premises, being an interest in reversion expectant (whether immediately or not) on the tenancy;

'reversioner's mortgagee in possession' means any person being a mortgagee in possession in respect of such an interest; and

'sub-tenant' includes a person retaining possession of any premises by virtue of the Rent (Agriculture) Act 1976 or the Rent Act 1977 after the coming to an end of a sub-tenancy, and 'sub-tenancy' includes a right so to retain possession.'.

Section 40 duties in transfer cases

24. After section 40 insert the following sections—

'Duties in transfer cases

40A.—(1) If a person on whom a notice under section 40(1) or (3) of this Act has been served has transferred his interest in the premises or any part of them to some other person and gives the appropriate person notice in writing—

(a)   of the transfer of his interest; and

(b)   of the name and address of the person to whom he transferred it,

on giving the notice he ceases in relation to the premises or (as the case may be) to that part to be under any duty imposed by section 40 of this Act.

(2) If—

(a)   the person who served the notice under section 40(1) or (3) of this Act ('the transferor') has transferred his interest in the premises to some other person ('the transferee'); and

(b)   the transferor or the transferee has given the person required to give the information notice in writing—

(i)   of the transfer; and

(ii)   of the transferee's name and address,

the appropriate person for the purposes of section 40 of this Act and subsection (1) above is the transferee.

(3) If—

(a)   a transfer such as is mentioned in paragraph (a) of subsection (2) above has taken place; but

(b)   neither the transferor nor the transferee has given a notice such as is mentioned in paragraph (b) of that subsection,

any duty imposed by section 40 of this Act may be performed by giving the information either to the transferor or to the transferee.

Proceedings for breach of duties to give information

40B. A claim that a person has broken any duty imposed by section 40 of this Act may be made the subject of civil proceedings for breach of statutory duty; and in any such proceedings a court may order that person to comply with that duty and may make an award of damages.'.

Miscellaneous amendments

Termination by tenant of tenancy

25.—(1) After section 27(1) (termination by tenant of fixed term tenancy at end of term) insert—

'(1A) Section 24 of this Act shall not have effect in relation to a tenancy for a term of years certain where the tenant is not in occupation of the property comprised in the tenancy at the time when, apart from this Act, the tenancy would come to an end by effluxion of time.'.

(2) In section 27(2) (termination by tenant of fixed term tenancy continuing by virtue of section 24)—

(a)   after 'of this Act' insert 'shall not come to an end by reason only of the tenant ceasing to occupy the property comprised in the tenancy but'; and

(b)   omit the word 'quarter'.

(3) After that subsection insert—

'(3) Where a tenancy is terminated under subsection (2) above, any rent payable in respect of a period which begins before, and ends after, the tenancy is terminated shall be apportioned, and any rent paid by the tenant in excess of the amount apportioned to the period before termination shall be recoverable by him.'.

Maximum duration of new tenancy

26. In section 33 (duration of new tenancy) for the word 'fourteen' substitute the word 'fifteen'.

Divided reversions

27.—(1) In section 44(1) (meaning of 'landlord'), for 'the next following subsection,' substitute 'subsections (1A) and (2) below,'.

(2) After section 44(1) insert—

' (1A) The reference in subsection (1) above to a person who is the owner of an interest such as is mentioned in that subsection is to be construed, where different persons own such interests in different parts of the property, as a reference to all those persons collectively.'.

(3) In section 35(1) (other terms of new tenancy), after the word 'thereunder)' insert ', including, where different persons own interests which fulfil the conditions specified in section 44(1) of this Act in different parts of it, terms as to the apportionment of the rent,'.

Final provisions

Consequential amendments, repeals and subordinate provisions

28.—(1) Schedule 5 to this Order, which contains amendments consequential on the provisions of this Order, shall have effect.

(2) The enactments specified in Schedule 6 to this Order are repealed to the extent mentioned in the third column of that Schedule.

(3) Schedules 1 to 4 to this Order are designated as subordinate provisions for the purposes of section 4 of the Regulatory Reform Act 2001.

(4) A subordinate provisions order relating to the subordinate provisions designated by paragraph (3) above shall be subject to annulment in pursuance of a resolution of either House of Parliament.

(5) The power to make a subordinate provisions order relating to those provisions is to be exercisable in relation to Wales by the National Assembly for Wales concurrently with a Minister of the Crown.

(6) Paragraph (4) above does not apply to a subordinate provisions order made by the National Assembly for Wales.

(7) The notices and statutory declarations set out in Schedules 1 to 4 to this Order shall be treated for the purposes of section 26 of the Welsh Language Act 1993 (power to prescribe Welsh forms) as if they were specified by an Act of Parliament; and accordingly the power conferred by section 26(2) of that Act may be exercised in relation to those notices and declarations.

Transitional provisions

29.—(1) Where, before this Order came into force—

(a)   the landlord gave the tenant notice under section 25 of the Act; or

(b)   the tenant made a request for a new tenancy in accordance with section 26 of the Act,

nothing in this Order has effect in relation to the notice or request or anything done in consequence of it.

(2) Nothing in this Order has effect in relation—

(a)   to an agreement—

    (i)   for the surrender of a tenancy which was made before this Order came into force and which fell within section 24(2)(b) of the Act; or

    (ii)   which was authorised by the court under section 38(4) of the Act before this Order came into force; or

(b)   to a notice under section 27(2) of the Act which was given by the tenant to the immediate landlord before this Order came into force.

(3) Any provision in a tenancy which requires an order under section 38(4) of the Act to be obtained in respect of any subtenancy shall, so far as is necessary after the coming into force of this Order, be construed as if it required the procedure mentioned in section 38A of the Act to be followed, and any related requirement shall be construed accordingly.

(4) If a person has, before the coming into force of this Order, entered into an agreement to take a tenancy, any provision in that agreement which requires an order under section 38(4) of the Act to be obtained in respect of the tenancy shall continue to be effective, notwithstanding the repeal of that provision by Article 21(2) of this Order, and the court shall retain jurisdiction to make such an order.

(5) Article 20 above does not have effect where the tenant quit the holding before this Order came into force.

(6) Nothing in Articles 23 and 24 above applies to a notice under section 40 of the Act served before this Order came into force.

Signed by authority of the First Secretary of State

Keith Hill
Minister of State, Office of the Deputy Prime Minister

1st December 2003

SCHEDULE 1   Article 22(2)

FORM OF NOTICE THAT SECTIONS 24 TO 28 OF THE LANDLORD AND
TENANT ACT 1954 ARE NOT TO APPLY TO A BUSINESS TENANCY

To:

[*Name and address of tenant*]
From:

[*Name and address of landlord*]

IMPORTANT NOTICE

**You are being offered a lease without security of tenure. Do not commit yourself
to the lease unless you have read this message carefully and have discussed it
with a professional adviser.**

Business tenants normally have security of tenure – the right to stay in their business
premises when the lease ends.

**If you commit yourself to the lease you will be giving up these important legal
rights.**

- You will have **no right** to stay in the premises when the lease ends.

- Unless the landlord chooses to offer you another lease, you will need to leave the
  premises.

- You will be unable to claim compensation for the loss of your business premises,
  unless the lease specifically gives you this right.

- If the landlord offers you another lease, you will have no right to ask the court to
  fix the rent.

It is therefore important to get professional advice – from a qualified surveyor, lawyer
or accountant - before agreeing to give up these rights.

If you want to ensure that you can stay in the same business premises when the
lease ends, you should consult your adviser about another form of lease that does
not exclude the protection of the Landlord and Tenant Act 1954.

If you receive this notice at least 14 days before committing yourself to the lease, you
will need to sign a simple declaration that you have received this notice and have
accepted its consequences, before signing the lease.

**But if you do not receive at least 14 days notice, you will need to sign a
"statutory" declaration. To do so, you will need to visit an independent
solicitor (or someone else empowered to administer oaths).**

Unless there is a special reason for committing yourself to the lease sooner, you may
want to ask the landlord to let you have at least 14 days to consider whether you wish
to give up your statutory rights. If you then decided to go ahead with the agreement
to exclude the protection of the Landlord and Tenant Act 1954, you would only need
to make a simple declaration, and so you would not need to make a separate visit to an
independent solicitor.

SCHEDULE 2   **Article 22(2)**

REQUIREMENTS FOR A VALID AGREEMENT THAT SECTIONS 24 TO 28 OF
THE LANDLORD AND TENANT ACT 1954 ARE NOT TO APPLY TO A
BUSINESS TENANCY

1. The following are the requirements referred to in section 38A(3)(b)
of the Act.

2. Subject to paragraph 4, the notice referred to in section 38A(3)(a) of
the Act must be served on the tenant not less than 14 days before the
tenant enters into the tenancy to which it applies, or (if earlier) becomes
contractually bound to do so.

3. If the requirement in paragraph 2 is met, the tenant, or a person duly
authorised by him to do so, must, before the tenant enters into the tenancy
to which the notice applies, or (if earlier) becomes contractually bound to
do so, make a declaration in the form, or substantially in the form, set out
in paragraph 7.

4. If the requirement in paragraph 2 is not met, the notice referred to
in section 38A(3)(a) of the Act must be served on the tenant before the
tenant enters into the tenancy to which it applies, or (if earlier) becomes
contractually bound to do so, and the tenant, or a person duly authorised
by him to do so, must before that time make a statutory declaration in the
form, or substantially in the form, set out in paragraph 8.

5. A reference to the notice and, where paragraph 3 applies, the declaration or, where paragraph 4 applies, the statutory declaration must be contained in or endorsed on the instrument creating the tenancy.

6. The agreement under section 38A(1) of the Act, or a reference to the
agreement, must be contained in or endorsed upon the instrument creating the tenancy.

7. The form of declaration referred to in paragraph 3 is as follows:—

I

(*name of declarant*) of

(*address*) declare that—
1. I/

(*name of tenant*) propose(s) to enter into a tenancy of premises at

(*address of premises*) for a term commencing on

2. I/The tenant propose(s) to enter into an agreement with

(*name of landlord*) that the provisions of sections 24 to 28 of the Landlord and Tenant Act 1954 (security of tenure) shall be excluded in relation to the tenancy.

3. The landlord has, not less than 14 days before I/the tenant enter(s) into the tenancy, or (if earlier) become(s) contractually bound to do so served on me/the tenant a notice in the form, or substantially in the form, set out in Schedule 1 to the Regulatory Reform (Business Tenancies) (England and Wales) Order 2003. The form of notice set out in that Schedule is reproduced below.

4. I have/The tenant has read the notice referred to in paragraph 3 above and accept(s) the consequences of entering into the agreement referred to in paragraph 2 above.

5. (*as appropriate*) I am duly authorised by the tenant to make this declaration.

DECLARED this

day of

To:

[*Name and address of tenant*]
From:

[*name and address of landlord*]

IMPORTANT NOTICE

<u>**You are being offered a lease without security of tenure. Do not commit yourself to the lease unless you have read this message carefully and have discussed it with a professional adviser.**</u>

Business tenants normally have security of tenure – the right to stay in their business premises when the lease ends.

<u>**If you commit yourself to the lease you will be giving up these important legal rights.**</u>

- You will have **no right** to stay in the premises when the lease ends.

- Unless the landlord chooses to offer you another lease, you will need to leave the premises.

- You will be unable to claim compensation for the loss of your business premises, unless the lease specifically gives you this right.

- If the landlord offers you another lease, you will have no right to ask the court to fix the rent.

It is therefore important to get professional advice – from a qualified surveyor, lawyer or accountant - before agreeing to give up these rights.

If you want to ensure that you can stay in the same business premises when the lease ends, you should consult your adviser about another form of lease that does not exclude the protection of the Landlord and Tenant Act 1954.

If you receive this notice at least 14 days before committing yourself to the lease, you will need to sign a simple declaration that you have received this notice and have accepted its consequences, before signing the lease.

But if you do not receive at least 14 days notice, you will need to sign a "statutory" declaration. To do so, you will need to visit an independent solicitor (or someone else empowered to administer oaths).

Unless there is a special reason for committing yourself to the lease sooner, you may want to ask the landlord to let you have at least 14 days to consider whether you wish to give up your statutory rights. If you then decided to go ahead with the agreement to exclude the protection of the Landlord and Tenant Act 1954, you would only need to make a simple declaration, and so you would not need to make a separate visit to an independent solicitor.

8. The form of statutory declaration referred to in paragraph 4 is as follows:—

I

(*name of declarant*) of

(*address*) do solemnly and sincerely declare that—
1. I

(*name of tenant*) propose(s) to enter into a tenancy of premises at

(*address of premises*) for a term commencing on

2. I/The tenant propose(s) to enter into an agreement with (name of landlord) that the provisions of sections 24 to 28 of the Landlord and Tenant Act 1954 (security of tenure) shall be excluded in relation to the tenancy.
3. The landlord has served on me/the tenant a notice in the form, or substantially in the form, set out in Schedule 1 to the Regulatory Reform (Business Tenancies) (England and Wales) Order 2003. The form of notice set out in that Schedule is reproduced below.
4. I have/The tenant has read the notice referred to in paragraph 3 above and accept(s) the consequences of entering into the agreement referred to in paragraph 2 above.

5. (*as appropriate*) I am duly authorised by the tenant to make this declaration.

To:

[*Name and address of tenant*]
From:

[*name and address of landlord*]

IMPORTANT NOTICE

You are being offered a lease without security of tenure. Do not commit yourself to the lease unless you have read this message carefully and have discussed it with a professional adviser.

Business tenants normally have security of tenure – the right to stay in their business premises when the lease ends.

If you commit yourself to the lease you will be giving up these important legal rights.

- You will have **no right** to stay in the premises when the lease ends.

- Unless the landlord chooses to offer you another lease, you will need to leave the premises.

- You will be unable to claim compensation for the loss of your business premises, unless the lease specifically gives you this right.

- If the landlord offers you another lease, you will have no right to ask the court to fix the rent.

It is therefore important to get professional advice – from a qualified surveyor, lawyer or accountant - before agreeing to give up these rights.

If you want to ensure that you can stay in the same business premises when the lease ends, you should consult your adviser about another form of lease that does not exclude the protection of the Landlord and Tenant Act 1954.

If you receive this notice at least 14 days before committing yourself to the lease, you will need to sign a simple declaration that you have received this notice and have accepted its consequences, before signing the lease.

But if you do not receive at least 14 days notice, you will need to sign a "statutory" declaration. To do so, you will need to visit an independent solicitor (or someone else empowered to administer oaths).

> Unless there is a special reason for committing yourself to the lease sooner, you may want to ask the landlord to let you have at least 14 days to consider whether you wish to give up your statutory rights. If you then decided to go ahead with the agreement to exclude the protection of the Landlord and Tenant Act 1954, you would only need to make a simple declaration, and so you would not need to make a separate visit to an independent solicitor.

AND I make this solemn declaration conscientiously believing the same to be true and by virtue of the Statutory Declaration Act 1835.

DECLARED at

this

day of

Before me

(*signature of person before whom declaration is made*)
A commissioner for oaths or A solicitor empowered to administer oaths or (*as appropriate*)

Article 22(2)   **SCHEDULE 3**

FORM OF NOTICE THAT AN AGREEMENT TO SURRENDER A BUSINESS
TENANCY IS TO BE MADE

To:

[*Name and address of tenant*]
From:

[*name and address of landlord*]

IMPORTANT NOTICE

You are being offered a lease without security of tenure. Do not commit yourself to the lease unless you have read this message carefully and have discussed it with a professional adviser.

Business tenants normally have security of tenure – the right to stay in their business premises when the lease ends.

If you commit yourself to the lease you will be giving up these important legal rights.

- You will have **no right** to stay in the premises when the lease ends.

- Unless the landlord chooses to offer you another lease, you will need to leave the premises.

- You will be unable to claim compensation for the loss of your business premises, unless the lease specifically gives you this right.

- If the landlord offers you another lease, you will have no right to ask the court to fix the rent.

It is therefore important to get professional advice – from a qualified surveyor, lawyer or accountant - before agreeing to give up these rights.

If you want to ensure that you can stay in the same business premises when the lease ends, you should consult your adviser about another form of lease that does not exclude the protection of the Landlord and Tenant Act 1954.

If you receive this notice at least 14 days before committing yourself to the lease, you will need to sign a simple declaration that you have received this notice and have accepted its consequences, before signing the lease.

But if you do not receive at least 14 days notice, you will need to sign a "statutory" declaration. To do so, you will need to visit an independent solicitor (or someone else empowered to administer oaths).

Unless there is a special reason for committing yourself to the lease sooner, you may want to ask the landlord to let you have at least 14 days to consider whether you wish to give up your statutory rights. If you then decided to go ahead with the agreement to exclude the protection of the Landlord and Tenant Act 1954, you would only need to make a simple declaration, and so you would not need to make a separate visit to an independent solicitor.

Article 22(2)   SCHEDULE 4

REQUIREMENTS FOR A VALID AGREEMENT TO SURRENDER A BUSINESS TENANCY

1. The following are the requirements referred to in section 38A(4)(b) of the Act.

2. Subject to paragraph 4, the notice referred to in section 38A(4)(a) of the Act must be served on the tenant not less than 14 days before the tenant enters into the agreement under section 38A(2) of the Act, or (if earlier) becomes contractually bound to do so.

3. If the requirement in paragraph 2 is met, the tenant or a person duly authorised by him to do so, must, before the tenant enters into the agreement under section 38A(2) of the Act, or (if earlier) becomes contractually bound to do so, make a declaration in the form, or substantially in the form, set out in paragraph 6.

4. If the requirement in paragraph 2 is not met, the notice referred to in section 38A(4)(a) of the Act must be served on the tenant before the tenant enters into the agreement under section 38A(2) of the Act, or (if earlier) becomes contractually bound to do so, and the tenant, or a person duly authorised by him to do so, must before that time make a statutory declaration in the form, or substantially in the form, set out in paragraph 7.

5. A reference to the notice and, where paragraph 3 applies, the declaration or, where paragraph 4 applies, the statutory declaration must be contained in or endorsed on the instrument creating the agreement under section 38A(2).

6. The form of declaration referred to in paragraph 3 is as follows:—

I

(*name of declarant*) of

(*address*) declare that—
1. I have/

(*name of tenant*) has a tenancy of premises at

(*address of premises*) for a term commencing on

2. I/The tenant propose(s) to enter into an agreement with

(*name of landlord*) to surrender the tenancy on a date or in circumstances specified in the agreement.

3. The landlord has not less than 14 days before I/the tenant enter(s) into the agreement referred to in paragraph 2 above, or (if earlier) become(s) contractually bound to do so, served on me/the tenant a notice in the form, or substantially in the form, set out in Schedule 3 to Regulatory Reform (Business Tenancies) (England and Wales) Order 2003. The form of notice set out in that Schedule is reproduced below.

4. I have/The tenant has read the notice referred to in paragraph 3 above and accept(s) the consequences of entering into the agreement referred to in paragraph 2 above.

5. (*as appropriate*) I am duly authorised by the tenant to make this declaration.

DECLARED this

day of

To:

[Name and address of tenant]
From:

[name and address of landlord]

IMPORTANT NOTICE

<u>**You are being offered a lease without security of tenure. Do not commit yourself to the lease unless you have read this message carefully and have discussed it with a professional adviser.**</u>

Business tenants normally have security of tenure – the right to stay in their business premises when the lease ends.

<u>**If you commit yourself to the lease you will be giving up these important legal rights**</u>.

- You will have **no right** to stay in the premises when the lease ends.

- Unless the landlord chooses to offer you another lease, you will need to leave the premises.

- You will be unable to claim compensation for the loss of your business premises, unless the lease specifically gives you this right.

- If the landlord offers you another lease, you will have no right to ask the court to fix the rent.

It is therefore important to get professional advice – from a qualified surveyor, lawyer or accountant - before agreeing to give up these rights.

If you want to ensure that you can stay in the same business premises when the lease ends, you should consult your adviser about another form of lease that does not exclude the protection of the Landlord and Tenant Act 1954.

If you receive this notice at least 14 days before committing yourself to the lease, you will need to sign a simple declaration that you have received this notice and have accepted its consequences, before signing the lease.

<u>**But if you do not receive at least 14 days notice, you will need to sign a "statutory" declaration.   To do so, you will need to visit an independent solicitor (or someone else empowered to administer oaths).**</u>

Unless there is a special reason for committing yourself to the lease sooner, you may want to ask the landlord to let you have at least 14 days to consider whether you wish to give up your statutory rights. If you then decided to go ahead with the agreement to exclude the protection of the Landlord and Tenant Act 1954, you would only need to make a simple declaration, and so you would not need to make a separate visit to an independent solicitor.

---

7. The form of statutory declaration referred to in paragraph 4 is as follows:—

I

(*name of declarant*) of

(*address*) do solemnly and sincerely declare that—
1. I have/

(*name of tenant*) has a tenancy of premises at

(*address of premises*) for a term commencing on

2. I/The tenant propose(s) to enter into an agreement with

(*name of landlord*) to surrender the tenancy on a date or in circumstances specified in the agreement.
3. The landlord has served on me/the tenant a notice in the form, or substantially in the form, set out in Schedule 3 to the Regulatory Reform (Business Tenancies) (England and Wales) Order 2003. The form of notice set out in that Schedule is reproduced below.
4. I have/The tenant has read the notice referred to in paragraph 3 above and accept(s) the consequences of entering into the agreement referred to in paragraph 2 above.
5. (*as appropriate*) I am duly authorised by the tenant to make this declaration.

To:

[*Name and address of tenant*]
From:

[*name and address of landlord*]

IMPORTANT NOTICE

You are being offered a lease without security of tenure. Do not commit yourself to the lease unless you have read this message carefully and have discussed it with a professional adviser.

Business tenants normally have security of tenure – the right to stay in their business premises when the lease ends.

If you commit yourself to the lease you will be giving up these important legal rights.

- You will have **no right** to stay in the premises when the lease ends.

- Unless the landlord chooses to offer you another lease, you will need to leave the premises.

- You will be unable to claim compensation for the loss of your business premises, unless the lease specifically gives you this right.

- If the landlord offers you another lease, you will have no right to ask the court to fix the rent.

It is therefore important to get professional advice – from a qualified surveyor, lawyer or accountant - before agreeing to give up these rights.

If you want to ensure that you can stay in the same business premises when the lease ends, you should consult your adviser about another form of lease that does not exclude the protection of the Landlord and Tenant Act 1954.

If you receive this notice at least 14 days before committing yourself to the lease, you will need to sign a simple declaration that you have received this notice and have accepted its consequences, before signing the lease.

But if you do not receive at least 14 days notice, you will need to sign a "statutory" declaration. To do so, you will need to visit an independent solicitor (or someone else empowered to administer oaths).

Unless there is a special reason for committing yourself to the lease sooner, you may want to ask the landlord to let you have at least 14 days to consider whether you wish to give up your statutory rights. If you then decided to go ahead with the agreement to exclude the protection of the Landlord and Tenant Act 1954, you would only need to make a simple declaration, and so you would not need to make a separate visit to an independent solicitor.

AND I make this solemn declaration conscientiously believing the same to be true and by virtue of the Statutory Declarations Act 1835

DECLARED at

this

day of

Before me (*signature of person before whom declaration is made*)

A commissioner for oaths or A solicitor empowered to administer oaths *or* (*as appropriate*)

Index

Unreasonably withheld consent—*contd*
  subletting—*contd*
    conditions deemed reasonable,
      7–21—7–22
    generally, 7–08
    reasonableness, 7–15—7–16
    remedies, 7–23—7–24
    unreasonableness, 7–17—7–19
Upholstery materials
  user, 5–18—5–19
User
  and see under individual headings
  advertising control
    landlords, by, 5–24
    statutory, 5–25—5–28
  change of
    landlords' consent, 5–10—5–11
    planning control, 5–13—5–14
    variation of lease terms, 5–12
  commonhold units, 5–01
  dangerous trades, 5–07—5–08
  development, 5–13—5–14
  enforcement, 5–09
  farm business tenancies, 5–16
  introduction, 5–01—5–02
  limitations on, 5–03—5–05
  mixed residential and business, 5–29
  nuisance, 5–07—5–08
  offensive trades, 5–07—5–08
  positive covenants, 5–06
  regulation
    animals, 5–23
    entertainment, 5–21
    introduction, 5–17
    licensing, 5–17
    manufacturing processes, 5–18
    registration, 5–17
    sale or storage of goods,
      5–19—5–20
    services, 5–21
    welfare, 5–22

User—*contd*
  residential
    employee accommodation, 5–31
    exclusive, 5–30
    partial, 5–29
    prohibition, 5–29
    restraint of trade, 5–15
    specific, 5–06
    Sunday trading, 5–09
Valuation
  renewal of business tenancies, 13–10
  rent review, 4–08—4–09
Variable rent
  formulae, 3–04—3–05
  index-linked, 3–04
  introduction, 3–03
Variation of lease terms
  recovery of rent, 3–15
  renewal of business tenancies,
    13–11—13–12
  user
    generally, 5–12
    taxation, 9–07
VAT
  generally, 9–05
Visiting forces service authorities
  renewal of business tenancies, 10–26

Waste
  alterations, 6–01
Welfare services
  user, 5–22
Whale oil treatment
  user, 5–18
Willing tenant/willing landlord
  renewal of business tenancies, 13–08
  rent review, 4–12

Zoos
  user, 5–23